THE VICTORIAN EIGHTEENTH CENTURY

The Victorian Eighteenth Century

An Intellectual History

B. W. YOUNG

OXFORD
UNIVERSITY PRESS

Great Clarendon Street, Oxford OX2 6DP

Oxford University Press is a department of the University of Oxford. It furthers the University's objective of excellence in research, scholarship, and education by publishing worldwide in

Oxford New York

Auckland Cape Town Dar es Salaam Hong Kong Karachi Kuala Lumpur Madrid Melbourne Mexico City Nairobi New Delhi Shanghai Taipei Toronto

With offices in

Argentina Austria Brazil Chile Czech Republic France Greece Guatemala Hungary Italy Japan Poland Portugal Singapore South Korea Switzerland Thailand Turkey Ukraine Vietnam

Oxford is a registered trade mark of Oxford University Press in the UK and in certain other countries

Published in the United States by Oxford University Press Inc., New York

First published 2007

British Library Cataloguing in Publication Data
Data available

Library of Congress Cataloging in Publication Data
Data available

Typeset by Laserwords Private Limited, Chennai, India
Printed in Great Britain
on acid-free paper by
Biddles Ltd., King's Lynn, Norfolk

ISBN 978–0–19–925622–8

1 3 5 7 9 10 8 6 4 2

To my siblings–Roselyn, Deborah, and Stuart

Contents

Acknowledgements

I owe an immense amount to a great number of people and to several institutions in my work on this book. The original idea for the book dates back to my time as a British Academy postdoctoral fellow at Jesus College, Oxford, and it took something like its final shape and conception during the years I spent in the History Subject Group at the University of Sussex. Research on the book was aided by a British Academy Small Grant which enabled me to spend the summer months of 2003 as a visiting fellow at Clare Hall, Cambridge; I am grateful to the Academy and to the President and Fellows of Clare Hall for making that productive and restorative stay possible. The book was largely written at Christ Church, Oxford. I would like to thank the librarians at the Bodleian Library, the British Library, Cambridge University Library, and the London Library; many books have also been fetched for me from the Wing Wing of Christ Church library. The book has been read in typescript by several friends and colleagues: John Walsh and John Burrow read most of the book, and chapters were also read and commented upon by Ruth Scurr, Donald Winch, Blair Worden, and Norman Vance. An earlier version of chapter 3 appeared in David Womersley ed., Edward Gibbon: Bicentenary Essays (Oxford, 1997). My debts to individuals are enormous, and I wish to thank in particular the members of my family who kept faith in the project, and also those of its members who simply reminded me of the important things: the Youngs (Brian, Joyce, Deborah, Stuart, Claire, Jacob, and Olivia); the Aherns (Adam and Ann); the Dewars (Roselyn, Peter, Helen, and Sophie); and the Robinsons (Faye, Nicholas, Phoebe, and Jemima). The debt I owe to my siblings is incalculable, and my dedication of the book to them is an inadequate acknowledgement of this fact. Mishtooni Bose was a great friend and support at all times, and so also has been Noël Sugimura. Christ Church is an ideal environment in which to work, and I am deeply grateful to my friends and colleagues for helping to sustain this project to its completion.

B. W. Y.

Christ Church,
Oxford,
November 2006

Abbreviations

CHAPTERS 1 AND 2

Thomas Carlyle

CME	*Critical and Miscellaneous Essays* (5 vols., London, 1899)
FG	*History of Friedrich II. of Prussia, Called Frederick the Great* (6 vols., London, 1858–65)
FR	*History of the French Revolution* (1837: Oxford Worlds Classics edition, ed. K. J. Fielding and David Sorensen, 2 vols. in one, 1989)
HE	*Historical Essays*, ed. Chris R. Vanden Bossche (Berkeley, 2002)
LDP	*Latter Day Pamphlets* (London, 1855)
OC	*The Letters and Speeches of Oliver Cromwell* (1845: 3 vols., ed. S. C. Lomas, London, 1904)
OH	*On Heroes, Hero-Worship and the Heroic in History*, ed. Carl Niemeyer (Lincoln, Neb., 1964)
PP	*Past and Present*, ed. Richard D. Altick (New York, 1965)

CHAPTER 3

Edward Gibbon

A	*Autobiographies*, ed. John Murray (London, 1896)
DF	*History of the Decline and Fall of the Roman Empire*, ed. David Womersley (3 vols., Harmondsworth, 1994)

John Henry Newman

Apol.	*Apologia pro vita sua, Being a History of his Religious Opinions*, ed. Martin J. Svaglic (Oxford, 1967)
Arians	*The Arians of the Fourth Century, their Doctrine, Temper, and Conduct, Chiefly as Exhibited in the Councils of the Church, between A.D. 325, and A.D. 381* (London, 1833)

ECH	*Essays Critical and Historical* (London, 1871)
EM	*An Essay on the Miracles Recorded in the Ecclesiastical History of the Early Church* (Oxford, 1843)
GA	*An Essay in Aid of a Grammar of Assent*, ed. I. T. Ker (Oxford, 1985)
Idea	*The Idea of a University*, ed. Martin J. Svaglic (Notre Dame, Ind., 1982)
LD	*The Letters and Diaries of John Henry Newman*, ed. Charles Stephen Dessain et al. (London, 1961–84)
Lectures	*Lectures on the History of the Turks, in their Relation to Europe*, in *Historical Sketches* (London, 1894), i. 1–238
PN	*The Philosophical Notebook*, ed. Edward J. Sillem, rev. A. J. Boekraak (Leuven, 1970)

CHAPTER 4

Caroline Emelia Stephen

LA	*Light Arising: Thoughts on the Central Radiance* (Cambridge, 1908)
QS	*Quaker Strongholds* (London, 1890)

Sir James Stephen

Essays	*Essays in Ecclesiastical Biography* (2 vols., London, 1849)
Lectures	*Lectures on the History of France* (2 vols., London, 1851)
Letters	*The Right Honourable Sir James Stephen K.C.B., LL.D. Letters with Biographical Notes*, ed. Caroline Emelia Stephen (London, 1906)

James Fitzjames Stephen

EB	*Essays by a Barrister* (London, 1862)
HS	*Horae Sabbaticae* (3 vols., London, 1892)
LEF	*Liberty, Equality, Fraternity* (1873), ed. Richard A. Posner (Chicago, 1991)

Leslie Stephen

AA	*An Agnostic's Apology and Other Essays* (London, 1873)
ELS	*English Literature and Society in the Eighteenth Century* (London, 1904)
EU	*The English Utilitarians* (3 vols., London, 1900)
History	*History of English Thought in the Eighteenth Century* (2 vols., London, 1876)
HL	*Hours in a Library* (3 vols., London, 1874)
JFS	*The Life of Sir James Fitzjames Stephen* (London, 1895)
MB	*The Mausoleum* Book, ed. Quentin Bell (London, 1977)
SB	*Studies of a Biographer* (4 vols., London, 1902)
SE	*The Science of Ethics* (London, 1882)
SEI	*Some Early Impressions* (London, 1923)
SRD	*Social Rights and Duties: Addresses to Ethical Societies* (2 vols., London, 1896)

Introduction

> There is a period in history which has a peculiar interest for all of us. It is that which lies upon the borderland between the past and present; which has gathered some romance from the lapse of time, and yet is not so far off but that we have seen some of the actors, and can distinctly realise the scenes in which they took part.[1]

Leslie Stephen's remark about the eighteenth century could equally be said of our own relation with the nineteenth century. In his last major work, *The English Utilitarians* (1900), Stephen was engaged in historicizing his own nineteenth century for a new generation, and one of the major points he was making was how rooted in its immediate predecessor culture the nineteenth century was. A cultural mediator between the Victorian generations and his children's generation, Stephen articulated much of the interest that his own mid-Victorian generation (to use Theodore Hoppen's useful phrase) felt in its own predecessor culture.[2] Indeed, John Burrow's remark that the origins of intellectual history in English culture lie in the reactions of the Victorians to the eighteenth century is strongly borne out by Stephen's *History of English Thought in the Eighteenth Century* (1876), the first sustained study in this nascent field.[3]

The present study has as its guiding principle a conviction voiced by James Fitzjames Stephen, Leslie Stephen's elder brother. Writing about Conyers Middleton, a once deeply controversial eighteenth-century divine, James Fitzjames Stephen declared that: 'Nothing can help us

[1] Leslie Stephen, 'Defoe's Novels', in *Hours in a Library* (3 vols., London, 1874), i. 1–41, at p. 26.

[2] K. Theodore Hoppen, *The Mid-Victorian Generation, 1846–1886* (Oxford, 1998).

[3] John W. Burrow, 'Intellectual history in English academic life: reflections on a revolution', in Richard Whatmore and Brian Young (eds.), *Palgrave Advances in Intellectual History* (Basingstoke, 2006), 8–24, at p. 9.

to understand the nineteenth century better than some familiarity with the writers of the eighteenth.'[4] This insight informs my argument throughout this book at every point, confirming as it does that, in order to understand the Victorians, modern historians will have increasingly to seek to understand how the Victorians familiarized themselves with their own immediate predecessor culture. Just as societal generations tend to compete with their elders, or else conservatively preserve what they think of as their legacy of sustaining values, so different (if not always evidently distinct) periods of history can be defined in terms of what had gone before, both by those who lived during them, and by those who directly succeed them. This is a complex cultural process, and this book explores such dynamics in general, as well as offering a firmly defined study of the Victorian relationship with the eighteenth century. It does so using the methods and procedures of intellectual history; other approaches to the problem would, of course, yield equally suggestive results.

The idea for this book originated in an essay I contributed to a Festschrift for John Walsh in 1993. My own studies in eighteenth-century religious and intellectual history had revealed (and continue to reveal) just how indebted we remain to pioneering studies in the field written by Victorian authors, whether it be from a secular and secularizing perspective, as in the writings of the Stephen brothers, or from a religiously motivated point of view, as demonstrated in the work of such Church historians as John H. Overton and Charles J. Abbey.[5] That essay was a preliminary exploration of a much larger field, and this book represents a wider and deeper interpretation of the subject. It offers an evaluation of the Victorians as interpreters of the eighteenth century, opening up in the process a plurality of narratives. The Victorians were the first to engage with a historicist interpretation of the past, and modern historians and literary scholars have shown how this affected their examination of a large number of cultures, from ancient Greece and Rome, and forward to the medieval period, whose art and ethos they so often simultaneously looked back to and sought to re-create; and thence to the Renaissance and the troubled political and

[4] James Fitzjames Stephen, 'Miscellaneous Works of Conyers Middleton', *Horae Sabbaticae* (3 vols., London, 1892), ii. 351.

[5] B. W. Young, 'Knock-kneed giants: Victorian representations of eighteenth-century thought', in Jane Garnett and Colin Matthew (eds.), *Revival and Religion since 1700: Essays for John Walsh* (London, 1993), 79–93.

religious legacies of the seventeenth century.[6] My examination of their relations with the eighteenth century takes this exploration forward into the Victorian engagement with the eighteenth century, as a period in both European and British history.

The book is organized chronologically and thematically, encompassing a long nineteenth century, beginning with the contribution of an author born in the mid-1790s, and ending as the consciously Victorian generation began to die out in the 1930s. It begins, in the 1830s, with a pre-Victorian, Thomas Carlyle, whose religious doubts and affirmations informed his entire career as a writer and social prophet; and it ends, in the 1930s, with an exploration of the eighteenth century offered by M. R. James, an etiolated Evangelical and self-conscious Victorian survivor, and by Vernon Lee, a militantly unbelieving art historian and cultural commentator, whose later writings veer on the fringes of Modernism. Each of the chapters is paradigmatic of the issues raised by the book as a whole, fundamental to which is the reaction of the Victorian age, a culture in which religion was of paramount importance, to one in which religion seemed much less certain of itself (at least according to Victorian commentators). There are many avenues which have not been explored here—the history of philosophy, of political thought and political economy, of the arts, and of literature—but the authors selected provide a means of achieving coherence that such wider exploration might have compromised.[7]

The most damningly influential account of the eighteenth century to appear in Victorian Britain, definitively marking the political and regnal

[6] Richard Jenkyns, *The Victorians and Ancient Greece* (Oxford, 1980); Frank M. Turner, *The Greek Heritage in Victorian Britain* (New Haven, 1981); Norman Vance, *The Victorians and Ancient Rome* (Oxford, 1997); R. J. Smith, *The Gothic Bequest: Medieval Institutions in British Thought, 1688–1863* (Cambridge, 1987); Mark Girouard, *The Return to Camelot: Chivalry and the English Gentleman* (New Haven, 1981); Hilary Fraser, *The Victorians and Renaissance Italy* (Oxford, 1992); Timothy Lang, *The Victorians and the Stuart Heritage: Interpretations of a Discordant Past* (Cambridge, 1995).

[7] For excellent studies in the field of philosophy, see Hans Aarsleff, 'Locke's reputation in nineteenth-century England', in *From Locke to Saussure: Essays and Studies in Language and Intellectual History* (London, 1982), 120–45, and Jane Garnett, 'Bishop Butler and the *Zeigeist*: Butler and the development of Christian moral philosophy in Victorian Britain', in Christopher Cunliffe (ed.), *Joseph Butler's Moral and Religious Thought: Tercentenary Essays* (Oxford, 1992), 63–96. For a study concerning eighteenth- and nineteenth-century interrelations in the field of political thought, see J. W. Burrow, *Whigs and Liberals: Continuity and Change in English Political Thought* (Oxford, 1988); in the field of literary history, see Francis O'Gorman and Katherine Turner (eds.), *The Victorians and the Eighteenth Century: Reassessing the Tradition* (Aldershot, 2004).

shift from the Hanoverian to the Victorian age, was published in the very year in which the young queen ascended the throne. Carlyle published his *French Revolution* in 1837, thereby helping to instigate the intellectual shift from the remains of what he disparagingly called the '*Sceptical* Century' to a new age of secularized if still recognizably religious faith.[8] As Peter H. Fritzsche has recently argued, the French Revolution marked a decisive shift in European and North American culture, a rupture in which the modern age defined itself against the *ancien régime*.[9] Similarly, in the study of national memory as a historical agent edited by Pierre Nora, the French Revolution is identified as a considerable site of historical memory in the evolution of modern France; it was also, not coincidentally, the moment at which the idea of the generation as a historical actor first emerged.[10] Carlyle's contribution to that appreciation of the impact of the Revolution was profound, and it had an immediate literary resonance in Dickens's novel *A Tale of Two Cities*. Carlyle hated the eighteenth century, but he was also obsessed by it. As the future Liberal politician John Morley (who venerated the eighteenth century—especially as experienced in France—as a generator of progress) remarked in an essay on Carlyle's contribution to English intellectual life:

> Take out of the mind of the English reader of ordinary cultivation and the average journalist, a degree or two lower than this, their conceptions of the French Revolution and the English Rebellion, and their knowledge of German literature and history, as well as most of their acquaintance with the prominent men of the eighteenth century, and we shall see how much work Mr. Carlyle has done simply as schoolmaster.

The centrality of the eighteenth century to Carlyle's collected writings led to Morley's reflection on the 'fact that to the eighteenth century belong the subjects of more than half of these thirty volumes . . . a proof of the fascination of the period for an author who has never ceased

[8] Thomas Carlyle, *On Heroes, Hero-Worship and the Heroic in History* (1841: Lincoln, Neb., 1966), 170.

[9] Peter H. Fritzsche, *Stranded in the Present: Modern Time and the Melancholy of History* (Cambridge, Mass., 2004).

[10] Pierre Nora, 'Generation', in Nora (ed.), *Realms of Memory: The Construction of the French Past*, trans. Arthur Goldhammer (3 vols., New York, 1998), i: *Conflicts and Divisions*, 499–531; Michelle Vovelle, 'Le Marseillaise: war or peace', Mona Ozouf, 'Liberty, equality, fraternity', and Christian Amalvi, 'Bastille Day: from *Dies Irae* to holiday', in *Realms of Memory*, iii: *Symbols*, 29–74, 77–114, 116–59. For studies of three nineteenth-century historians of the French Revolution—Alphonse de Lamartine, Jules Michelet, and Louis Blanc—see Ann Rigney, *The Rhetoric of Historical Interpretation: Three Narrative Histories of the French Revolution* (Cambridge, 1990).

to vilipend it'.[11] Carlyle was intent on recording his own century's intimate and pervasive connection with the predecessor cultures of the eighteenth century, noting at the opening of his life of Frederick the Great, the subject of my second chapter, that:

> It is the ground out of which we ourselves have sprung; whereon now we have our immediate footing, and first of all strike down our roots for nourishment:—and, alas, in large sections of the practical world, it (what we specially mean by *it*) still continues flourishing round us! To forget it quite is not yet possible, nor would be profitable.[12]

Carlyle was interested in the problem of generations in history, 'a perennial controversy' richly illustrated in relations between Frederick the Great and his father, concluding in Carlyle's account with the metaphor of change in its most obviously rewarding and homely form:

> This Fritz ought to fashion himself according to his Father's pattern, a well-meant honest pattern; and he does not! Alas, your Majesty, it cannot be. It is the new generation come; which cannot live quite as the old one did. A perennial controversy in human life; coeval with the genealogies of men. This little Boy should have been the excellent paternal Majesty's exact counterpart; resembling him, at all points, 'as a little sixpence does a big half-crown:' but we perceive he cannot. This is a new coin, with a stamp of its own. A surprising *Friedrich d'or* this; and may prove a good piece yet; but will never be the half-crown your Majesty requires![13]

Something of his native Calvinism informs Carlyle's depiction of humankind's limited freedoms in seeking to shape itself; Frederick the Great may have contradicted the eighteenth century, but he was shaped and directed by it nonetheless. Leslie Stephen rightly appreciated that Carlyle's investment in 'the German idea', namely his commitment to the new historical philosophies offered by the German Renaissance, meant that:

> a new light had dawned upon the world: that an escape was opened up from that wicked old eighteenth century, with its scepticism and its materialism, and that real survey must correspond to some appreciation of the great spiritual revolution of the age.[14]

[11] John Morley, 'Carlyle' in *Critical Miscellanies* (2 vols., London, 1886), i. 135–201, at pp. 141, 158.

[12] Thomas Carlyle, *History of Friedrich II of Prussia, Called Frederick the Great* (6 vols., London, 1858–65), i. 13.

[13] Ibid., 513.

[14] Stephen, 'The importation of German', in *Studies of a Biographer* (4 vols., London, 1902), ii. 38–75, at p. 71.

Notoriously, the Oxford Movement had little to do with German thought or historicism, and could instead be defined as a largely reactionary intellectual movement. It is to the leading light of that movement, John Henry Newman, and his lifelong engagement with the historian and religious sceptic Edward Gibbon, that the third chapter of this book is devoted. As an intellectually precocious schoolboy, Newman had enjoyed his own engagement with the sceptical eighteenth century, later recording in his *Apologia* how, in the year of Waterloo:

> When I was fourteen, I read Paine's Tracts against the Old Testament, and found pleasure in thinking of the objections which were contained in them. Also, I read some of Hume's Essays; and perhaps that on Miracles. So at least I gave my Father to understand; but perhaps it was a brag. Also, I recollect copying out some French verses, perhaps Voltaire's in denial of the immortality of the soul, saying to myself something like 'How dreadful, but how plausible!'

Leslie Stephen was quick to impute scepticism to Newman, as more recently has Frank M. Turner, who claims a closer relationship to Hume's scepticism on Newman's part than one might initially suspect, thus further deepening Newman's relations with eighteenth-century thought.[15] Newman, born in the 1800s, was closer to the eighteenth century than many scholars allow, and nowhere more so than in his admiring, if troubled, relationship with Gibbon's brand of ecclesiastical history. In tracing that relationship, the third chapter of this study demonstrates how enriching and lively intellectual relations were between the nineteenth and eighteenth centuries, even when the thoughts and individuals in question were, in many ways, unsympathetic to one another.

Leslie Stephen, his older brother James Fitzjames Stephen, and their father Sir James Stephen, were all fascinated by the eighteenth century. Sir James Stephen, a Colonial Office official who went on to hold the Regius Chair of Modern History at Cambridge, wrote about the period from a liberal Evangelical position in his *Essays in Ecclesiastical Biography*; Leslie and James Fitzjames chronicled the same age in essays and books from a position of religious unbelief. James Fitzjames Stephen was so preoccupied by the reach of the eighteenth century into his own experience that he wrote a two-volume study rebutting the charges of corruption against Warren Hastings and Elijah Impey made by

[15] J. H. Newman, *Apologia pro vita sua*, ed. Martin J. Svaglic (Oxford, 1967), 17; Leslie Stephen, 'Newman's theory of belief', in *An Agnostic's Apology and Other Essays* (London, 1893), 168–241; Frank M. Turner, *John Henry Newman: The Challenge to Evangelical Religion* (New Haven, 2002), 263, 330, 475–6, 504, 565.

Edmund Burke and Richard Brinsley Sheridan, a study originating in his own service as a legal official in colonial India.[16] Similarly, for Leslie Stephen a sometime priest who abandoned his profession for a lay career as a journalist and man of letters, the prehistory of Victorian agnosticism could be traced in the history of eighteenth-century deism and religious scepticism; this was not exactly Whiggish intellectual history, but it was decidedly a story with a beginning and a mid-point: the future of religion, however, was not a subject to which he gave much of his interpretative energy. The Stephen brothers moved some way from liberal Evangelicalism into principled unbelief, whilst their sister, Caroline Emelia, sought refuge in Quakerism, producing pioneering studies in both its history and its distinctive spirituality. For all three siblings, the eighteenth century maintained its fascination as an era in which much that preoccupied them as Victorian thinkers could be found to parallel their own contemporary experience, not least as a new age of faith, and also of unbelief, could be traced, as it was in Leslie Stephen's *History of English Thought in the Eighteenth Century*, alongside its earlier parallels with the age of Evangelical Revival and of a religiously sceptical experience of Enlightenment.

Leslie Stephen, so often engaged in highly serious analysis of what he called the 'history of opinion' during the eighteenth century, sometimes escaped to a lighter side of that period in his studies. Such an escape was one that led away from the complications of Victorian life to an allegedly simpler eighteenth century, and it was one in which the issue of class was, nonetheless, of serious and fundamental importance. In an essay on Gibbon, Stephen traced the 'peculiar pleasure of transplanting ourselves to the middle of the eighteenth century, when political revolutions and mechanical inventions had not yet turned things topsy-turvy'. The Victorian man of letters could thus imagine himself as a 'fine gentleman':

> When I indulge in day-dreams, I take flight with the help of Gibbon, or Boswell, or Horace Walpole, to that delightful period. I take the precaution, of course, to be born the son of a prime minister, or, at least, within the charmed circle where sinecure offices may be the reward of a judicious choice of parents. There, methinks, would be enjoyment, more than in this march of mind, as well as more than in the state of nature on the islands where one is mated with a squalid savage. There I can have philosophy enough to justify at once my self-complacency in my wisdom and acquiescence in established

[16] James Fitzjames Stephen, *The Story of Nuncomar and the Impeachment of Sir Elijah Impey* (London, 1885).

abuses. I make the grand tour for a year or two on the Continent, and find myself at once recognised as a philosopher or a statesman simply because I am an Englishman. I become an honorary member of the tacit cosmopolitan association of philosophers, which formed Parisian *salons*, or collected round Voltaire at Ferney. I bring home a sufficient number of pictures to ornament a comfortable villa on the banks of the Thames; and form a good solid library in which I write books for the upper circle, without bothering myself about the Social Question or Bimetallism, or swallowing masses of newspaper and magazine articles to keep myself up to date.[17]

Unfortunately, as Stephen the Darwinist knew, one could not choose one's parents, let alone heredity, and, as Stephen the literary journalist knew all too well, one had to read a lot of what he would have called 'chaff' in order to keep up to date. Was it this very Victorian reaction against Victorianism in favour of the eighteenth century part of the heredity that would inform Virgina Woolf when writing about the two periods in such contrasting registers in *Orlando*? As Chapter 4 in the present study, which is devoted to the Stephen family, will demonstrate, generational change was a subject of some moment in the consideration given to intellectual and literary history by the Stephen family as a whole.

The grandfather of Violet Paget, who acquired fame when she assumed the pen name of Vernon Lee, had abandoned England in the eighteenth century precisely because of his own Voltairian commitments to religious unbelief. Vernon Lee, who had a consciously lay education, inherited this commitment, and promoted it in several volumes of philosophical reflection, as well as shadowing it more obliquely in her ghost stories and studies in art history. In the final chapter of the present study, Lee's interests in the ghostly eighteenth century are traced alongside those of her Christian contemporary Montague Rhodes James, who rose to become Provost of King's College, Cambridge, and who knew the Stephen family through his friendship with J. K. Stephen, the son of James Fitzjames Stephen. (Vernon Lee would also become associated with the family, publishing as she ultimately did with the Hogarth Press, which had been founded and was managed by Virginia and Leonard Woolf.) The ghost story as a literary form provided a locus of sceptical reflection, and several of its practitioners, including Lee and Grant Allen, were decided secularists who used the form sceptically; James used it in quasi-religious terms, sceptical though he was about

[17] Leslie Stephen, 'Gibbon's autobiography', *Studies of a Biographer* (4 vols., London, 1902), i. 147–87, at pp. 152–3.

the actual existence of ghosts. As this chapter demonstrates, Victorians, especially late Victorians, were haunted by the eighteenth century, and this ghostly commingling of the eighteenth and nineteenth centuries continued well into the 1930s. Where Carlyle had sought to contain the eighteenth century in the 1830s, Lee and James were to demonstrate that its contagious presence was still to be felt as late as the 1930s, when it was to begin to enjoy a new lease of life freed from the ambivalences the Victorians felt about their own predecessor culture. It is to an exploration of these ambivalences that this book is devoted, and the plurality of narratives it analyses is a testimony to the strength that the eighteenth century held over the imaginations of Victorian thinkers. There are moments in this story when the eighteenth and nineteenth centuries meld almost imperceptibly together, and it is precisely for this reason that I have chosen to call the study *The Victorian Eighteenth Century*.

1

Carlyle and the 'Distracted Century'

> Immortality, mortality:—there were certain runaways whom Fritz the Great bullied back into the battle with a: '*R—, wollt ihr ewig leben*, Unprintable Offscouring of Scoundrels, would ye live for ever!'
>
> Thomas Carlyle, *The French Revolution*[1]

In *The Times* of 3 August 1837, an anonymous review appeared of a book whose narrative style and intellectual content definitively marked the end of the long dominant eighteenth-century register of historical writing. The reviewer, William Makepeace Thackeray, then a young man of 26, was to develop his own complex engagements with the Hanoverian period, as can be appreciated in the tone of his references to eighteenth-century historical eminences:

> But never did a book so grievously from outward appearance, or a man's style so mar his subject and dim his genius. It is stiff, short, and rugged, it abounds with Germanisms and Latinisms, strange epithets, and choking double words, astonishing to the admirers of simple Addisonian English, to those who love history as it gracefully runs in Hume, or struts pompously in Gibbon—no such style is Mr. Carlyle's. A man, at the first outset, must take breath at the end of a sentence, or, worse still, go to sleep in the midst of it. But those hardships become lighter as the traveller grows accustomed to the road, and he speedily learns to admire and sympathize; just as he would admire a Gothic cathedral in spite of the quaint carvings and hideous images on door and buttress.[2]

Something of the peculiarity of the style of the book so reviewed, Thomas Carlyle's *The French Revolution*, can be appreciated from the praise Carlyle had himself devoted in an essay published ten years

[1] *FR*, i. 331.

[2] William Makepeace Thackeray, unsigned review, *The Times*, 3 Aug. 1837, in Jules Paul Seigel (ed.), *Thomas Carlyle: The Critical Heritage* (London, 1971), 69–75, at p. 69.

earlier to Jean-Paul Richter, a German Romantic writer whom he much admired. It is a passage worth quoting in full, so close is the parallel to what the uninitiated reader faces when first confronting Carlyle's equally idiosyncratic prose style; it is as if Carlyle had alerted his readers in 1827 to what would confront them when they turned to his own magnum opus in 1837:

He is a phenomenon from the very surface; he presents himself with a professed and determined singularity; his language itself is a stone of stumbling to the critic; to critics of the grammarian species, an unpardonable, often an insuperable rock of offence. Not that he is ignorant of grammar, or disdains the sciences of spelling and parsing; but he exercises both in a certain latitudinarian spirit; deals with astonishing liberality in parentheses, dashes, and subsidiary clauses; invents hundreds of new words, alters old ones, or by hyphen chains and pairs and packs them together into most jarring combination; in short, produces sentences of the most heterogeneous, lumbering, interminable kind. Figures without limit; indeed the whole is one tissue of metaphors and similes, and allusions to all the provinces of Earth, Sea and Air; interlaced with epigrammatic breaks, vehement bursts, or sardonic turns, interjections, quips, puns, and even oaths! A perfect Indian jungle it seems; a boundless, unparalleled imbroglio; nothing on all sides but darkness, dissonance, confusion worse confounded![3]

Demanding, frequently startling, and complex though Carlyle's own prose style undoubtedly is, the contours of his response to the eighteenth century (during which his hero Richter wrote) can readily be traced throughout his historical writings. Expository exploration of the terrain so charted reveals a consistent response on Carlyle's part to the eighteenth century. What rapidly becomes evident is a series of interlocking convictions concerning the eighteenth century: a deep suspicion of its lack of heroism, either religious or political; its place as a historical rupture between the heroic age of the Reformation and the hollowness of modernity; the starkly contrasting roles played by France, Germany, and Britain in these developments; and, related to all of these aspects, the need for the prophet-historian to undo the secularizing worldliness of eighteenth-century philosophy if the soul of the nineteenth century were to be saved from this compromised inheritance. These themes will be explored in this and the following chapter chiefly, but not exclusively, in

[3] 'Jean Paul Friedrich Richter' in *CME*, i. 1–25, at pp. 11–12. For discussion of Carlyle's indebtedness to Richter's prose style, see Albert J. la Valley, *Carlyle and the Idea of the Modern: Studies in Carlyle's Prophetic Literature and its Relation to Blake, Nietzsche, Marx, and Others* (New Haven, 1968), 35–6, and Elizabeth M. Vida, *Romantic Affinities: German Authors and Carlyle: A Study in the History of Ideas* (Toronto, 1993), 170–80.

relation to the monumental works he devoted early and late in his career to what he called the sceptical eighteenth century: *The French Revolution* and his *History of Friedrich II of Prussia, Called Frederick the Great* (1858–65). It is remarkable that his historical career was propelled by reflection on the eighteenth century, and that it effectively ended with an extended meditation on its occasional glories and rather more frequent failings. Carlyle dominated British understanding of the eighteenth century in the reign of Victoria, and any greater understanding of that aspect of Victorian thought needs to consider Carlyle with becoming care and attention.[4]

It was not just as an interpreter of cultures joined by time, but also as a mediator between those linked through language and inheritance, that Carlyle promoted his self-appointed task as the leading poet-prophet of nineteenth-century British culture. Carlyle was the greatest and most effective catalyst of the 'German Idea' in the England of his day, and it is fitting that a pronouncedly critical account of France's impact on the world, as evinced in *The French Revolution*, should ultimately have been succeeded by a sustained hymn of epic praise to the Prussia of Frederick the Great, sustained over six lengthy volumes.[5] The history of the German language as a sacred tongue, a genuinely poetic language, was one of the great themes of Carlyle's writings, in which suspiciously easy fluency is always contrasted with the truthful complications of less facile world tongues. It resonates with what he claimed regarding his great English hero Cromwell's language:

> He that works and *does* some Poem, not he that merely *says* one, is worthy of the name of Poet. Cromwell, emblem of the dumb English, is interesting to me

[4] He is a pervasive presence in a recent collection of essays concerning the Victorian appreciation of eighteenth-century literary culture: 'Thomas Carlyle stood out as the most vocal of the Victorians to have apparently spurned the period, and to have constructed an image of moral and spiritual poverty, defined neither by heroes nor by faith but by "*spiritual paralysis.*"' Francis O'Gorman and Katherine Turner, 'Introduction' to O'Gorman and Turner (eds.), *The Victorians and the Eighteenth Century: Reassessing the Tradition* (Aldershot, 2004), 1–13, at p. 2.

[5] In addition to Vida, *Romantic Affinities*, for discussion of Carlyle's role as a translator and advocate of German literature and thought, see Rosemary Ashton, *The German Idea: Four English Writers and the Reception of German Thought, 1800–1860* (Cambridge, 1980), 67–104, and G. B. Tennyson, 'Carlyle as mediator of German language and thought', in Horst W. Drescher (ed.), *Thomas Carlyle 1981: Papers Given at the International Thomas Carlyle Centenary Symposium* (Frankfurt-am-Main, 1993), 263–79. For a useful placing of the history of Frederick within Carlyle's oeuvre, see John Clive, 'Carlyle's *Frederick the Great*', in *Not by Fact Alone: Essays on the Writing and Reading of History* (London, 1989), 86–106.

by the very inadequacy of his speech. Heroic insight, valour and belief, without words,—how noble is it in comparison to the adroitest flow of words without heroic insight![6]

Likewise, Carlyle's deep familiarity with the German language accorded with his own self-image as the poet-prophet of his age, and the close relationship of his custodianship of German literature with this imagined role is visible throughout the work with which he closed his writing career, *The History of Friedrich II of Prussia.* This is very apparent in the following pivotal linguistic moment in the first of the six volumes that constitute the final major work he published during his lifetime:

German, to this day, is a frightful dialect for the stupid, the pedant and dullard sort! Only in the hands of the gifted does it become supremely good. It had not yet been the language of any Goethe, any Lessing; though it had stood on the eve of becoming such. It had already been the language of Luther, of Ulrich Hutten, Friedrich Barbarossa, Charlemagne and others. And several extremely important things had been said in it, and some pleasant ones even sung in it, from an old date, in a very appropriate manner,—had Crown-Prince Friedrich known all that. But he could not reasonably be expected to know:—and the wiser Germans now forgive him for not knowing, and are even thankful that he did not.[7]

If the golden age of German literature was to emerge in the second half of the eighteenth century, its spiritual legacy had been laid down in the Reformation, and its political potential in the early middle ages: Frederick the Great was to incarnate all that was best in this legacy, giving life to later generations. Reading these volumes makes one realize that, if Frederick is the god (a 'new Phoebus Apollo risen in his wrath'), then Carlyle is the prophet of a German Renaissance which will necessarily encompass the English-speaking lands.[8] That Frederick emerged in the eighteenth century which Carlyle hated so much is one sign of his world-historical standing for Carlyle, whose political testimony is contained in these volumes as much as it is in the more famous, and rather more frequently consulted, *Latter-Day Pamphlets* (1850). Frederick's eighteenth century thus had much to teach Carlyle's nineteenth century. The Prussia in which Frederick emerged had also had much to teach others, and it was with something very like pride that Carlyle wrote of the impact of Prussian military lessons on the Russia of Peter the Great, noting that 'the Russian Art of War has a tincture

6 *OC*, i. 69. 7 *FG*, i. 390. 8 *FG*, v. 54.

of *German* in it (solid German, as contradistinguished from unsolid Revolutionary-French); and hints to us of Friedrich Wilhelm and the Old Dessauer, to this hour'.[9]

Not that everything German was so reliably exported: Carlyle's sarcasms about the House of Hanover in England are frequent and telling, as when he observes of their looking to George I for heroism that the English are: 'Always a singular People!'[10] This was a remarkable claim to be making in the middle years of Victoria's reign; it was also, of course, a remark made by a Scotsman. It is also remarkable how Scotsmen prosper in that unlikely source for their appearance, his life of Frederick. Thus Tobias Smollett's account of a battle in Silesia was like that 'of a highly intelligent Eyewitness, credible and intelligible in every way'. A Prussian scholar is celebrated as 'the Berlin Hugh Blair that then was'. Sir Andrew Mitchell, a diplomat, was

> by far the ablest Excellency England ever had in that Court. An Aberdeen Scotchman, creditable to his Country: hard-headed, sagacious; sceptical of shows; but capable of recognising substances withal; and of standing loyal to them, stubbornly if needful; who grew to a great mutual regard with Friedrich, and well deserved to do so; constantly about him, during the next seven years; and whose Letters are among the perennially valuable Documents on Friedrich's History.[11]

It is as if Mitchell were the precursor of Carlyle himself, another Scotsman possessing Scottish virtues interpreting a Prussian monarch to his English audience. Carlyle was also honest regarding those Scotsmen who were perceived to have failed in England, as when he declared that the 'great Pitt' had been thrown out and 'perverse small Bute come in'.[12]

Pitt the Elder was the solitary great English hero in the history of Frederick. Comparable with Frederick himself, he was also a superbly gifted speaker who just failed to make the Cromwellian grade. Carlyle observed that his speech was 'lively, ingenious, and though not quitting the Parliamentary tone for the Hebrew-Prophetic, far more serious than the modern reader thinks'.[13] It was important for Carlyle's anti-democratic politics that this was so, allowing him to conclude that Pitt's speeches 'are not Parliamentary Eloquences, but things which, with his whole soul he means, and is intent to *do*'.[14] Carlyle was to be Pitt's interpreter, finding in his words an insight into the providential

[9] *FG*, i. 461. [10] *FG*, i. 532–3. [11] *FG*, iii. 368; iv. 406, 538.
[12] *FG*, vi. 234. [13] *FG*, iv. 68, 65. [14] *FG*, iv. 67.

role assigned to England, as he concluded that: 'In a dialect different from Cromwell's or Pitt's, but with a sense true to theirs, I call it the Eternal Destinies knocking at England's door again.'[15] Critical though he frequently was of England, and occasionally keen to assert the superior insights of the Scots, Carlyle constantly repeated the particular role his adopted country had been set up to achieve: he was the apostle of German culture within the English nation, and his championing of Pitt—'a despotic sovereign, though a temporary one'—in a life of Frederick is symptomatic of this role, as is his fear that the English will fail to recognize this for themselves, as attested in their earlier failure to appreciate Pitt: 'Oh my English brothers, Oh my Yankee half-brothers, how oblivious are we of those that have done us benefit!'[16]

I

In pursuing Carlyle's fascination with the eighteenth century, it is first necessary to ask what sort of a narrator he was, since narrative was the very foundation of his conception of history. Narrative was, for Carlyle, at the centre of what it was to be human, and the basic appetite for narrative progressed from everyday conversation to the supreme effort involved in understanding the totality of knowledge. This claim was instantiated in his essay 'On History', first published in *Fraser's Magazine* in 1830:

> Most men, you may observe, speak only to narrate; not in imparting what they have thought, which indeed were often only a very small matter, but in exhibiting what they have undergone or seen, which is a quite unlimited one, do talkers dilate. Cut us off from Narrative, how would the stream of conversation, even among the wisest, languish into detached handfuls, and among the foolish utterly evaporate! Thus, as we do nothing but enact History, we say little but recite it; nay, rather, in that widest sense, our whole spiritual life is built thereon. For, strictly considered, what is all Knowledge too but recorded Experience, and a product of History; of which, therefore, Reasoning and Belief, no less than Action and Passion, are essential materials?[17]

[15] *FG*, iv. 65.

[16] *FG*, v. 492, 561; vi. 334. Characteristically, when eulogizing Pitt, Carlyle adverts to his solemn conviction that there would be no more Pitts in England's parliament: *FG*, vi. 555–7.

[17] 'On History', *HE*, 3–13, at p. 4.

Carlyle's conception of history was uniquely personal and decidedly capacious, and this affected the form as well as the content of his historical writings. He was constantly playing with genres, from his first major work, *Sartor Resartus* (1833–4), to his last major piece of writing to be published during his lifetime, his history of Frederick the Great. As Alastair Fowler notes, 'No satirist is more self-conscious, or more communicative, about his art's farragolike character than Carlyle.' As Fowler also goes on to notice, Carlyle's work reaches a sublime point at which its constituent elements of several mixed genres attain the status of epic:[18] this observation holds true of both Carlyle's work on the French Revolution and that concerning Frederick. Indeed, the daring presumption of the implied comparison drawn by Carlyle at the close of *The French Revolution* is quite startling: 'Homer's Epos, it is remarked, is like a Bas-Relief sculpture: it does not conclude, but merely ceases. Such, indeed, is the Epos of Universal History itself.'[19] The whole work ceases in an almost bardic manner, with its echoes of the disputed origins of the Homeric epic and of Jeremiah, as the written becomes the oral, and then the oral in turn becomes the written:

And so here, O Reader, has the time come for us two to part. Toilsome was our journeying together; not without offence; but it is done. To me thou wert as a beloved shade, the disembodied or not yet embodied spirit of a Brother. To thee I was but as a Voice. Yet was our relation a kind of sacred one; doubt not that! For whatsoever once sacred things become hollow jargons, yet while the Voice of Man speaks with Man, hast thou not there the living fountain out of which all sacrednesses sprang, and will yet spring? Man, by the nature of him, is definable as 'an incarnated Word'. Ill stands it with me if I have spoken falsely: thine also it was to hear truly. Farewell.[20]

It was Carlyle's obsession with speech and with time that informed so much of his play with genres, as can be appreciated from his fleeting meditation on the theme in *The French Revolution*:

What unutterable things the stone-walls spoke, during these five years! But it is all gone; To-day swallowing Yesterday, and then being in its turn swallowed

[18] Alastair Fowler, *Kinds of Literature: An Introduction to the Theory of Genres and Modes* (Oxford, 1982), 123–6, 190, 228.

[19] *FR*, ii. 451. For a reading of the work as a mock epic, demonstrating the impossibility of a modern, historical epic for Carlyle, see Chris R. Vanden Bossche, *Carlyle and the Search for Authority* (Columbus, Oh., 1991), 40–89.

[20] *FR*, ii. 453.

of To-morrow, even as Speech ever is. Nay what, O thou immortal Man of Letters, is writing itself but Speech conserved for a time?[21]

This was something he could satirize, as in a speech from June 1790 uncertainly reported in a revolutionary periodical, the *Moniteur*:

A long-flowing Turk, for rejoinder, bows with Eastern solemnity, and utters articulate sounds: but owing to his imperfect knowledge of the French dialect, his words are like spilt water; the thought he had in him remains conjectural to this day.[22]

It could also lead him to contemplate the stern pathos of silence: 'one's heart flutters on the verge of dread unutterabilities'.[23] The silence of death could also be supremely articulate, as in his evocation of the corpse of Jerôme l'Héritier, a member of the National Guard killed by the Maenad-like 'insurrection of women' at Versailles: 'there shall the livid face and smashed head, dumb for ever, *speak*'.[24] Speech and writing are of the essence in Carlyle's double conception of history as event and of history as record: hence much of the power of his description of Louis XV as 'a solecism incarnate', and the mordant satire of his frequently repeated topos of constitution-making as the construction of a theory of irregular verbs.[25] Words were redolent both of pathos and of power, both living and extinct. Their deployment *in* time, Carlyle insisted, was also an aspect of human psychology at its most basic:

For indeed it is a most lying thing that same Past Tense always: so beautiful, sad, almost Elysian-sacred, 'in the moonlight of Memory', it seems; and *seems* only. For observe, always one most important element is surreptitiously (we not noticing it) withdrawn from the Past Time: the haggard element of Fear! Not *there* does Fear dwell, nor Uncertainty, nor Anxiety; but it dwells *here*; haunting us, tracking us; running like an accursed ground-discord through all the music-tones of our Existence;—making the Tense a mere Present one![26]

His play on the resonances of the word 'tense' is indicative of the sort of linguistic watchfulness that pervades his writings. It is, therefore, at once surprising that Carlyle was not subjected to the tropological readings of nineteenth-century historical writing famously laid out by Hayden White, and also not surprising at all, since it would be hard to pin down

[21] *FR*, i. 331. [22] *FR*, i. 355.

[23] *FR*, i. 479, 481. On the importance of speech and silence in Carlyle, see John D. Rosenberg, 'Carlyle: history and the human voice', in *Elegy for an Age: The Presence of the Past in Victorian Literature* (London, 2005), 13–31.

[24] *FR*, i. 289. [25] *FR*, i. 23, 225, 230, 233, 320, 438. [26] *FR*, ii. 204.

the sheer generic verve of Carlyle according to any of the somewhat halting procedures promoted by White. White's fleeting reference to Carlyle as a historian whose work rests on the nostalgia of recovering the past as a wholly integrated entity, in which nothing is missing, allowing the wholeness of a concert of individual lives to be heard in the poetic reconstruction of the past, is, nevertheless, a valuable contribution to understanding this most literary of historians.[27]

White's characterization of Carlyle's self-imposed task offers a lucid insight into the construction of *The French Revolution*, which can be read as a poem; similarly, when writing about Frederick and his people, Carlyle was also and consciously very much their self-appointed poet, since 'the Prussian Muse of History, choked with dry military pipeclay, or with husky cobwebbery and academic pedantry', is allegedly incapable of celebrating her heroes, whose sacrifice is celebrated by Carlyle in language redolent of neoclassical homoeroticism:

> They lie there, with their blond young cheeks and light hair; beautiful in death;—could not have done better, though the sacred poet has said nothing of them hitherto,—nor need, till times mend with us and him. Adieu, my noble young Brothers; so brave, so modest, no Spartan, nor no Roman more; may the silence be blessed to you![28]

The city of Frankfurt, likewise, had suffered an 'Iliad of miseries'.[29] There are echoes here of his claim, made some twenty years before, that the 'Puritan Revolt' might be considered as a '*Cromwelliad*'.[30] Both the Frankfurt *Iliad* and the English *Cromwelliad* were the heroic products of Protestantism; the seeds of Prussian nationhood had germinated in the Reformation, and were as real as *ancien régime* France had proved unreal. It was, then, with a strong edge of irony that Carlyle had noted that the epithet 'Great' was 'not uncommon among petty German nations'.[31] Parallels with Carlyle's Scottish experience are not too hard to find in this praise for Prussia, one of whose greatest virtues was that of thrift, the general secret of which 'is lost from the world'. Furthermore, when Carlyle praises the Prussian peasant poet Frau Karsch, echoes of his own history are discernible for the informed reader. The wistfulness of this passage is deeply felt:

[27] Hayden White, *Metahistory: The Historical Imagination in Nineteenth-Century Europe* (Baltimore, 1973), 146. Carlyle, disappointingly, does not merit a mention in either *Tropics of Discourse: Essays in Cultural Criticism* (Baltimore, 1978), or in *The Content of the Form: Narrative Discourse and Historical Representation* (Baltimore, 1987). Carlyle would seem to be supremely resistant to theories of narrative.

[28] *FG*, v. 141, 306. [29] *FG*, v. 459. [30] *OC*, i. 10. [31] *FG*, i. 343.

The child of utterly poor Peasants there; whose poverty, shining out as thrift, unwearible industry and stoical valour, is beautiful to me, still more their little girl's bits of fortunes, 'tending three cows' in the solitudes there, and gazing wistfully into Earth and Heaven with her ingenuous little soul,—desiring mainly one thing, that she could get Books, any Book whatever; having half-accidentally picked up the art of reading, and finding hereabouts absolutely nothing to read.[32]

There are many registers in Carlyle's *Friedrich*, and this brief pastoral interlude is of a piece with the nostalgia which pervades this consciously ramshackle epic. John Holloway interpreted it as an 'attempted epic', reading it as an extended exercise in cosmology, a gallery of acute and deeply felt psychological portraits whose complementary diversity accumulated into Carlyle's richest and most detailed work as 'moral sage'.[33] If one were to seek a catch-all genre for the work one could well lift his description of some 6,000 of the 'lawless heroic' of Frederick's soldiers, thereby christening the volumes as specimens of what he called the 'bastard heroic'.[34] What is certain, however, is that an implicit contrast has to be drawn between Carlyle's nineteenth-century conception of the epic, and that represented by Voltaire's much-admired *Henriade,* whose status Carlyle sarcastically devalued in his use of quotation marks around 'Epic' in his own text.[35]

Carlyle is a narrator who uses many modes, many genres, one of which is distinctly and appropriately eighteenth century in character. Ruth apRoberts has read the history of Frederick the Great as an exercise in Shandean humour, making much of the fleeting appearances made in the text by Laurence Sterne's ensign father.[36] There is indeed much to be said for this reading; its comedy is dark, however, and there is an echo of Marx's famous dictum in *The Eighteenth Brumaire of Louis Napoleon* regarding tragedy being replayed as farce, when Carlyle declares, towards the very close of his six volumes, that: 'Something of Farce will often enough, in this irreverent world, intrude itself on the most solemn Tragedy; but, in pity even to the Farce, there ought at

[32] *FG*, v. 397; vi. 606.

[33] John Holloway, *The Victorian Sage: Studies in Argument* (London, 1953), 75–85.

[34] *FG*, vi. 327. [35] *FG*, ii. 7.

[36] Ruth apRoberts, 'The historian as Shandean humorist: Carlyle and Frederick the Great', in David R. Sorensen and Rodger L. Tarr (eds.), *The Carlyles at Home and Abroad* (Aldershot, 2004), 14–26. For references to Sterne and his military father, see *FG*, i. 560; ii. 4.

least to be closed doors kept between them.'[37] It is also the work of a self-conscious poet-historian, who, when describing the Battle of Prague in 1757, states that at its height there was, 'as the old *Niebelungen* has it, a "murder grim and great" going on'.[38] Something of the epic poet's task is indicated when, in attempting to describe the battle, Carlyle, like Tolstoy after him, is forced to declare:

> but in what sequence done, under what exact vicissitudes of aspect, special steps of cause and effect, no man can say; and only imagination, guided by these few data, can paint to itself. Such a chaotic whirlwind of blood, dust, mud, artillery-thunder, sulphurous rage, and human death and victory,—who shall pretend to describe it, or draw, except in the gross, the scientific plan of it?[39]

What Carlyle says of battle might be said of any attempt to understand his own *Friedrich*; and all readers will sympathize with a moment of authorial insight which occurs mid-way through the third of the six volumes comprising the work: 'Alive to any considerable degree, in the poor human imagination, this Editor does not expect or even wish the Austrian-Succession War to be. Enough for him if it could be understood sufficiently to render his poor History of Friedrich intelligible.'[40] The desire to write history as the experience of life had informed Carlyle's efforts since the 1830s, as when he declared in his essay on 'The Diamond Necklace' in 1837 that 'the Romance of Life' had gone 'wholly out of sight', leaving

> all History degenerating into empty invoice-lists of Pitched Battles and Changes of Ministry; or, still worse, into 'Constitutional History,' or 'Philosophy of History,' or 'Philosophy teaching by Experience,' is become dead, as the Almanacks of other years,—to which species of composition, indeed, it bears, in several points of view, no inconsiderable affinity.[41]

The historical genre was not, then, for Carlyle exactly heroic when left in the hands of mere historians.

Carlyle, the poet-historian perpetually chafing at the bit imposed by the disciplinary boundaries of history writing and the requirements of historical intelligibility, also saw in the written word glimpses of the heroic at least as much as he saw it manifested in political actions. Carlyle was a supremely literary historian.[42] In his edition of *The Letters*

[37] *FG*, vi. 690 [38] *FG*, v. 39. [39] *FG*, v. 41 [40] *FG*, iii. 334

[41] 'The Diamond Necklace', *HE*, 86.

[42] Philippa Levine excused her lack of discussion of Carlyle in her account of the professionalization of history in the nineteenth century by emphasizing his place within

and Speeches of Oliver Cromwell (1845), Carlyle constantly adverted to this equivalent importance of word and deed, pointing out that the day on which Cromwell was admitted a fellow-commoner at Sidney Sussex College, Cambridge, was also the day on which Shakespeare had died, that Milton's burial took place in the same church in which Cromwell had married his wife, and even that both Samuel Johnson and Cromwell were hypochondriacs (what the Tory Johnson would have made of this comparison with Cromwell is sensibly left unremarked by Carlyle).[43] He also saw in the inspired writings of the historian as prophet a spiritual analogue to the task of the theologian, as instanced in his critique of the merely academic historian figured as Dryasdust, a constant butt of his ire:

> Modern Dryasdust, interpreting the mysterious ways of Divine Providence in this Universe, or what he calls writing History, has done uncountable havoc upon the best interests of mankind. Hapless godless dullard that he is; driven and driving on courses that lead only downward, for him as for us!'[44]

His work on Cromwell had also confirmed his self-image as the editor, a pose played out in *Sartor Resartus* and which has been traced back to his review of John Wilson Croker's much-disputed edition of Boswell's *Life of Johnson*;[45] an early nineteenth-century version of the greatest work of eighteenth-century biography was to prove pivotal for Carlyle, as can be appreciated from the editorial imagery of all of his subsequent book-length narratives, from *Past and Present* (1843), with its reflections on Jocelin of Brakelond's life of Abbot Samson, to Carlyle's own life of Frederick the Great, littered as it is with remarks on the editorial labours of himself and the other editors whose work informed his monumental study. He was always ready to play a game with his readers on this score, as when he excuses the sheer size of his six-volume history of Frederick: 'Brevity, this Editor knows, is extremely desirable, and that the scissors should be merciless on those sad paper-Heaps, intolerable to the modern mind; but, unless the modern mind chanced to prefer ease and darkness, what can an Editor do?'[46]

an older, essayistic, belle-lettrist tradition: *The Amateur and the Professional: Antiquarians, Historians and Archaeologists in Victorian England 1838–1886* (Cambridge, 1986), 3, 24.

[43] *OC*, i. 35, 41, 44. [44] *FG*, i. 202–3.

[45] Vanessa L. Ryan, 'The unreliable editor: Carlyle's *Sartor Resartus* and the art of biography', *Review of English Studies*, 54 (2003), 287–307. There are also German influences at work in Carlyle's deployment of the editor image: see Vida, *Romantic Affinities*, 45–51.

[46] *FG*, iii. 604.

As his edition of Cromwell's speeches and letters also demonstrated, Carlyle's editorial practice assumed the form of narrative, a narrative in this instance which affected all subsequent study of his subject; one can only infer that he had sought the same for his biography of Frederick, but the subsequent effect was absolutely nothing like so powerful or influential. A large proportion of these differing receptions can be attributed to the fact that Carlyle was a fervent champion of the English experience of the seventeenth century; stating that English Puritanism was 'the last of all our Heroisms', he had hoped to make a bridge between that heroic past and the singularly unheroic present, transcending the 'Philosophical Histories' and 'torpedo narratives' that had intervened—in the eighteenth and early nineteenth centuries—in the process.[47] It was those philosophical histories and the atmosphere in which they had emerged that made it neither possible nor desirable to bridge the eighteenth century with its successor age; the eighteenth century was about as unheroic as it was possible for an age to be in Carlyle's estimation, yet it was the age with which he was most determinedly engaged in his writings. Why was this? What did Carlyle hope would emerge from such labour? The answers to these questions reveal much about the Victorian eighteenth century, and about the conceptions of history and religion that emerged in their preoccupation with their predecessor culture.

The fundamental development that marked out the seventeenth from the eighteenth century for Carlyle was the growth of unbelief—a fundamental view that he might well have derived from the German author Novalis—as when he remarked in 1845 of English Puritanism, that it had been 'A practical world based on belief in God;—such as many centuries had seen before, but as never any century since has been privileged to see. It was the last glimpse of it in our world, this of English Puritanism: very great, very glorious; tragical enough to all thinking hearts that look on it from these days of ours.'[48] The Victorians

[47] *OC*, 1–3. For a magisterial reading of Carlyle's edition and its place in the development of English historiography, see Blair Worden, 'Thomas Carlyle and Oliver Cromwell', *Proceedings of the British Academy*, 105 (2000), 131–70. On the wider context of Carlyle's Cromwellian thinking, see Blair Worden, 'The Victorians and Oliver Cromwell', in Stefan Collini, Richard Whatmore, and Brian Young (eds.), *History, Religion, and Culture: British Intellectual History, 1750–1950* (Cambridge, 2000), 112–35.

[48] *OC*, i. 71. On Carlyle and Novalis's view of the eighteenth century as an age of unbelief, see René Wellek, 'Carlyle and the philosophy of history', *Philological Quarterly*, 23 (1944), 555–76, at p. 561.

were divided from the glory days of English Puritanism by 'the dead ashes of some six unbelieving generations'.[49] The eighteenth century had thus opened up the tragic momentum that the nineteenth century seemed destined to maintain; it was a period that looked very like a second Fall to Carlyle the sceptical Scottish Puritan, the chronicler not only of Cromwell's Puritanism, but also, and no less heroically, of Robert Baillie's Scottish Covenanters.[50] Its attempts at salvation were always compromised by its distance from the religious energies of the seventeenth century, a situation made explicit in his Cromwell edition when comparing the divinely orientated aspirations of the Puritan Revolt with the subject of his earlier historical masterpiece: 'In other somewhat sadly disfigured form, we have seen the same immortal hope take practical shape in the French Revolution, and once more astonish the world.'[51] Cromwell would also appear in his final history in a section concerning the 'meaning of the Reformation', as Carlyle observed that Cromwell and the Puritans had made England 'habitable even under Charles-Second terms for a couple of centuries more'.[52] It was in the reign of Charles II that heroism had died in Carlyle's moralizing chronology, a theme first elaborated in *Past and Present* and shortly thereafter constantly reiterated, as a *leitmotif*, of political and religious corruption, in the *Latter-Day Pamphlets*.[53] The Restoration of all that Cromwell had battled with marked for Carlyle the essentially intertwined declension of both politics and religion.

Carlyle's histories thus enact his early estimation of the primary role accorded to the political historian, whose labours are but a part of the wider enterprise shaped by historians, and:

> Foremost among these comes the Ecclesiastical Historian; endeavouring, with catholic or sectarian view, to trace the progress of the Church, of that portion of the whole establishments, which respects our religious condition, as the other portion does our civil, or rather, in the long run, our economical condition. Rightly conducted, this department were undoubtedly the more important of the two; inasmuch as it concerns us more to understand how man's moral well-being had been and might be promoted, than to understand in the like sort his physical well-being; which latter is ultimately the aim of all Political arrangements.

[49] *OC*, i. 3.

[50] 'Baillie the Covenanter', *HE*, 239–69. On the supposed superiority of the defenders of the Solemn League and Covenant over French revolutionaries, see *FR*, i. 345, 351.

[51] *OC*, i. 72. [52] *FG*, i. 264. [53] *PP*, 149.

This sense of the proper prevalence of the religious aspect of man's being precluded conventional ecclesiastical history from performing a primary role in shaping man's historical understanding, as it was all too frequently concerned only with the outward appearances of religion, its churches and its access to political power, and all too infrequently with the spiritual core of belief. His own shaping of the religious within his histories is shadowed in his consequent assertion that 'The History of the Church is a History of the Invisible as well as of the Visible Church; which latter, if disjoined from the former, is but a vacant edifice; gilded, it may be, and overhung with old votive gifts, yet useless, nay pestilentially unclean; to write whose history is less important than to forward its downfall'.[54] This pessimistic assessment is at the core of Carlyle's chronicle of the history of European humanity; it is a decidedly postlapsarian account.

Carlyle had written four essays concerning the French eighteenth century in addition to his major work on the theme, one of which appeared four years before the publication of his *French Revolution*, the remaining three essays appearing the same year, 1837, and all of which concentrated on what he called, in his essay on the 'Parliamentary History of the French Revolution', 'the event of these modern ages'.[55] His aversion to the eighteenth century was markedly present in his 1833 essay devoted to 'Count Caglisotro', 'the most perfect scoundrel that in these latter ages has marked the world's history'. Characterizing his anti-hero as 'the Quack of Quacks', Carlyle denounced eighteenth-century Europe as an age of quackery and worse than quackery, as an alleged age of reason gave vent to an outburst of the Gothic:

It was the very age of impostors, cut-purses, swindlers, double-goers, enthusiasts, ambiguous persons; quacks and quackeries of all colours and kinds. How many Mesmerists, Magicians, Cabalists, Swedenborgians, Illuminati, Crucified Nuns, and Devils of Loudun! To which the Inquisition Biographer adds Vampires, Sylphs, Rosicrucians, Freemasons, and an *Etcetera*. Consider your Schröpfers, Cagliostros, Casanovas, Saint-Germains, Dr. Grahams; the Chevalier d'Eon, Psalmanazar, Abbé Paris, and the Ghost of Cock-lane! As if Bedlam had broken loose; as if rather, in that 'spiritual Twelfth-hour of the Night,' the everlasting Pit had opened itself, and from *its* still blacker bosom had issued Madness and all manner of shapeless Misbirths, to masquerade and chatter there.[56]

54 'On history', *HE*, 10–11.

55 'Parliamentary history of the French Revolution', *HE*, 219–38, at p. 219.

56 'Count Cagliostro', *HE*, 23–83, at pp. 26, 52, 82, 41. On Carlyle and Cagliostro, see Iain McCalman, *The Seven Ordeals of Count Cagliostro: The Many Lives of the Greatest Adventurer of the Eighteenth Century* (London, 2003), 3, 242–44.

Cagliostro flourished in an atmosphere of 'prurient brute-mindedness' in 'the most deceivable of modern ages'; it was in this credulous epoch that the French Revolution, 'the stern Avatar of DEMOCRACY', first stirred.[57] In the 'Memoirs of Mirabeau', Carlyle was explicit about the purpose and reach of his study of the Revolution, detailing the shift in generational perspective that made his perspective both possible and desirable:

A second generation, relieved in some measure from the spectral hallucinations, hysterical opthalmia, and natural panic-delirium of the first contemporary one, is gradually coming to discern and measure what its predecessor could only execrate and shriek over: for, as our Proverb said, the dust is sinking, the rubbish-heaps disappear; the built house, such as it is, and was appointed to be, stands visible, better or worse.[58]

It was the duty of the young of the nineteenth century to reject the work that had been undertaken by the young in 1789, thereby promoting the intergenerational dialectic that constituted history.[59] By turning the French Revolution into a history, Carlyle was marking out the territory between the eighteenth and the nineteenth centuries, a space in which much of the destruction that it had caused, particularly of religion, might yet be undone. His writing of that history was, in its own creative way, part of that vitally necessary undoing of much that the Revolution had spawned.

II

Carlyle's *The French Revolution* was the historical masterpiece which inaugurated the reign of Victoria in 1837, marking out the Victorian from the Hanoverian generations; an awareness of its intellectual and

[57] 'Count Cagliostro', *HE*, 63, 40.

[58] 'Memoirs of Mirabeau', *HE*, 153–217, at p. 158.

[59] Thus *FR*, i. 149, on the procession to the Estates General, with its complicatedly generative appeal to classical precedent, and its implied relations with Carlyle's reader: 'Till thirty the Spartans did not suffer a man to marry; but how many people here under thirty; coming to produce not one sufficient citizen, but a nation and a world as such! The old to heap up rents; the young to remove rubbish:—which latter, is it not, indeed the task here?' In this context, 'here' would seem to connote both the task facing the youthful regeneration of revolutionary France, and that in which Carlyle colluded with his young, newly Victorian readers in undoing its negative achievements For an instance of generational revenge, see *FR*, i. 216, and for a critique of an 'irrational generation', see *FR*, i. 315.

cultural primacy in the years that followed is, as Carlyle says of the history of Frederick the Great's family in his extraordinary *Schwanengesang*, 'another hook to hang Chronology upon'.[60] It was effectively a generational revolt in print, as the newly begun Victorian era immediately interrogated the defining revolutionary moment that separated *ancien régime* Europe from a self-consciously industrial and commercial modernity. Two further points can be made in relation to this foundational affirmation of this distance between two cultures, as this was elaborated in Carlyle's great history.

The first and more obvious point to be made is that Carlyle, the preeminent Victorian sage, was not himself a Victorian, but a product of the closing years of the Scottish Enlightenment and of the international atmosphere of late Romanticism. Born in 1795, he was over 40 when Victoria ascended the throne.[61] When he claimed in his *History of Friedrich II of Prussia*, the work of a self-conscious old man, that events dating back to 1791 were 'almost our own day',[62] he was quietly drawing attention to the fact that he had been born in the middle of that decade, and was therefore part of an older dispensation than that to which many, if not most, of his later readers belonged.[63] Few historians have been as conscious of their audience as Carlyle proved to be, and few have been as influential in shaping the historical tastes of that audience.

The second less obvious, but no less significant point, is that *The French Revolution* heralded a new and revolutionary conception of historical writing as unlike that operating in the work of historians writing immediately before its appearance as could readily be conceived. The style of history writing initiated by Carlyle was to prove deeply influential on the way history was composed and thought about throughout Victoria's reign. As Thackeray had immediately appreciated, it was a long way from the historical styles initiated by David Hume, William Robertson, and Edward Gibbon; it was also distant from the historical

60 *FG*, i. 320.

61 He shared his year of birth with John Keats, and the complications that result for the periodization of literary and intellectual history can begin to be appreciated in C. C. Barfoot (ed.), *Victorian Keats and Romantic Carlyle: The Fusions and Confusions of Literary Periods* (DQR Studies in Literature, 27) (Amsterdam, 1999).

62 *FG*, i. 226.

63 It is worth remembering that when Carlyle published his entry on Pitt the Younger for the *Edinburgh Encyclopaedia*, he could remind his readers that Bishop Tomline of Winchester, Pitt's sometime Cambridge tutor, was still producing his multi-volume biography of his illustrious pupil: 'William Pitt, the Younger', *CME*, v. 152–67, at p. 153.

style of T. B. Macaulay, who was much more obviously (if ambivalently) indebted to the late Enlightenment, both conceptually and in terms of literary taste and judgement, than was Carlyle.[64] The Victorian epoch was born as a historical age with Carlyle's reflection on the defining rupture of modernity, and consideration of that rupture demonstrated how strongly present the eighteenth century was in much of the thought of the Victorian era.[65] John Stuart Mill's perceptive and (for him) rhapsodic review of the work made much of the fact that here was a new style of history, defiantly distant from the neoclassical models promoted by the British eighteenth-century masters. It was distant from, and superior to, those models, both conceptually and stylistically, as Mill emphasized in the telling opening to his appreciation in the *London and Westminster Review* for July 1837:

> This is not so much a history, as an epic poem; and notwithstanding, or even in consequence of this, the truest of histories. It is the history of the French Revolution, and the poetry of it, both in one; and on the whole no work of greater genius, either historical or poetical, has been produced in this country for many years.[66]

In order to situate the originality of Carlyle's text, not least its peculiar narrative status as an epic poem that somehow, and somewhat strangely, made its historical character even stronger, it is important to bear in mind the slightly earlier, contemporaneous, and later appearances of the various essays on the early period of the Revolution written by John Wilson Croker, the Tory politician, confidant of Sir Robert Peel, and literary journalist. Croker's essays appeared over a thirty-year period, beginning ten or so years before Carlyle's history was published, continuing into the next two decades, and were finally published together in 1857, shortly after his death. As with Carlyle, Croker, a slightly older man, traced his own interest in the French Revolution and its aftermath to its having been (in his case, literally) contemporaneous

64 Peter Ghosh, 'Macaulay and the heritage of the Enlightenment', *English Historical Review*, 112 (1997), 358–95. On which traditions, and in particular, Carlyle's self-conscious distance from them, see Mark Salber Phillips, *Society and Sentiment: Genres of Historical Writing in Britain, 1740–1820* (Princeton, 2000), 345–6, 349.

65 For an understanding of Carlyle's unique place in such historical meditation, see Hedva Ben-Israel, *English Historians of the French Revolution* (Cambridge, 1968), 127–47, 275–82.

66 John Stuart Mill, 'Carlyle's French Revolution', in *The Collected Works of John Stuart Mill*, xx: *Essays on French History and Historians*, ed. John M. Robson (Toronto, 1985), 131–66, at p. 133. For Mill's distancing of Carlyle from Hume, Robertson, and Gibbon, see pp. 136–7.

with his birth, and to the allied fact that the modern history of France into the mid-nineteenth century was very much a contemporary history of the longevity of the revolution. As an Anglo-Irishman, Croker looked on France with even more passionate eyes than would a contemporary Englishman, and just as Carlyle, a Scot, sought to teach the English about the true nature of the political cataclysm across the Channel, so Croker thought it his duty to remind his readers of the political lessons to be drawn from it, lessons that had been drawn immediately by his fellow Irishman, Edmund Burke (referred to, intriguingly, by Carlyle as 'English Burke').[67]

What is also interesting, however, is the scant notice that Croker gave to Carlyle's *French Revolution.* Writing as late as 1856, Croker described the French statesman Thiers (whose studies of the French Revolution he had noticed very critically in the *Quarterly Review* in 1845), as seeming to be 'now the most popular, and I fear the most influential historian' of those events.[68] In this, Croker was at one with Peel, who, writing to Croker a year after Carlyle's history had appeared, made the following observations:

> I have a new thought—at least new to me—with respect to the French Revolution, or rather to publications on that inexhaustible subject. I have just been reading Thiers again, and I think, considering his position, and the advantages it must have given him, there will be no call for a new history for some time; with the exception of his evident partiality towards the Gironde, and particularly Roland, I think his work is well done. He makes good use of the records of the Jacobin Club. But what think you of a 'Revolutionary Encyclopaedia'?[69]

For Peel (who acquired heroic stature in Carlyle's *Latter-Day Pamphlets*), there was, after the publications of Thiers, patently no need for the sort of narrative Carlyle had written; what was needed, in Peel's opinion, was a work detailing the prosopography, topography, and

[67] John Wilson Croker, *Essays on the Early Period of the French Revolution* (London, 1857), 'Preface', pp. v–vii, and *passim*; Carlyle, *FR* i. 325. On Croker as a historian, especially of the French Revolution, see William Thomas, *The Quarrel of Macaulay and Croker: Politics and History in the Age of Reform* (Oxford, 2000), 36, 42, 48–9, 52, 162–209, 253–54.

[68] Croker, 'Preface', and 'Thiers' Histories', in *Essays*, pp. vii, 1–71.

[69] Peel to Croker, 1 Nov. 1838, in Louis J. Jennings (ed.), *The Croker Papers: The Correspondence and Diaries of the Late Right Honourable John Wilson Croker, LL.D., F.R.S., Secretary to the Admiralty from 1809 to 1830* (3 vols., London, 1884), ii. 334.

chronology of the Revolution for British readers.[70] Tories were naturally interested in understanding the Revolution, and the ambiguous politics of Carlyle's account, more sympathetic to a radical such as John Stuart Mill, were to play no part in the immediate evolution of such an understanding. Croker's own preference was for contemporaneous studies of the Revolution, as in the praise meted out by him in 1835 to John Adolphus's *Biographical Memoirs of the French Revolution* (1799), which he economically eulogized as 'the best English work—indeed, we may say the best work—on the subject'.[71]

Adolphus's account was decidedly Tory, replete with a dedication to William Windham, Pitt's secretary of state for war: 'whose early discernment of the real tendency, and uniform opposition to the progress of the French Principles, have entitled you to the gratitude of your Country, and to the admiration of Europe.' The tone of the work was immediately apparent in Adolphus's preface, with its disavowal of the 'sanguine innovators, who, under a pretence of ameliorating the condition of mankind, meditated the subversion of social order'. Adolphus's regrets for France ten years after the outbreak of the Revolution betray the counter-revolutionary temper that would come to inform so much British reflection; Croker's views were deeply rooted in such instinctive distaste:

> The historian . . . may, without prescribing the precise line of conduct pursued by every individual, speak in terms of appropriate abhorrence of the tyranny and hypocrisy of the Government: he may portray with the energy of indignant virtue, the fraud, rapacity, cruelty, and general profligacy of that system which exposes a nation, evinced in the social arts, in politeness, and in every branch of useful and elegant knowledge, whom situation and science have qualified to enlighten and protect, the scourge and stigma of the human race.[72]

Interestingly, in the light of Carlyle's developing enthusiasm for Cromwell in the years in which he was composing his *French Revolution*, Adolphus had referred to Carlyle's greatest English hero no fewer than three times in his memoir of Robespierre, first disapprovingly, but then

[70] Jules Seigel, 'Carlyle and Peel: The prophet's search for a heroic politician and an unpublished fragment', *Victorian Studies*, 26 (1983), 181–95. Intriguingly, Carlyle had echoed Peel's neologism 'popularize' in the work Peel ignored: 'and so by substance and show, shall Royalty, if man's art can popularize it, be popularized'. Louis was also 'getting popularized at Paris'. *FR*, i. 305, 337, and editorial note at ii. 479.

[71] Croker, 'Robespierre', in *Essays*, 299–430, note to p. 348.

[72] John Adolphus, *Biographical Memoirs of the French Revolution* (2 vols., London, 1799), i. pp. iii, v–viii.

more approvingly. First, he compared the superficial appeal to the texts and ideals of ancient Greece and Rome that were ritually invoked by French republicans as having been 'as hypocritically descanted on, as the Holy Bible was during the civil commotion of Charles I and the usurpation of Cromwell'. Secondly, praise for Cromwell outweighed grudging acknowledgement of Robespierre's ability, as Adolphus observed that 'He possessed considerable vigour of mind, though not sufficient to entitle him to a comparison with Cromwell.' Finally, noting Robespierre's posthumous reputation, Adolphus adverted to the fact that 'after his fall he was denominated Cataline, and has been compared to Cromwell; but he is not worthy to associate with either character'.[73] Carlyle, likewise, had manifestly enjoyed citing Mirabeau's nickname for Lafayette, combining as it did the name of his greatest English hero with the eponymous hero of a novel by an eighteenth-century writer, Samuel Richardson: 'whose name shall be Cromwell-Grandison, and fill the world'.[74] Plainly, Carlyle's interest in political personality had been anticipated by the likes of Adolphus, but where they and their fellow conservatives had sought to contain the energies so described, Carlyle sought to liberate and celebrate them, and even so dangerous a political agent as Robespierre was to be appreciated accordingly. There is a radical continuity between his depiction of Robespierre in the *French Revolution* and his subsequent re-evaluation of Cromwell; in order to appreciate the logic of the *French Revolution* it has to be read alongside its British predecessors and contemporaries, of which the texts of Adolphus and Croker mark the conservative edge.

Interpretative possession of the Revolution mattered politically, and Carlyle's sympathetically radical narrative faced stiff competition in Croker's meticulously minded surveys of the history of the Revolution, where his conservative judgements were laid out with Olympian authority. That Croker's essays were prosaic in the deepest sense of the term also mattered fundamentally in both their conception and reception, as British empiricism self-consciously undid the political fancies of a disputatious nation. That Carlyle had composed an epic poem was likewise testimony to the powerfully radical climacteric in the life of Europe that was the French Revolution. Tragedy and the epic were integral to his vision of 1789, as in his remarks on the hero of the work, Mirabeau (who was also celebrated in Adolphus's account):

[73] Adolphus, *Biographical Memoirs*, ii. 365–446, at pp. 367, 444, 445.
[74] *FR*, i. 152.

Alas is not the life of every such man already a poetic Tragedy; made up 'of Fate and of one's own Deservings', of *Schicksal und eigene Schuld*; full of the elements of Pity and Fear? This brother man, if not Epic for us, is world-large in his destinies.[75]

As Peter Fritzsche has perceptively observed of the narrative challenge the Revolution posed to Carlyle—the peculiar style of whose history corresponded, in Fritzsche's reading, to 'the radical contingency of events'—the endeavour 'to understand the revolution validated ideas of history as an ongoing process that destroyed the past'.[76] Conservatism, comfortable or otherwise, was not an option in Carlyle's radically contingent conception of the past, evoked so memorably in his biblically resonant injunction: 'call not the Past Time, with all its confused wretchednesses, a lost one.'[77] His separation from Croker was, then, stylistic and political, and is reminiscent of the differences in style, message, and intended audience that separated the stark directness of Thomas Paine's welcome of the Revolution in *The Rights of Man* from the altogether more intricate and stylized critique of it offered in Edmund Burke's *Reflections on the Revolution in France*, albeit their nineteenth-century successors reversed the styles for their political purposes. The conservative counter-revolutionary prose championed by Croker was chaste and simple, while radical ambivalence about the revolution in Carlyle's account was stylistically intense and densely fluid, its language struggling for accuracy in describing a chaotic and constantly shifting landscape, alluding to a sea of repeated images, and to a host of languages and a litany of literary allusions in the frequently disappointed hope of conveying the inner realities of the contingency of the events characterized as the French Revolution.

Equally, for Carlyle, the visual could both stimulate and obscure, as when he notes, with knowing anachronism, of a moment of revolutionary brigandage early in the Revolution, that it was 'a picture for Salvator!'[78] The ambiguities of the visual, and the relativities to which it gives rise, are memorably inscribed in his famous exclamation regarding a philosopher who had been much given to the problems of vision:

[75] *FR*, i. 453. For Adolphus's appreciation of Mirabeau, see *Biographical Memoirs*, ii. 62–139. On the failure of Mirabeau, Danton, and Napoleon as epic heroes, but the success of Goethe in the role, see John Clubbe, 'Epic heroes in the *French Revolution*', in Drescher, *Thomas Carlyle 1981*, 165–85.

[76] Peter Fritzsche, *Stranded in the Present: Modern Time and the Melancholy of History* (Cambridge, Mass., 2004), 46–7.

[77] *FR*, i. 10. [78] *FR*, i. 279.

'To Newton and to Newton's Dog Diamond, what a different pair of Universes; while the painting on the optical retina of both was, most likely, the same!'[79] One has to remember Carlyle's scientific training at Edinburgh when reading such intensely visual passages, as when interpreting his description of Kepler's use of a camera obscura, which likewise opens up our sight of the opening of the Thirty Years War in the work on Frederick the Great.[80]

What was politically implicit in 1837, however, became explicit with the publication of Carlyle's *Latter-Day Pamphlets* in collected form in 1850. In the course of a harangue on political corruption in eighteenth-century England, Carlyle had listed the sources which made evident how patronage was systematically abused by predecessor generations:

> But how those Offices in Downing Street were made; who made them, or for what kind of objects they were made, would be hard to say at present. Dim visions and phantasmagories gathered from the Books of Horace Walpole, Memoirs of Bubb Doddington, Memoirs of my Lady Sundon, Lord Fanny Hervey, and innumerable others, rise on us, beckoning fantastically towards, not an answer, but some conceivable intimations of an answer, and proclaiming very legibly the old text '*Quam parva sapientia*', in respect of this hard-working, much-subduing British Nation;—giving rise to endless reflections in a thinking Englishman of this day.[81]

In 1848, Croker had brought out an admiring edition of Lord Hervey's *Memoirs of the Reign of George II*, complete with a sympathetic, politically astute introduction.[82] Carlyle's denunciation of such authorities served to undermine Croker's confidently assumed and frequently practised intellectual authority, and competing conceptions of eighteenth-century political history thus powerfully demonstrated their purchase in the ideologies active in nineteenth-century political history. Division in regard to eighteenth-century English political history drew to the fore the division latent in their competing interpretations of the French Revolution, equally powerfully placing thereby the continuing presence of the revolution in the politics of nineteenth-century England.

Burke made an occasional appearance in Carlyle's argument, but always fleetingly, as when 'Burke and Toryism eye askance' the National

[79] *FR*, i. 7. [80] *FG*, i. 321–2.

[81] Carlyle, 'Downing Street', *LDP*, 19.

[82] John Wilson Croker, 'Prefatory and biographical notice', in *Memoirs of the Reign of George the Second, from his Accession to the Death of Queen Caroline, by John, Lord Hervey* (2 vols., London, 1848), i. pp. ix–lxvi.

Assembly, or as morbidly fearing Jacobinism.[83] Burke also appears positively, as a progenitor of Carlyle's critique of the Revolution: 'Great Burke has raised his great voice long ago; eloquently demonstrating that the end of an Epoch is come, to all appearance the end of Civilized Time.' On the very same page, however, he is also present negatively, as it was Burke's role as the ideologue who had helped to launch the European war with revolutionary France that led to the depredations facing France, both externally and internally, so that Carlyle could write with a strong sense of irony, and quoting perhaps the most celebrated phrase in the *Reflections,* that '"the Age of Chivalry *is* gone", and could not but go, having now produced the still more indomitable Age of Hunger'.[84] He also included Paine, 'the rebellious Needleman', in his ironies: both Burke and Paine appear implicitly in Carlyle's narrative as simplifying observers, both on the Right, and on the Left, whose theoretical analyses of the Revolution are so much less valuable, so much less worth examination, than the experiential domains explored by Carlyle the poet-historian.[85] There is, however, a major paradox at work here, in that one of Carlyle's favoured metaphors for unreality, that of 'paper', is also one that litters Burke's *Reflections*. Rather than being an 'Age of Gold', as contemporaries had thought it, Carlyle saw the 1770s as an 'Age of Paper'; so it was that 'an Era of Hope' was actually an age of paper, and Talleyrand would later come to preside over an 'Age of Paper, and of the Burning of Paper'. The alleged rights of man would prove themselves to be the 'true paper basis of all paper Constitutions'. Newspapers and journals, the very stuff of paper, would merely promote unreality.[86] Similarly, what J. G. A. Pocock has called the political economy of Burke's critique of the French Revolution, likewise seems, however obliquely, to inform the rhetoric of Carlyle's history of 'this distracted eighteenth century'.[87] Just as Burke despised the *assignat* as unreal, purely speculative, and hence entirely worthless paper money, so Carlyle derided such money as 'a standing miracle'. The spiritual and the

[83] *FR*, i. 324, ii. 53. [84] *FR*, ii. 36. [85] *FR*, ii. 324–5, 473.

[86] *FR*, i. 31, 41, 154, 229, 245–6.

[87] J. G. A. Pocock, 'The political economy of Burke's analysis of the French Revolution', in *Virtue, Commerce, and History: Essays on Political Thought and History, Chiefly in the Eighteenth Century* (Cambridge, 1985), 193–212. Carlyle, *FR*, i. 246. Carlyle was also, like Burke, suspicious of the political consequences of religious Enthusiasm: witness his reference to the 'enthusiast complexion' of revolutionary brigands: *FR*, i. 133–4. For a rather more theoretically orientated description of Carlyle's distance from Burke, see Mary Desaulniers, *Carlyle and the Economics of Terror: A Study of Revisionary Gothicism in* The French Revolution (Montreal, 1995), 30–3, 90.

real were elided by this phenomenon, as he had earlier declared regarding the political economy of immediately pre-revolutionary France: 'It is Spiritual Bankruptcy, long tolerated; verging now towards Economical Bankruptcy, and become intolerable.'[88] (Where, arguably, Carlyle parted company with Burke, is that Burke, an admirer of Adam Smith, actually understood political economy, whereas Carlyle, who decried the modern world—'with its Wealth of Nations, Supply-and-demand and such like'—merely hated, misunderstood, and condemned it.)[89]

Carlyle's relationship with Burke is, then, complicated, but essentially, and interpretatively, it is a close, but deeply critical one; it is as if Carlyle is dealing with a foreshadowing of his argument that needs to be distanced from his own if his originality is to be felt and appreciated by Carlyle's readers. In common with Burke, Carlyle condemned the spirit of *philosophism*, but he did so from a complex post-Christian perspective, which allows him to exercise rather more irony than Burke ever indulged on the subject. Carlyle, who gave the unchristian Louis XV the benefit of his having at least believed in the Devil, noted that 'enlightened Philosophism' was not 'given to prayer'; he also noted the manner in which, once the old orthodoxies of the Sorbonne had sunk into an intellectual dotage, rationality and irrationality could compete on equal terms, so that a 'nameless innumerable multitude of ready Writers, profane Singers, Romancers, Players, Disputators, and Pamphleteers . . . now form the Spiritual Guidance of the world'. Here lies the kernel of Carlyle's semi-religious critique of all that followed in the Enlightenment's wake: 'French Philosophism has arisen; in which little word how much do we include! Here, indeed, lies properly the cardinal symptom of the whole wide-spread malady. Faith is gone out; Scepticism has come in.'[90] Two abbés, Raynal and Sieyès, were consequently condemned for abandoning religion for mere worldly philosophy; the condemned clergy (condemned explicitly by the revolutionaries, and implicitly by Carlyle) troop by, but they too are the occasion of Carlyle's snarling, post-Calvinist wrath, as he identified the religious declension of the age, with 'the Cant of Catholicism, raging on the one side, and sceptic Heathenism on the other'.[91] By the early 1790s, France was 'rent asunder' by religion, 'or with the

[88] *FR*, i. 311, 84.

[89] *PP*, 26. In placing Burke and Carlyle in this context, the work of Donald Winch is uniquely informative: see *Riches and Poverty: An Intellectual History of Political Economy in Britain, 1750–1834* (Cambridge, 1996).

[90] *FR*, i. 6, 13, 16.

[91] *FR*, i. 58, 61, 123, 151–2, 155, 312–13.

cant and Echo of Religion'; Catholicism had been—in one of Carlyle's beloved scientific metaphors—'*galvanized* into the detestablest death-life', but then, however 'skilfully galvanized', it had ambiguously become both 'hideous, and even piteous, to behold!' Appealing (unspokenly) to a mildly misogynistic witticism of Bishop Warburton, Carlyle felt enabled to look on with the disinterested yet passionate commitment of a post-Christian, yet deeply religious, gaze (and note the power of his relentless repetition of earlier imagery, a stylistic feature which marks all his writings): 'In such an extraordinary manner does dead Catholicism somersault and caper, skilfully galvanized. For, does the reader inquire into the subject-matter of controversy in this case; what the difference between Orthodoxy or *My-Doxy* and Heterodoxy and *My-Doxy* might be here?'[92]

Nevertheless, it is the power of religion that matters to Carlyle, rather more than its fragmentation by philosophy, as in his dismissal of Voltairian scoffing, but religion's genuine power had also been undone by the worldly clergy:

> Shall we say then: Woe to Philosophism, that it destroyed Religion, what it called 'extinguishing the abomination (*écraser l'infame*)'? Woe rather to those that made the Holy an abomination, and extinguishable; woe to all men that live in such a time of world-abomination and world-destruction![93]

What is more, at least one *philosophe*, Mirabeau, is accorded the status of a great man by Carlyle. What Voltaire had been to his generation, so Mirabeau was to his, 'the Type-Frenchman of this Epoch'; but, unlike Voltaire and his colleagues, Mirabeau, the sole saving grace in Carlyle's gallery of Enlightenment extremists, was not a man of systems, but 'a man of instincts and insights'. His very faults contrived to make him attractive to Carlyle the hater of philosophical and moral abstractions; Mirabeau was 'A man not with *logic-spectacles*; but with an *eye*! Unhappily without Decalogue, moral Code or Theorem of any fixed sort; yet not without a strong living Soul in him, and Sincerity there: a Reality, not an Artificiality, not a Sham!' Mirabeau had the heroic attribute above all others, for 'had Mirabeau lived, the History of France and of the World had been different'.[94] Mirabeau's authenticity and humanity marked him out in the age of the sham and the quack, the age

[92] *FR*, i. 425, 457, 461, 462. For a parallel instance of the galvanized metaphor, witness this assault on Tractarianism: 'But of our Dilettantisms, and galvanized Dilettantisms, of Puseyism—O Heavens, what shall we say of Puseyism, in comparison to Twelfth-Century Catholicism?' *PP*, 119–20.

[93] *FR*, i. 60.

[94] *FR*, i. 144, 147, 444.

of sentimentalism, 'twin-sister to Cant'.[95] In this important particular, Mirabeau is distinguished from the philosopher Carlyle despised above all others in the eighteenth century, Voltaire included.

It is Rousseau who is constantly lambasted in the pages of the *French Revolution*. Rousseau, the pseudo-religious 'Evangel of a *Contrat Social*' provides the very antithesis of Carlyle's historicized, experiential conception of the political and the social, as it is economically dispatched in his pregnant, recognizably post-Burkean phrase regarding Rousseau's political thought: 'Theories of Government!' Carlyle enjoyed inverting the would-be naturalistic imagery favoured by Rousseau, as when he observed that the worst of the constitutional innovators had been 'nursed more or less on the milk of the *Contrat Social*'. Returning once again to his contest between the genuine power of religion and the compromised energies of philosophy, Carlyle repeatedly dismissed 'the Gospel according to Jean-Jacques!' and 'the new Church of Jean-Jacques Rousseau'; he savoured the reburial of 'Evangelist Jean-Jacques', alongside Voltaire, in the new 'Pantheon of the Fatherland'.[96] A few years after the publication of *The French Revolution*, Carlyle extended this discussion of Rousseau, whom he saw, in *On Heroes and Hero Worship* (1841), alongside Johnson and Robert Burns, as a heroic man of letters principally because of his earnestness, but whose sensuality and fanatical egoism he continued to condemn; he remained the 'Evangelist' of Revolution.[97]

Above all, the Revolution had given birth to democracy, a political system Carlyle associated both with buffoonery and with violence, as in its quickly limned annunciation in America in the mid-1770s, a darkly comic prelude to the French Revolution:

> Boston Harbour is black with unexpected Tea; behold a Pennsylvanian Congress gather; and ere long, on Bunker-Hill, DEMOCRACY announcing, in rifle-volleys, death-winged, under her Star Banner, to the tune of Yankee-doodle-doo, that she is born, and, whirlwind-like, will envelop the whole world![98]

Feudalism had gradually extinguished itself in France, and with the summoning of the Estates General had come the great theme of Carlyle's history, as also of his political writings, and with it the present-centred nature of his dialogue with the immediate past, in which the eighteenth century was identified as the birthplace of modernity. Hence his powerful invocation of Monday, 4 May 1789:

[95] *FR*, i. 57. [96] *FR*, i. 56, 66, 156, 227, 230, 340, 344, 345, 411, 451.
[97] 'The hero as man of letters', *OH*, 154–95, at pp. 168, 184–6. [98] *FR*, i. 9.

It is the baptism day of Democracy; sick Time has given birth, the numbered months being run . . . What a work, O Earth and Heavens, what a work! Battles and bloodshed, September Massacres, Bridges of Lodi, retreats of Moscow, Waterloo, Peterloos. Tenpound Franchises, Tarbarrels and Guillotines;—and from this present date, if one might prophesy, some two centuries of it still to fight! Two centuries; hardly less; before Democracy go through its due, most baleful, stages of *Quacko*cracy; and a pestilential World be burnt up, and have begun to grow green and young again.[99]

This was the terrain marked out by the Revolution, the triumph of democracy, against which Carlyle was to write again and again, not least in his political testimony, his *Latter-Day Pamphlets*, where he had declared, in his essay on 'The Present Time', that:

Democracy, it may be said everywhere, is here:—for sixty years now, ever since the grand or *First* French revolution, that fact has been terribly announced to all the world; in message after message, some of them very terrible indeed; and now at last all the world ought really to believe it.[100]

It was in his history of Frederick that Carlyle traced the last noble attempt to withstand that unwelcome democratic climacteric, as a land of Reformation sobriety attempted, under its heroic and absolutist leader, to withstand the enticements of unheroic modernity. A reading of his gargantuan study of Frederick is thus vitally necessary in order to appreciate the counters of his influential repudiation of the eighteenth century, a century whose demise in the French Revolution was seemingly preordained by its corrupt and compromised nature. The history of Frederick has to be understood, therefore, as being in fundamental dialogue with Carlyle's history of the French Revolution, and this dialogue reveals just how central to Carlyle's philosophy was his lifelong fascination with the much loathed eighteenth century.

[99] *FR*, i. 139–40. One wonders whether Carlyle would have found this a happy or an unhappy hit to have made regarding the revolutions of 1989.

[100] *LDP*, 10.

2

Carlyle, *Friedrich*, and the 'Bastard Heroic'

> After long reading, with Historical views, in this final section of the Friedrich–Voltaire Correspondence, at first so barren otherwise and of little entertainment, one finds that this too, when once you *can* read it (that is to say, when the scene and its details are visible to you), becomes highly dramatic, Shakespearean-comic or more, for this is Nature's self, who far excels even Shakespeare;—and that the inextricably dark condition of these Letters is a real loss to the ingenuous reader, and especially to the student of Friedrich.
>
> Thomas Carlyle, *History of Friedrich*[1]

If revolutionary France is for Carlyle the morally and spiritually perplexing confusion out of which modernity emerged, then Frederick the Great's Prussia offered, by contrast, a far nobler example of the heroic somehow contriving to flourish (albeit temporally) in a base age. His heroic portrait of Frederick allowed Carlyle to construct and indulge a nostalgic politics from afar. Writing of the Battle of Prague in 1757, for example, Carlyle discerned some dim hope for his English readers, albeit only through the act of tracing linguistic consanguinity:

> Gradually, in stirring up those old dead pedantic record-books, the fact rises on us: silent whirlwinds of old Platt-Deutsch fire, beautifully held down, dwell in those mute masses; better human stuff there is not than that old Teutsch (Dutch, English, Platt-Deutsch, and other varieties); and so disciplined as here it never was before or since.[2]

The language of epic is held appropriate for such a people, and Carlyle is their self-appointed poet; his life of Frederick is a history whose hero lived during an unheroic age: hence the peculiar nature of

[1] *FG*, v. 607–8. [2] *FG*, v. 35–6.

the epic which results. Where the epoch in which it occurred provided much of the atmospheric argument of *The French Revolution*, so the eighteenth century is just as much the major character in the argument of the life of Frederick—outflanking even Frederick himself—as it is also merely the period during which it is set. Both histories are extended meditations on the eighteenth century. Whereas, however, the *French Revolution* acquired a mass of readers and devotees, the work on Frederick was never to achieve anything like the same popularity; readers had grown tired of Carlyle's explorations of the eighteenth century, and also, it would seem, of his very particular style: as an erstwhile admirer, George Gilfillan, put it in a review of the first two volumes published in the *Scottish Review* in 1859, they were 'Carlyle's own caricature of his *History of the French Revolution*'.[3] They seemed too full of Carlyle's mannerisms, and too full of Carlyle himself: indeed, the other major character in the later work, alongside the eighteenth century itself, is not so much Frederick as Carlyle himself, whose labours are constantly referred to over the course of six volumes, and this near identification of Carlyle with Frederick is made very clear when he adverts to the chance which kept alive an ancestor of his royal subject:

> And indeed it must be owned, had the shot taken effect as intended, the whole course of human things would have been surprisingly altered;—and for one thing, neither *Friedrich the Great*, nor the present *History of Friedrich*, had ever risen above ground, or troubled an enlightened public or me![4]

I

The century in which Frederick reigned is itself a vivid presence throughout the study, a century perpetually foreshadowing its dramatic closure in the French Revolution which so preoccupied Carlyle. The Revolution was the climacteric with which he began his successful writing career, and with which he chose to complete it, in as much as so much of his history of Frederick is taken up with considerations of the Revolution and its world-historical consequences. Within pages of opening the first volume of his final history, Carlyle's imagination

[3] George Gilfillan review of *FG*, reproduced in Jerome Paul Siegel (ed.), *Thomas Carlyle: The Critical Heritage* (London, 1971), 427–38, at p. 432.

[4] *FG*, i. 289.

erupts with the geological intensity that so marks his writing, especially when he is narrating revolutionary events:

When he died, in 1786, the enormous phenomenon since called FRENCH REVOLUTION was already growing audibly in the depths of the world; meteoric-electric coruscations heralding it, all round the horizon. Strange enough to note, one of Friedrich's last visitors was Gabriel Honoré Riquetti, Comte de Mirabeau. These two saw one another; twice, for half-an-hour each time. The last of the old Gods and the first of the modern Titans;—before Pelion leapt on Ossa; and of the foul earth taking fire at last, its vile mephitic elements went up in volcanic thunder. This also is one of the peculiarities of Friedrich, that he is hitherto the last of the Kings; that he ushers in the French Revolution, and closes an epoch of World-History. Finishing off forever, think many; who have grown profoundly dark as to Kingship and him.[5]

Frederick's memory has to be rescued from the post-revolutionary world, where 'he is found defaced under strange mud-incrustations', and the two poles of Carlyle's career as historian are also to be found there, since 'This is one of the difficulties in dealing with his History;—especially if you happen to believe both in the French Revolution and in him; that is to say, both that Real Kingship is eternally indispensable, and also that the destruction of Sham Kingship (a frightful process) is occasionally so.'[6]

The 'formidable Explosion, and Suicide of his Century' left Frederick 'eclipsed amid the ruins of that universal earthquake, the very dust of which darkened all the air and made of day a disastrous midnight'.[7] As the chronicler of that explosion, Carlyle was making his claim to be the rescuer of Frederick's reputation as the bearer of the last vestige of true kingship; in the process he had to disavow the competing status of another claimant, both demonized and idolized by the Romantic generation preceding Carlyle: [8]

It must be owned the figure of Napoleon was titanic; especially to that generation that looked on him, and that waited shuddering to be devoured by him. In general, in that French Revolution all was on a huge scale; if not greater than anything in human experience, at least more grandiose.[9]

[5] *FG*, i. 8; Rebecca Stott, 'Thomas Carlyle and the crowd: revolution, geology, and the convulsive nature of time', *Journal of Victorian Culture*, 4 (1999), 1–24; John Burrow, 'Images of time: from Carlylean Vulcanism to sedimentary gradualism', in Stefan Collini, Richard Whatmore, and Brian Young (eds.), *History, Religion, and Culture: British Intellectual History, 1750–1950* (Cambridge, 2000), 198–223.

[6] *FG*, i. 8. [7] *FG*, i. 8–9.

[8] See Simon Bainbridge, *Napoleon and English Romanticism* (Cambridge, 1995).

[9] *FG*, i. 9.

The eighteenth century had no history in Carlyle's severe estimation until the outbreak of the Revolution abolished it, with all its 'accumulated falsities', overwhelming a period 'opulent in that bad way as never Century was before!' Frederick flourished in a period that was false to the bone; that he maintained his veracity in such an age, and that he did this as a king, was 'doubly remarkable'. Carlyle thus presented his readers with the challenge awaiting them at the very outset of his mammoth exercise in historical resuscitation: 'How show the man, who is a Reality worthy of being seen, and yet keep his Century, as a Hypocrisy worthy of being hidden and forgotten, in the due abeyance?'[10] This, we are informed, was a huge task, since the eighteenth century was unlovely to Carlyle, its only grandeur occurring in its 'grand universal Suicide, named French Revolution', erupting in flames and volcanic explosions, and fitly terminating a 'fraudulent-bankrupt' century.[11] Frederick was a genius 'born into the purblind rotting Century', a hero living out his life in a sensual, unheroic era; consequently, he had had to labour 'as no man of his Century had': 'the World all round one's Hero is a darkness, a dormant vacancy'.[12] A moralizing purpose undoubtedly informed Carlyle's narrative, as he observed: 'How this man officially a King withal, comported himself in the Eighteenth Century, and managed *not* to be a Liar and a Charlatan as his Century was, deserves to be seen a little by men and kings, and may silently have didactic meanings in it.'[13]

The eighteenth century encompassed 'those dull old years of European history', fast making their way 'towards vacant Oblivion and eternal Night;—which (if some few articles were once saved out of them) is their just and inevitable portion from afflicted human nature'.[14] Something was indeed to be pulled from the wreckage of the eighteenth century, albeit the exemplary career of a man atypical of his age; in this way the past spoke to the present, and this was especially true when Carlyle reflected on the medium through which he revived his model king: 'Curious enough, Friedrich lived in the Writing Era,—morning of that strange Era which has grown to such a noon for us;—and his favourite society, all his reign, was with the literary or writing sort.'[15]

Narrating the life of Frederick could help to justify Carlyle in his tacit identification of himself as a heroic man of letters; it is interesting to note that Frederick is introduced as a hero, a veritable Samson, along with another Samson Agonistes, namely Samuel Johnson, one of

[10] *FG*, i. 10–11. [11] *FG*, i. 11. [12] *FG*, i. 27–8; iii. 37–8, 236, 237.
[13] *FG*, i. 18. [14] *FG*, i. 470. [15] *FG*, i. 14.

Carlyle's select few, but fervently admired, eighteenth-century heroes.[16] The closeness of the suicidal century in which Frederick and Johnson lived is constantly reiterated in Carlyle's account, as he negotiates his readers through to 'the other side of that still troubled atmosphere of the Present and immediate Past'.[17] This border country of past and present encouraged Carlyle in his penchant for prolepsis, so that the future death of a Prussian prince at Jena is first foretold seventy-six years before the event;[18] when discoursing on an eighteenth-century 'braggart of the histrionic-heroic sort', he could satisfyingly point out that this favourite of the Prussian Princess Amelia was eventually to be guillotined by Robespierre:[19] the long shadow of the guillotine peremptorily pervades the six volumes of Frederick's history, linking past and present, whilst also literally severing all connections between them with unequalled ferocity. Frederick's hopes were to be realized, but darker things lay in the wings:

> and how high his hopes go for mankind and for himself? Yes, surely;—and introducing, we remark withal, the 'new Era', of Philanthropy, Enlightenment and so much else; with French Revolution, and a 'world well suicided' hanging in the rear! Clearly enough, to this young ardent Friedrich, foremost man of his Time, and capable of *doing* its inarticulate or dumb aspirings, belongs that questionable honour; and a very singular one it would have seemed to Friedrich, had he lived to see what it meant![20]

Again and again, Frederick is seen as an unexpected harbinger of the French Revolution, and Carlyle happily refers to Burke's famous declaration regarding the social mores of the Revolution when he observes that the 'Age of Chivalry' was all but dead in the eighteenth century.[21] Just as the French Revolution is introduced early in the first volume, so its nature and consequences are elaborated in the closing volume. The French look towards 'Spontaneous Combustion, in the year 1789, and for long years onwards!' The Revolution is humanity's next milestone after the reign of Frederick; it constitutes the 'New Act in World-History'. It burns up 'Sham-Governors and Sham-Teachers', slouching towards the millennium due two centuries later; tracing its progress, Carlyle sees its apocalyptic qualities as overwhelming its

[16] *FG*, i. 7, 411, 473. On Carlyle's heroic reading of Frederick, and his mirroring of himself in the monarch, see John D. Rosenberg, *Carlyle and the Burden of History* (Oxford, 1985), 159–72.

[17] *FG*, i. 19. [18] *FG*, ii. 177, 639, and 687. [19] *FG*, i. 540.

[20] *FG*, iii. 20. [21] *FG*, iii. 35; iv. 316.

interpretative usefulness in his life of Frederick, so that 'World-History, eager to be at the general Funeral-pile and ultimate Burning-up of Shams in this poor World, will have less and less to say of small tragedies and premonitory symptoms'.[22] It burns its way through the closing volume of Frederick's history into the silences of Carlyle's later years.

Next to geological metaphors, clothes constitute the great source of imagery in Carlyle's writings, as demonstrated in *Sartor Resartus* and its 'clothes philosophy'.[23] He relished, in the *French Revolution*, the fabled detail of Mirabeau's having briefly opened up a clothes-shop; in death, Mirabeau was himself a reality, 'walking sorrowful in a world mostly of "Stuffed Clothes-suits"'.[24] The Sanscullote, 'Destitute-of-Breeches', 'the Sans-indispensables', were a metaphorical godsend; how he enjoyed inverting the anarchic era of Sanscullotic anarchy into that of 'a new singular system of Culottism and Arrangement'.[25] Similarly, clothes often denote falseness in his work on Frederick, as when, describing the failures of the Congress of Cambrai, Carlyle denounces its 'wiggeries' in a 'nightmare-vision in Human History'.[26] Such was the sight witnessed by 'Arouet *le Jeune* . . . as a contemporary Fact, drinking champagne in ramilies wigs, and arranging comedies for itself'.[27] Similarly, Frederick was capable of shaking the eighteenth century 'out of its stupid refuges of lies, and ignominious wrappages and bed-clothes, which will be its grave-clothes otherwise'; and we recognize the elderly Frederick as a worthy monarch in the opening page of the history precisely because he is not dressed as such: 'He is King every inch of him, though without the trappings of a King.'[28] In this way he is unlike Louis XIV, who had set Europe ablaze for 'the sake of one poor mortal in periwig' (and whose decayed form was dangerously transformed by such dress, an image economically illustrated in a celebrated cartoon by Thackeray).[29]

Likewise, in contrast with the French monarchs, Carlyle makes an unlikely hero out of Frederick's father, the blustering bully Friedrich Wilhelm, precisely because he is out of step with the eighteenth century. This 'Squire Western of the North' was

[22] *FG*, vi. 339–41. The French Revolution destroyed 'Sham Kingship'; Frederick incarnated 'Real Kingship': *FG*, i. 8.

[23] On Carlyle's indebtedness to Jean-Paul Richter and other German authors for this idea, see Elizabeth M. Vida, *Romantic Affinities: German Authors and Carlyle: A Study in the History of Ideas* (Toronto, 1993), 91–107.

[24] *FR*, i. 131, 452.

[25] *FR*, i. 428, ii. 70, 418, 421, 441.

[26] *FG*, i. 563. On Frederick's opposition to wigs, see *FG*, vi. 630.

[27] *FG*, i. 565.

[28] *FG*, iii. 320; i. 3.

[29] *FG*, i. 371.

like no other King that then existed, or had ever been discovered. Wilder Son of Nature seldom came into the artificial world; into a royal throne there, probably never. A wild man; wholly in earnest, veritable as the old rocks,—and with a terrible volcanic fire in him, too. He would have been strange anywhere; but among the dapper Royal gentlemen of the Eighteenth Century, what was to be done with such an Orson of a King?—Clap him in Bedlam, and bring out the ballot-boxes instead? The modern generation, too, still takes its impression of him from these rumours,—still more now from Wilhelmina's Book; which paints the outside savagery of the royal man, in a most striking manner; and leaves the inside vacant, undiscovered by Wilhelmina or the rumours.[30]

One is left to infer that Carlyle will succeed where Friedrich Wilhelm's daughter Wilhelmina and rumour had supposedly failed: he will enter the soul of this man, whose very antipathy to the eighteenth century through which he stormed is what made him so attractive to the counter-suggestible narrator of his son's life. Similarly, while it was difficult for a Frenchman to be 'real' during the reign of Louis XV, Carlyle would do his best to find the reality behind the life of the diplomat Belleisle.[31] The Victorian historian can see beneath the soil of the eighteenth century, and, by digging into the surrounding rocks, he can aim to reveal the geological reality that preceded the lava flows of the French Revolution.

As the author of *Past and Present,* Carlyle was forever aware of the need to link both elements if history was to live and to instruct, and this sense of the historian's moral task strongly informs the history of Frederick. Both irony and pathos endure in such insights, as he declares, 'So different is present tense from past, in all things, especially in things like these!'[32] This tone affects his presentations of the now dead liveliness of the past, as in his remark concerning a regular social event of the mid-eighteenth century: 'The Roucoulles Soirees,—gone all to dim buckram for us, though once so lively in their high periwigs and speculations—fall on Wednesday.'[33] The tangible pleasure Carlyle felt in adducing the pastness of that event by emphasizing the present tense of 'fall on Wednesday' is a masterly narrative detail. As with so many of his contemporaries, Carlyle was fascinated by survivals from the eighteenth century into the 'mechanical age';[34] thus he recalled recollections of the Battle of Prague 'fought May 6th 1757; which sounded through all the world,—and used to deafen us in drawing-rooms within man's

[30] *FG*, ii. 441; i. 405. Rosenberg has claimed that Carlyle's portrait of Friedrich Wilhelm presents one of 'the few credible monsters in modern literature'. *Carlyle and the Burden of History*, 164.

[31] *FG*, iii. 247. [32] *FG*, ii. 655. [33] *FG*, ii. 6. [34] *FG*, iv. 430.

memory'.[35] Princess Elizabeth of Brunswick, the king's niece, 'survived all her generation, and the next and the next, and indeed into our own'.[36] Frederick's idea for secularizing seven Austro-Bavarian bishoprics was held to be 'A bright idea; but had come a century too soon.'[37] Likewise, a military textbook written by Frederick was still used by Prussian cadet-schools when Carlyle's history was being written; other texts were identified by their modern equivalents, so that the *Bibliothèque raisonnée* was extolled as the 'mild-shining Quarterly Review of those days' (the *Quarterly Review* had been Croker's Tory journal).[38]

Carlyle was usually critical of the present, drawing on the past to expose it. Thus, to their great shame, the English and their soldiers no longer knew anything of the Seven Years War, and its various calamities.[39] Writing of Frederick's ancestors as heroes of the Reformation era, Carlyle tartly observes that 'Readers of this enlightened gold-nugget generation can form to themselves no conception of the spirit that then possessed the nobler kingly mind.'[40] The love of truth of such an ancestor makes a strong contrast with 'the vague maunderings, flutings; indolent, impotent day-dreaming and tobacco-smoking, of poor modern Germany'; where Truth led Heavenwards for the reformers, the temptations of 'Sophistry, Virtù, the Aesthetic Arts, and perhaps (for a short while) Book-keeping by Double Entry' will lead modernity to the Devil.[41] Small wonder, then, that he was happy to condemn a history of the Thirty Years War as 'a trivial modern book'.[42] Most telling for Carlyle's historical philosophy is the observation, made at the end of a chapter in the final volume, that 'the sins of the fathers are visited upon the children in a frightful and tragical manner, little noticed in the Penny Newspapers and Periodical Literatures of this generation. Oh my friends—!'[43]

History was to recover the grand, the noble, the heroic for the sake of the present, but even it had first to make its way through the miasma of the present in order to find the vital light of the past. This is made plain

[35] *FG*, v. 47. [36] *FG*, vi. 377. [37] *FG*, iii. 667.

[38] *FG*, iv. 33, 429. On the journal alluded to by Carlyle, see William Thomas, 'Religion and politics in the *Quarterly Review*, 1809–1853', in Collini, Whatmore, and Young, *History, Religion, and Culture*, 136–55. The review that appeared there of the volumes on Frederick was not particularly admiring, and this is not surprising given that the author, H. M. Merivale, had been professor of political economy at Oxford, and hence an exponent of the 'dismal science' Carlyle loathed so much, and which Merivale defended in his review: Merivale in the *Quarterly Review*, 118 (1865), 225–54.

[39] *FG*, iii. 333. [40] *FG*, i. 241. [41] *FG*, i. 261, 265. [42] *FG*, i. 326.

[43] *FG*, i. 348.

at the outset of the history, where Carlyle adverted to the problems endemic to the sources he used, and thus alerted his readers to his own manfully heroic task as historian:

Truth is, the Prussian Dryasdust, otherwise an honest fellow, and not afraid of labour, excels all other Dryasdusts yet known: I have often sorrowfully felt as if there were not in Nature, for darkness, dreariness, immethodic platitude, anything comparable to him. He writes big Books wanting in almost every quality; and does not even give an *Index* to them. He has made of Friedrich's History a wide-spread, inorganic, trackless matter; dismal to your mind, and barren as a continent of Brandenburg sand!—Enough, he could do no other: I have striven to forgive him. Let the reader now forgive me; and think sometimes what probably my raw-material was![44]

Pointing out that, with the single exception of Mirabeau (who saw Frederick for only an hour), no man of 'genius, or with an adequate power of human discernment', ever looked on Frederick—where this leaves Voltaire will be discussed later—Carlyle concluded that:

Had many such men looked successively on his History and him, we had not found it in such a condition. Still altogether chaotic as a History; fatally destitute even of the Indexes and mechanical appliances: Friedrich's self, and his Country, and his Century, still undeciphered; very dark phenomena, all three, to the intelligent part of mankind.[45]

Plainly, one can only infer that Carlyle considers himself a man of genius with a more than adequate power of human discernment, and it is certainly the case that his indexes are excellent.[46] Whatever one might be led to deduce from Carlyle's complaint, there can be no doubt that he had little time for Prussian Dryasdusts: 'the German Dryasdust is a dull dog, and seldom carries anything human in those big wallets of his!'[47] Carlyle the self-employed, self-mastering historian did not lose his opportunity, through the character of Smelfungus, bitterly to berate the academic historians, personified in the Prussian Dryasdust 'sitting comfortable in his Academies, waving sublimely his long ears as he tramples human Heroisms into unintelligible pipeclay and dreary continents of sand and cinders, with the Doctors all applauding'.[48]

[44] *FG*, i. 13–14. [45] *FG*, i. 14.

[46] It is an obsession that surfaced early in his Cromwell edition, when a Carlylean alter ego admonishes Dryasdust: 'Surely at least you might have made an Index for these huge books!' *OC*, i. 3.

[47] *FG*, i. 197. [48] *FG*, v. 236.

The Dryasdust was supremely an editor, usually of the most arcane and useless material; he would publish from 'those sad Prussian Repositories', 'these Dryasdust labyrinths', rubbish '*in extenso*'.[49] A supreme instance lay in the Nosi–Grumkow correspondence:

likely to be published by the Prussian Dryasdust in coming time: but a more sordid mass of eavesdroppings, kitchen-ashes and floor-sweepings, collected and interchanged by a pair of treacherous Flunkies (big bullying Flunky and little trembling cringing one, Grumkow and Reichenbach), was never got together out of a gentleman's household. To no idlest reader, armed even with barnacles, and holding mouth and nose, can the stirring-up of such a dustbin be long tolerable. But the amazing problem was this Editor's, doomed to spell the Event into clearness if he could, and put dates, physiognomy and outline to it, by help of such Flunky-Sanscrit![50]

Once again, the heroic labours of Carlyle quietly triumph over crabbed information, and his powers of imagination are held to be incomparably superior to those of 'lazy Dryasdust'.[51] He loudly lamented 'the dark Dryasdustic Ages, gone all spectral under Dryasdust's sad handling'.[52] Even the most heroic of modern ages in Carlyle's eyes, the seventeenth century, was subject to the attentions of the pedantically academic as opposed to the genuinely gifted historian, and he regretted that the appalling experiences of the Thirty Years War had become only 'the most intricate of modern Occurrences in the domain of Dryasdust'.[53]

Irony accordingly prevails in Carlyle's evocations of the most celebrated of his Prussian contemporaries in the historical field, not least in regard to the familiarly pedantic claims of the Dryasdusts: 'Accurate Professor Ranke has read somewhere,—does not comfortably say where, nor comfortably give the least date,—this passage, or what authorises him to write it.'[54] Carlyle was thus one of the first to accuse Ranke of publishing incompletely referenced researches, although he was equally happy to ridicule his celebrated desire for achieving verisimilitude in his writings:

Ingenious Herr Professor Ranke,—whose *History of Friedrich* consists mainly of such matter excellently done, and offers mankind a wondrously distilled '*Astral-Spirit*,' or ghost-like facsimile (elegant gray ghost, with stars dim-twinkling through), of Friedrich's and other people's Diplomatisings in this

[49] *FG*, iv. 236; iii. 556; ii. 168. [50] *FG*, ii. 153. [51] *FG*. v. 33.
[52] *FG*, iii. 601. [53] *FG*, i. 328. [54] *FG*, i. 188.

World,—will satisfy the strongest diplomatic appetite; and to him we refer such as are given that way.[55]

Here one might recall Carlyle's own testimony to an inaccuracy of his own, where he cites a history of the Seven Years War '(incidentally, somewhere)'.[56] The hint here is plainly to the tedious unimportance of such a necessarily fleeting reference: the inspired writer could afford, apparently, to forgo such merely scholarly niceties if his appreciation of truth was to triumph over the Dryasdust's passion for mere accuracy. This gloriously self-serving confession did not prevent him from relishing the errors of others, as in his criticism of a 1787 *Collection of Royal Letters*: 'one of the most curious Books on the Thirty-Years War; "edited" with a composed stupidity, and cheerful infinitude of ignorance, which still farther distinguish it.'[57] Small wonder, then, that it was, by implication, left to the reader when, citing Pöllnitz's *Memoiren*, Carlyle invited him to 'correct his many blunders'.[58]

In marked contrast with his remarks on Ranke and his compatriots, Carlyle's greatest praise for his predecessors in the art of historical writing, particularly as it related to a history of Frederick the Great, was reserved, intriguingly, for eighteenth-century writers. Chief of these was one Köhler, the author of a *Reichs-Historie* published in Frankfurt and Leipzig in 1737. Crucially for Carlyle's readers, Köhler is mainly used as an effective point of contrast with later Prussian Dryasdusts:

He seems to me by far the best Historical Genius the Germans have yet produced, though I do not find much mention of him in their Literary Histories and Catalogues. A man of ample learning, and also cheerful human sense, and human honesty; whom it is thrice pleasant to meet with in those ghastly solitudes, populous chiefly with doleful creatures.[59]

[55] *FG*, iii. 726. On Ranke's inaccuracies, see Elizabeth A. Clark, *History, Theory, Text: Historians and the Linguistic Turn* (Cambridge, Mass., 2004), 10.

[56] *FG*, iii. 511 n. [57] *FG*, i. 225 n. [58] *FG*, iii. 266 n.

[59] *FG*, i. 71 n. A less admired chronicle to that produced by Köhler was the *Helden-Geschichte . . . Friedrichs des Andern* (Frankfurt, 1758–60), which Carlyle described as: 'One of the most hideous imbroglios ever published under the name of Book,—without vestige of Index, and on paper that has no margin and cannot stand ink,—yet with many curious articles stuffed blindly into the awful belly of it, like jewels in a rag-sack, or into *ten* rag-sacks all in one; with far more authenticity than you could expect in such case.' *FG*, ii. 180. It is, nonetheless, significant that Carlyle decides to abbreviate the otherwise unmanageably bulky title of this work precisely to the *Helden-Geschichte*; the heroic is of the essence in his historical works. The reader of Carlyle's historical writings needs to be aware of such, usually well signposted, editorial interventions. Likewise, any reading, even the most cursory, of *The Letters and Speeches of Oliver Cromwell* or the

This is an extremely rare instance of an eighteenth-century predecessor being held superior to nineteenth-century successors in Carlyle's opinion, but it is well to emphasise that this is in the field of work in which Carlyle equally plainly held himself to excel all other efforts undertaken by his own contemporaries. Accordingly, it ought to come as no surprise that his greatest praise was for the witness of an unprofessional eighteenth-century writer, again adduced at least as much to help denigrate his own contemporaries as to celebrate the work for its own sake. Carlyle lauded the memoirs of Frederick's sister Wilhelmina as pointing up the contrast with the unimaginative work of later students of the period; his words are also redolent of the familial sentimentality common in the fiction of his own age:

Wilhelmina's Narrative, very loose, dateless or misdated, plainly wrong in various particulars, has still its value for us: human *eyes*, even a child's, are worth something in comparison to human want-of-eyes, which is too frequent in History-books and elsewhere![60]

The superiority inherent in Wilhelmina's memoirs was held to be especially true in regard to the sections relating to the early part of Frederick's life, when he and his sister shared in the frequently disorientating and never less than strange atmosphere of their father's dictatorial court. This was an experience which gave her account, in Carlyle's estimation, a great advantage over other sources:

Pull Wilhelmina *straight*, the best you can; deduct a twenty-five or sometimes even a seventy-five per cent, from the exaggerative portions of her statement; you will find her always true, lucid, charmingly human; and by far the best authority on this part of her Brother's History. State-Papers to some extent have also been printed on the matter; and of written State-Papers, here in England and elsewhere, this Editor has had several hundredweights distilled for him: but except as lights hung out over Wilhelmina nothing yet known, of published or manuscript, can be regarded as good for much.[61]

Again, note how Carlyle quietly undervalued the workmanlike toil of his assistants at this point, whilst simultaneously emphasizing his own editorial labours. His assistants merely distil documents for him, allowing

History of Friedrich II of Prussia reveals evidence of Carlyle's obsession with indexes. The act of recovery from works of the past is one of the many images of labour promoted by Carlyle in his historical works, hence something of the heroic language accorded to his self-image as an editor, something that is constant in his work, from *Sartor Resartus* and *Past and Present* to the *History of Friedrich II of Prussia*.

[60] *FG*, i. 453. [61] *FG*, i. 606.

him, by contrast, to accentuate his own almost intuitive understanding of the eighteenth century; it is as if he and Wilhelmina shared some mystic rapport over the intervening years. Likewise, although from a rather different perspective, if an experientially suggestive one, Carlyle critically appreciated Napoleon's remarks on Frederick's military campaigns as 'pleasant reading, though the fruit evidently of slight study' and which 'do credit to Napoleon perhaps still more than to Friedrich'.[62] Such a calculated evocation of the mind of Napoleon attests to Carlyle's own roots in the Romantic culture of an England by then long given over to Victorian sensibilities. In both cases, Carlyle preferred the words of elite sources, respectively those of a Prussian princess and a world-historical conqueror, to those of mere historians: his own self-appointed task as poet-historian was clearly felt by him as fitting him out as worthy to share the insights of such exalted company. It is in this way that his references to the 'titanic' figure of Napoleon are rapidly followed by the claims of his own heightened senses, through which he alerted his readers to the fact that 'the dark-whirlwind, and huge uproar of the last generation, gradually dies away again'.[63]

Such implied equality is evident in a rare instance of Carlyle's praising Voltaire, which he does in regard to Voltaire's work on a life of another monarch and military worthy, Charles XII. Note here, however, how the work of more workaday chroniclers is valued in higher terms than usual, albeit in order to qualify Carlyle's notably pinched praise for Voltaire:

> Now it was by questioning this Fabrice, and industriously picking the memory of him clean, that M. de Voltaire wrote another Book, much more of an 'Epic' than Henri IV.,—a *History*, namely, *of Charles XII.*; which seems to me the best-written of all his Books, and wants nothing but *truth* (indeed a dreadful want) to make it a possession forever. *Voltaire*, if you want fine writing; *Alderfeld* and *Fabrice*, if you would see the features of the Fact: these three are still the Books upon Charles XII.[64]

Voltaire, an earlier incarnation of the dual role of poet-historian was thus found wanting, both as a poet—'fine writing'—and as a historian—'wants nothing but *truth*'—and a rather different division of

[62] *FG*, v. 265 n.

[63] *FG*, i. 9, 10. On Napoleon's proleptic appearances in his earlier history, see *FR*, i. 112, ii. 380. He is placed alongside Cromwell and 'Modern Revolutionism' in 'The hero as king', *OH*, 196–244.

[64] *FG*, ii. 14–15.

labour from that Carlyle posited for himself had held for Voltaire and those Dryasdusts of an earlier epoch, Alderfeld and Fabrice. In such an apparently throwaway gesture, Carlyle made a major statement about his own task in the nineteenth century as compared with that of an altogether less worthy eighteenth-century predecessor. It is a moment that merits much reflection by the critical reader of Carlyle, and has to be read alongside his claims that Voltaire's *Vie privée du roi de Prusse* contains angrily mendacious calumnies.[65] A calculated gesture appearing early in the second volume, it offers a defiant statement about relations between Carlyle's own age and the eighteenth century that can be taken as a keynote of his own thoughts on this epochal matter.

Carlyle, indeed, made many statements about epochs in the course of his massively discursive life of Frederick, statements that demonstrate an exalted conception of history. In a passage pointed adroitly to the Berlin in which Hegel had taught, but nowhere mentioning the philosopher, Carlyle deflatingly referred to a witness of events there, Sir Jonas Hanway, as giving to Hanway's later readers the insights of 'an extinct Minerva's Owl': the Owl of Minerva does, however, move her wings more conventionally elsewhere in the text, ushering in a new age, as is her Hegelian wont, when Wolfe captures Quebec: 'which is itself, as the Decision that America is to be English and not French, is surely an Epoch in World-History!'[66] There is an almost Hegelian seriousness about history throughout the history of Frederick, even if the necessities of human life mean it is usually honoured in the breach rather than in the observation. Hence also something of the power of the ventriloquized commentators, such as Sauerteig, one of whose observations allows Carlyle to build up an incremental vision of history as a possible source of human spiritual improvement in otherwise despondent times:

> Alas, the Ideal of History, as my friend Sauerteig knows, is very high; and it is not one serious man, but many successions of such, and whole serious generations of such, that can ever again build up History towards its old dignity. We must renounce ideals. We must sadly take up with the mournfullest barren realities;—dismal continents of Brandenburg sand, as in this instance; mere tumbled mountains of marine-stores, without so much as an Index to them![67]

The political history of the eighteenth century was only to be glanced at when seeking to ferment such improvement: 'These are fields of History which are to be, so soon as humanly possible, *suppressed*; which only

[65] *FG*, ii. 270, 277 n. [66] *FG*, iii. 313. v. 560. [67] *FG*, i. 21.

Mephistopheles, or the Bad Genius of Mankind, can contemplate with pleasure.'[68] Spiritually pure history was to be promoted apart from such depressing periods, which are 'more worthy to be called Phenomena of Putrid Fermentation, than Struggles of Human Heroism to vindicate itself in this Planet, which latter alone are worthy of recording as "History" by mankind'.[69]

Just as 'History' was rigidly defined by Carlyle, so learning and culture were similarly held in check by his own standards. Noting that his father had ordered that Frederick was not to study Latin, a language of pedantry, Carlyle emphasized how Frederick's sense of reality made him superior to 'Men-of-Letters' who 'have made a reputation for themselves with but a fraction of the real knowledge, concerning men and things, past and present, which Friedrich was possessed of'. Book-men were 'generally pedants and mere bags of wind and folly', though occasionally 'rich mines of quizzability' for the historian. Even Frederick's father, Friedrich Wilhelm, was held superior to the merely book learned, such was Carlyle's preference for experience over theory.[70] Indeed, one can never be certain at whose expense the irony contained in his references to 'such' soldiers as 'read'—to 'soldier students, if there were among us any such species'—is directed: is it at the soldiers, or at the world of books?[71] What is certain, is that Frederick's well-known love of music was of remarkably little interest to Carlyle, whose only interest in one Fasch, 'a virtuoso on I know not what instrument', was that he was 'a man given to take note of things about him'. Musicians served their turn as sources, not as artists; Mendelssohn's revival of Bach had plainly had little or no impact on Carlyle. Frederick the soldier-musician was remembered by Carlyle for the former ability, not at all for the latter, as he referred contemptuously to his favoured monarch's 'flutings'. [72]

Carlyle's allusions to culture are sometimes philistine to a degree, and they often serve as an opportunity for him to praise the Germanic over the French in cultural terms. Even here his own claims regarding the epic nature of his study are evident, as he remarked of his hero

[68] *FG*, i. 544. [69] *FG*, i. 549.

[70] *FG*, i. 466, 520, 616, 624. Few figures are as cruelly presented in his *Friedrich* as the novel-writing Prince Anton Ulrich of Brunswick, described by Carlyle as a 'goodnatured old gentleman, of the idle ornamental species, in whose head most things, it is likely, were reduced to vocables, scribble and sentimentality' and in whom 'only a steady internal gravitation towards praise and pudding was traceable as very real'. *FG*, i. 547.

[71] *FG*, iii. 60, 550–1; vi. 17, 103. He recommended that soldiers should study Frederick's military art: *FG*, vi. 79.

[72] *FG*, vi. 148. He had, however, praised Gluck in his earlier history: *FR*, i. 203–4.

that 'he loved intellect as few men on the throne, or off it, ever did; and the little he could gather of it round him often seems to me a fact tragical rather than otherwise'.[73] Sadly exemplary in this regard was the Italian *philosophe* Algarotti, 'whose books seem to claim a reading, and do not repay it you when given'.[74] Even worse than the pseudo-French Algarotti was the despised Rousseau, whose *Confessions* showed him like 'many other poor waste creatures, going off in self-conflagration, for amusement of the parish, in that manner'.[75] Yet worse, predictably, was his eighteenth-century *bête-noire*, Voltaire, who had gradually overtaken Rousseau in Carlyle's list of eighteenth-century hates by the time he came to write his life of Frederick. Voltaire's presence in *Friedrich* is as historically disastrous as it was in the *French Revolution*.[76] Carlyle regretted his indebtedness to Voltaire for information on the Congress of Cambrai; he worried over Frederick's immersion in the 'Anarchic Republic of Letters', alluding with irony to 'Heaven's own Inspiration' in Voltaire's poem *Mahomet*, and 'such a terrestrial Doggery' lying at Frederick's heels.[77] Even Mirabeau's praise of free trade was similarly dispatched by Carlyle, whilst his dismissal of Helvetius allowed him to praise the Prussian writer Hamann, a Counter-Enlightenment figure, as being 'on modest terms a Literary man of real merit and originality';[78] Goethe is present throughout the text as the true type of the writer as genius. Never guilty of false modesty, Carlyle, about to descend into his own literary silence as he described Frederick's death, alluded to his own early essays when once again praising Goethe at the very close of this, his final, mammoth undertaking:

> In these final days of his, we have transiently noticed Arch-Cardinal de Rohan, Arch-Quack Cagliostro, and a most select Company of Persons and of Actions, like an Elixir of a Nether World, miraculously emerging into daylight; and all Paris, and by degrees all Europe, getting loud with the *Diamond-Necklace* History. And to eyes of deeper speculation,—World-Poet Goethe's, for instance,—it is becoming evident that Chaos is again big. As has not she proved to be, and is still proving, in the most teeming way! Better for a Royal Hero, fallen old and feeble, to be hidden from such things.[79]

Frederick disappears into a dark European night—and these passages were later to be read in an even darker, infinitely stranger moment in

[73] *FG*, ii. 572. [74] *FG*, ii. 663. [75] *FG*, iii. 445.
[76] The association is made late in the text: *FG*, vi. 599–600.
[77] *FG*, i. 562; iii. 634.
[78] *FG*, vi. 351, 368–9. [79] *FG*, i. 390; ii. 252; vi. 156–7, 574, 696.

European history, when, according to Hugh Trevor-Roper, they were read to Hitler during his last days by Goebbels (it was his favourite book).[80] Frederick dies, however, a hero, and his heroic status seems to run counter to most of the features of Carlyle's bankrupt and sceptical eighteenth century. What was it about Frederick that made him stand out from his decidedly unheroic epoch? What, indeed, does Carlyle's characterization of his latter-day hero tell readers about his broader conception of the eighteenth century? In answering these questions it is well to bear in mind how Frederick is understood antithetically in relation to Voltaire, his erstwhile friend, as when, in the opening stages of Carlyle's history, he condemns Voltaire's critical *Vie privée du roi de Prusse*:

> Our counsel is, Out of window with it, he that would know Friedrich of Prussia! Keep it awhile, he that would know François Arouet de Voltaire, and a certain numerous unfortunate class of mortals, whom Voltaire is sometimes capable of sinking to be spokesman for, in this world![81]

Intriguingly, he figured their relations in revealingly classical terms as those between 'the Sage Pluto of the Eighteenth Century and his Tyrant Dionysius'.[82]

So great was the dismissal of Voltaire's French world, that Carlyle even nominated the notoriously unbalanced martinet Friedrich Wilhelm as a man who showed the 'whims of genius', praising him as a 'Spartan King', and as 'the great Drill-sergeant of the Prussian nation'. Friedrich Wilhelm preferred German thrift to 'French sumptuosity', revealing himself to have been 'a North-German Spartan' in a world which had long lost its Spartans.[83] Martial virtues prevailed over intellectual ability in Carlyle's Prussian history, to a disturbing degree that all too accurately reflected his taste, at the end of his career, for the dictatorial as evincing the true virtues of statesmanship. With all the asperity of an intellectual, Carlyle celebrated Friedrich Wilhelm's honest lack of learning, as he declared him: 'A Spartan man, as we said,—though probably he knew

80 Hugh Trevor-Roper, *The Last Days of Hitler* (London, 1947; seventh edition, 1995), 87–8, 206–8. For a reading of Carlyle's Prussianism in his life of Frederick as 'proto-fascist', and comparable in this respect with Nietzsche, see Albert La Valley, *Carlyle and the Idea of the Modern: Studies in Carlyle's Prophetic Literature and its Relation to Blake, Nietzsche, Marx, and Others* (New Haven, 1968), 265–78.

81 *FG*, i. 17. 82 *FG*, ii. 597.

83 *FG*, i. 412–14, 422. He had earlier praised the Duke de Broglie as a 'veteran disciplinarian, of a firm drill-sergeant morality, such as may be depended on'. *FR*, i. 164.

as little of the Spartans as the Spartans did of him.'[84] When lamenting his death, Carlyle betrayed himself as the author both of a heroic life of Odin and as the anti-democratic prophet behind the *Latter-Day Pamphlets*. It is a digest of all of Carlyle's political peculiarities, and is but one of many occasions in which he inscribes himself within his own text:

No Baresark of them, nor Odin's self, I think, was a bit of truer human stuff;—I confess his value to me, in these sad times, is rare and great. Considering the usual Histrionic, Papin's-Digester, Truculent-Charlatan and other species of 'Kings,' alone attainable for the sunk flunky populations of an Era given up to Mammon and the worship of its own belly, what would not such a population give for a Friedrich Wilhelm, to guide it on the road *back* from Orcus a little? 'Would give,' I have written; but alas, it ought to have been '*should* give.' What *they* 'would' give is too mournfully plain to me, in spite of ballotboxes: a steady and tremendous truth from the days of Barabbas downwards and upwards![85]

In so praising Friedrich Wilhelm, Carlyle faced a difficult problem in doing similar justice to another eighteenth-century martial hero, Charles XII of Sweden, but one who was also praised by the hated Voltaire. Carlyle's solution was to praise the physical courage of Charles, a 'man of antique character', whilst disparaging Voltaire's celebrated portrait. Where the 'Open-hearted Antique populations' would have worshipped such a figure as a god: 'Voltaire, too, for the artificial Moderns, has made a myth of him, of another type; one of those impossible cast-iron gentlemen, heroically mad, such as they show in the Playhouses, pleasant but not profitable, to an undiscerning Public.'[86] Friedrich Wilhelm and Charles XII embodied many of the virtues that Carlyle would come to praise in Frederick, but it was vital for his purposes that the despised Voltaire was disposed of lest his relationship with the monarch be allowed to tarnish his image.[87] Whilst generally successful in distancing his monarch from the *philosophe*, the narrative pull of his story sometimes got the better of Carlyle, as when he openly described the two men when

[84] *FG*, i. 425. Interestingly, Carlyle's conception of Sparta has been read, by the leading authority on the subject, as very like that of Voltaire's: Elizabeth Rawson, *The Spartan Tradition in Western Thought* (Oxford, 1969), 360.

[85] *FG*, ii. 690. 'The hero as divinity', *OH*, 1–41.

[86] *FG*, i. 436–8.

[87] Carlyle was explicit in the matter, writing of Voltaire that 'Friedrich was not wise in his longing for him, or clasping him so frankly in his arms.' *FG*, iv. 375. For even more insinuating remarks about the relationship, see *FG*, iv. 381: 'Voltaire's flatteries to Friedrich, in those scattered little Billets with their snatches of verse, are the prettiest in the world,—and approach very near to sincerity, though seldom quite attaining it.'

they had finally fallen out as, 'A pair of Lovers hopelessly estranged and divorced; and yet, in a sense, unique and priceless to one another.'[88] It is of a piece with this otherwise usually strictly maintained strategy that one of the first images of Frederick that we glimpse as readers is also an opportunity for Carlyle to criticize the *cognoscenti*, as he heaps praise on a portrait of a young Frederick drumming, a work which ought to have encouraged collectors to forget 'the coreggiosity of Coreggio, and the learned babble of the sale-room and varnishing Auctioneer': praise for the painting also allowed Carlyle to give yet further evidence of the visceral racism that so frequently vitiates his later writings, as he detailed how, 'probably for the sake of colour and pictorial effect, a Blackamoor, aside with parasol in hand, grinning approbation, has been added'.[89] Frederick, in Carlyle's estimation, incarnated unassailable political and military values, and not the allegedly specious values of art and its votaries. Hence the power of his astonishingly self-assured remark that: 'Of Friedrich's Literary works, nobody, not even Friedrich himself, will think it necessary that we say much.'[90]

Frederick's relations with his father also revealed a major theme of much Victorian reflection on its relations with its predecessor culture, as Carlyle noted how, despite physical similarities, Frederick would not simply be a reproduction of his father, since: 'It is the new generation come; which cannot live quite as the old one did. A perennial controversy in human life; coeval with the genealogies of men.' However this might be, in the narrational logic of Carlyle's moralistic history, Frederick did prove himself 'in all manner of important respects, the filial sequel of Friedrich Wilhelm'.[91] Thus it was also that, due to the training instilled on the reluctant Crown Prince by his father, 'to his Athenian-French elegancies, and airy promptitudes and brilliances, there shall lie as basis an adamantine Spartanism and Stoicism; very rare but very indispensable, for such a superstructure'.[92] When Friedrich Wilhelm's distrust of his son's associate Lieutenant Katte led to his

[88] *FG*, v. 607. For more of the same, with talk of 'a Duet of estranged Lovers!' see *FG*, v. 611–12. On the implications of such remarks as interpreted by later historians, see David Wotton, 'Unhappy Voltaire, or "I shall never get over it as long as I live"', *History Workshop Journal*, 50 (2000), 137–55.

[89] *FG*, i. 445–6. [90] *FG*, iv. 290.

[91] *FG*, i. 513, 521. For a reading of *FG* as a work which parallels Carlyle with Frederick (and which usefully describes it as 'a non-epic history of the creation of an epic nation'), see Chris R. Vanden Bossche, *Carlyle and the Search for Authority* (Columbus, O.H., 1991), 151–62.

[92] *FG*, i. 576.

placing Frederick before a Court Martial and then executing his young friend, Carlyle excused such behaviour by insisting that his goal had been discipline, not revenge, and that the scene so described was 'a wild enough piece of humanity, not so much ludicrous as tragical'.[93] Carlyle, the omnipresent narrator of this royal history, insisted on his rights to choreograph the many genres that constituted his unique exercise in the 'bastard heroic'.

The military arts were the most praised in Carlyle's Prussian history, and experience always triumphed over theory, as in his reference to an attachment of Frederick's soldiers as being 'unconscious stoic-philosophers in buff', and his own declaration that Frederick's feats at Teintiz were 'didactic, admonitory to the military mind, nay to the civic reader that has sympathy with heroisms, with work done manfully, and terror and danger and difficulty well trampled under foot'.[94] What Carlyle would not allow was any survival of the traditional image of Frederick's 'mendacity', an attribute that was to be dismissed totally in favouring Frederick's heroic status as the truthful and practically minded 'Land-Father' and 'Sheperd' of his people, a man, supremely, of 'excellent practical sense'.[95] Such was the nature of Carlyle's appraisal of his hero that he concluded that 'Posterity is still striving for a view of [Frederick], as something memorable.'[96] Considering time in an almost Hegelian reverie, Carlyle discerned in Frederick a Promethean Titan, belittled by those who could not comprehend him, and stating his own position as a properly appreciative poet-historian accordingly: 'Friedrich does wonderfully, without sympathy from almost anybody; and the indifference with which he walks along, under such a cloud of sulky stupidities, of mendacities and misconceptions, from the herd of mankind is decidedly admirable to me.'[97]

Whilst praising Frederick's military prowess, Carlyle did not claim always to understand his abilities, and the reader who has kept in step with him through much marching over the six volumes is apt to accept rather readily his leave taking of such matters in the sixth and final volume:

> Hardly above two Battles more from him, if even two:—and mostly the wearied Reader's imagination left to conceive for itself those intricate strategies, and endless manouverings on the Diemel and the Dill, on the Ohm River and the Schwalm and the Lippe, or wherever they may be, with small help from a wearied Editor!—[98]

[93] *FG*, ii. 280. [94] *FG*, iv. 601, 54. [95] *FG*, iii. 419; iv. 372.
[96] *FG*, v. 23. [97] *FG*, v. 638–9. [98] *FG*, vi. 140.

For all his celebration of Frederick's military pre-eminence, Carlyle was nonetheless happy to record the end of 'these wearisome death-wrestlings'. With the completion of Frederick's 'Twelve Hercules-labours', one of which was the Seven Years War, 'his Seven-Years labour of Hercules', 'what was required of him in World-History is accomplished'.[99] Similarly, what was to become Hegel's State had flourished accordingly, since 'To have achieved a Friedrich the Second for King over it, was Prussia's grand merit.'[100]

A warrior—whose army was accorded high praise when likened by his historian to Cromwell's Ironsides—Frederick was nevertheless praised by Carlyle for being far from sanguinary as a head of state, and whilst signing death sentences, where he had to, 'rigorously well', he prided himself that only some fourteen to fifteen of Prussia's over five million citizens were executed in any one year.[101] His declining years were chronicled as those of a 'fine, unaffectedly vigorous, simple and manful old age', fitting for 'a mighty reformer . . . the greatest of his day', the opponent of 'monkeries, school-pedantries, trade-monopolies, serfages', all those things, notably, that would have troubled such an admittedly unusual product of the late Scottish Enlightenment as Carlyle.[102] Frederick had put into practical effect the better aims of the eighteenth century, and died before its worst features could be identified. He was both of his century and a figure that rose above it. Plainly, at the end of the work, Carlyle enjoyed making a monarch literally *his* subject, adopting his prophetic mantle to adjudicate the true nature of kingship, the Scottish peasant voicing the accents of eternity as voiced in scriptural echoes, and moralizing to the very end as he pointed to his readers and their shortcomings as part of his self-appointed, world-historical, not to say religious task:

I define him to myself as hitherto the Last of the Kings;—when the Next will be, is a very long question! But it seems to me as if Nations, probably all Nations, by and by, in their despair,—blinded, swallowed like Jonah, in such a whale's-belly of things brutish, waste, abominable (for is not Anarchy, or the Rule of what is Baser over what is Nobler, the one life's-misery worth complaining of, and, in fact, the abomination of abominations, springing from and producing all others whatsoever?)—as if the Nations universally and England too if it hold on, may more and more bethink themselves of such a Man and his Function and Performance, with feelings far other than are

[99] *FG*, vi. 298, 339, 389. [100] *FG*, vi. 347. [101] *FG*, v. 260; vi. 632.
[102] *FG*, vi. 637, 675.

possible at present. Meanwhile, all I had to say of him is finished: that too, it seems, was a bit of work appointed to be done. Adieu, good readers; bad also, adieu.[103]

The prophet who had inaugurated the reign of Queen Victoria with a lightning-lit display of republican horror went into silence at the mid-point of her reign, bemoaning the lack of kingship in the post-revolutionary world.

Prophets, especially post-Enlightenment prophets, often need at least a quasi-religious basis for their prophecies, and here the historian of Frederick's life faced a genuine problem. Most troubling for, and most evasively treated by, Carlyle the poet-prophet was a very particular feature of Frederick's version of Enlightened despotism: his religion, or rather his lack of it. Carlyle was reduced to saying that:

Atheism, truly, he never could abide: to him, as to all of us, it was flatly inconceivable that intellect, moral emotion, could have been put into *him* by an Entity that had none of its own. But there, pretty much, his Theism seems to have stopped.[104]

This had also been a problem facing an English predecessor of Carlyle, Thomas Campbell, who had been engaged in editing an anonymous biography of Frederick which celebrated, in 1840, the centenary of his accession to the Prussian throne, and which similarly tried to reclaim Frederick for Protestantism.[105] The difference between that work and Carlyle's is that this was a genuinely creative problem for a post-Christian thinker such as Carlyle, and the nature of that problem raises two related questions for readers of his biography of Frederick: what is the religion that can be found in the history of Frederick and his reign; and where did Carlyle's own theism stop? In seeking to answer this question it is well to reflect on a phrase Carlyle threw out in relation to the views of two female members of the Prussian royal house: 'Sceptico-Calvinistic' is an accurate description of much in Carlyle's own religious universe.[106] Where catechisms failed to instruct, only the piety of parents could succeed, and Frederick suffered from catechisms produced in an age of 'enlightened Protestantism' of which Carlyle was deeply suspicious, allowing him to blame the environment for Frederick's scepticism:

[103] *FG*, vi. 697–8. [104] *FG*, vi. 686–7.

[105] Thomas Campbell, *Frederick the Great, his Court, and Times* (4 vols., London, 1842–3), iv. 127–8, 132, 135, 137–9, 140, 168.

[106] *FG*, i. 44.

'Enlightened Edict-of-Nantes Protestantism, a cross between Bayle and Calvin; that was but indifferent babe's-milk to the little creature.' In maternal terms, Frederick lacked exactly the sort of 'Devoutness, pious Nobleness!' that could put into initial effect the growth of a lasting faith.[107]

There is something deeply ambiguous in Carlyle's evocation of the religion of Sophie Charlotte and her mother, as can be appreciated through his ambivalence concerning the light that illuminates Charlottenburg, but which is an unambiguously French light:

> French essentially, Versaillese, Sceptico-Calvinistic, reflex and direct,—illuminating the dark North; and indeed has never been so bright since. The light was not what we can call inspired; lunar rather, not of the genial or solar kind: but, in good truth, it was the best then going.

There is much, as it were, to reflect on here, since light is unambiguously presented as a good, albeit a limited version of the light, but the best then available implies some understanding of the appeal of French rationalism, or is it, rather, that anything French is put to better purpose in the northern lands? This ambiguity is affirmed in the irony around his appropriately chiaroscuro presentation of Sophie Charlotte's attempted meeting with 'that admirable sage, the doubter Bayle':

> Their sublime messenger roused the poor man, in his garret there [Rotterdam], in the Bompies,—after dark: but he had a headache that night; was in bed, and could not come. He followed them next day; leaving his paper imbroglios, his historical, philosophical, anti-theological marine-stores; and suspended his never-ending scribble, on their behalf;—but would not accept a pension, and give it up.[108]

Bayle may have been a sceptical scribbler, but he was an honest one; sceptics would seem acceptable to Carlyle when honest, and a subject of horror if merely cynical and self-serving. Bayle comes out of the volumes rather better than does the text's resident anti-hero, Voltaire. As Carlyle puts it, referring to his own favoured Icelandic saga image: 'Scepticism, which is there beginning at the very top of the world-tree, and has to descend through all the boughs with terrible results to mankind, is as yet pleasant, tinting the leaves with fine autumnal red.'[109]

[107] *FG*, i. 387, 507–10.

[108] *FG*, i. 44–5. He is much more critical of John Toland, a 'mere broken Heretic' in England, but a favourite in Sophie's Prussia: *FG*, i. 48–9.

[109] *FG*, i. 46.

Autumnal eighteenth-century scepticism, usually French, was forever contrasted with the vernal Reformation, usually German, in Carlyle's history; hence some of the polemical power of his creation of the 'Sceptico-Calvinist' category. He was conventionally critical of the Council of Constance—'one of the largest *wind-eggs* ever dropped with noise and travail in this world'—and properly admiring, accordingly, of the Reformed world which succeeded it, noting that Duke Albert of Brandenburg, a Hohenzollern ancestor of Frederick, was 'a profoundly religious man, as all thoughtful men then were'.[110] The theological wars of the sixteenth century constituted a world-historical moment in Carlyle's universe, as he noted that: 'The Reformation was the great Event of that Sixteenth Century; according as a man did something in that, or did nothing and obstructed doing, has he much claim to memory, or no claim, in this age of ours.'[111] It allowed him also to combine his religious views with his cultivated philistinism, as he observed of the Italians, very much the proto-French in this respect, that their removal from the Reformation into the world of art signalled the descent of a nation 'sunk from virtue to *virtù*', but the real contrast with the German lands was France, 'to which we constantly return for illustration'. France had come close to accepting the Reformation, but this was lost with the Massacre of St Bartholomew, and with it:

> the Writ of Summons had been served; Heaven's Messenger could not stay away forever. No he returned duly; with accounts run up, on compound interest to the actual hour in 1792;—and then, at last, there had to be a 'Protestantism;' and we know of what kind that was!

Nations were to heed the voice of Heaven, as the 'question of questions' in Europe in Frederick's time was: 'Will you obey the heavenly voice, or will you not?'[112] The revolutionary French plainly did not, whilst Friedrich Wilhelm did, for whilst he was 'a very arbitrary King', he found that his '*arbitrium,* or sovereign will, was that of the Eternal Heavens as well; and did exceedingly behove to be done, if the Earth would prosper'.[113]

Approbation of Protestantism is a constant in Carlyle's history. It was at the core of his meditations on the seventeenth century, about which he had declared that: 'The History of Europe, at that epoch, meant essentially the struggle of Protestantism against Catholicism,—a broader

[110] *FG*, i. 190, 254. [111] *FG*, i. 262. [112] *FG*, i. 266–7.
[113] *FG*, i. 409.

form of that same struggle, of devout Puritanism against dignified Ceremonialism, which forms the History of England then.'[114] In the history of Frederick, Protestantism was praised in the world-historical developmental manner so familiar in Carlyle's writing, a march of moral insight and religious profundity rather more significant for him than the familiar Scottish Enlightenment trope of the 'march of mind'. Thus Frederick's ancestor Joachim II had adopted the Confession of Augsburg in 1539 as 'the true Interpretation of this Universe, so far as we had as yet got'; there can be no doubt as to which side Carlyle supported in 'the grand Protestant-Papist Controversy, the general armed-lawsuit of mankind in that generation'.[115]

The presence of the Reformation remained strangely unobserved in the eighteenth century, and a young Frederick travelled through Saxony without 'thinking about Luther, which thou and I, good English reader, would surely have done, in crossing Wittenberg and the birthplace of Protestantism'. Yet, Frederick was also allegedly a believer in Calvinistic double-predestination, a notion held by 'many benighted creatures, this Editor among them'; avoiding the scene of long dead theological controversy—and Carlyle wondered whether it matters whether a Protestant theologian was a Socinian or not—he praised Frederick, somewhat bizarrely, as being, in his own way, a devout Protestant:

> Friedrich's Creed, or Theory of the Universe, differed extremely, in many important points, from that of Dr. Martin Luther: but in the vital all-essential point, what we may call the heart's-core of all Creeds which are human, human and not simious or diabolic, the King and the Doctor were with their whole heart at one: That it is not allowable, that it is dangerous and abominable, to attempt believing what is not true. In that sense, Friedrich, by nature and position, was a Protestant, and even the chief Protestant in the world.[116]

A tacit identification was thus made between Frederick's doctrinally minimal creed and that propounded by Carlyle, echoes of whose own position were voiced in his description of Frederick's non-clerical brand of piety, and in the sad, but consistent, creed by which he lived; the assumption that there was no Divine Justice or Providence in the world, but that things were overseen by an 'unfathomable Demiurgus' may not have been Carlyle's exact creed, but it was close enough for him to remark on Frederick's evident 'piety'.[117] Silence can, however, be

114 *OC*, i. 34.

115 *FG*, i. 274, 308–9.

116 *FG*, ii. 212, 278, 634; vi. 150; v. 586.

117 *FG*, vi. 346, 687.

religious gold in Carlyle, as in his claim regarding Frederick that: 'His religion, and he had in withered forms a good deal of it, if we will look well, being almost always in a strictly voiceless state,—nay, ultra-voiceless, or voiced the wrong way, as is too well known.'[118] Nonetheless, Frederick's reflections on the earthquake at Lisbon in 1755 'are stingy, snarling contemptuous, rather than valiant and pious, and need not detain us here'.[119] These remarks were Frederick at his most Voltairian; small wonder that Carlyle sought to distance not only himself from them, but even Frederick himself.

Where Carlyle felt closer to Frederick (and even to Voltaire) was in the repudiation of Roman Catholicism, but even here the campaign against the *Infâme* was fraught with dangers, as revolt against 'religious slavery' could easily have been followed by what neither Frederick nor Voltaire had foreseen, namely a general revolt against authority, so that their revolt against the 'Priestly Sham-Hierarchies' foreshadowed that staged in France in 1793 against 'the Social and Civic Sham-Hierarchies'.[120] Disapprobation of Catholicism took the form of a critique of its political pretensions, in which the Gothic language of the fantastic was deployed against the Holy Roman Empire and its satellites. Lapland witchcraft was invoked alongside satirical images of old cardinals riding on brooms through the sky to meet Satan; the Kaiser Karl continued to fight with 'Satan's Invisible World'; even the balance of power in Europe was described as 'a certain spectral something'.[121] The Kaiser Karl was 'unlucky, spectre-hunting, spectre-hunted'; huge spectres and 'absurd bugaboos' stalked Europe, all reflecting Karl's 'Imperial Necromancy', his 'Imperial Spectre-Politics'.[122] Nearer home, the Pretender was a 'World Spectre', and the superstitious intricacies of Catholic diplomacy in a time of war revealed that 'in an age of universal infidelity to Heaven, where the Heavenly Sun has *sunk*, there occur strange Spectre-huntings'.[123] Even Friedrich Wilhelm was captured by two diplomatic conjurors, entering into his employ 'as two devils would have done in the old miraculous times'; generally, however, the Protestantism of the Hohenzollerns stood its ground, as instanced by the story of a spectre haunting the royal palace resolving itself into a perfectly everyday explanation.[124]

'Devil-Diplomatists', both Catholic and Protestant, carried out 'Devil Diplomacy'; the battles that ensued were 'spurred on by spectralities of

[118] *FG*, v. 245. [119] *FG*, iv. 489. [120] *FG*, vi. 342–4.
[121] *FG*, i. 451, 500, 568. [122] *FG*, i. 569–70, 574, 600–1.
[123] *FG*, i. 530, 551. [124] *FG*, i. 604, 439–41.

the sick brain, by phantasms of hope, phantasms of terror'; 'phantasm and the babble of Versailles' maintained such warfare, but they also ushered in through their enterprise, 'by way of response, a *Ragnarök*, or Twilight of the Gods, which, as "French Revolution, or Apotheosis of *Sansculottism*," is now well known;—and that is something to consider of!'[125] Frederick had to withstand a 'general dance of Unclean Spirits with their intrigues and spectralities', a 'General Dance of the Furies': fortunately, Frederick was himself god-like, a Phoebus-Apollo, a man fit to keep company with the Muhammad Carlyle had done so much to glorify in his *On Heroes and Hero Worship* (1841).[126] Frederick and other warrior-kings were to be praised as the opponents of political anarchies, which 'to the Maker of this Universe . . . are eternally abhorrent':[127] Frederick thus played a major part in the final development of Carlyle's fundamentally religious, if 'Sceptico-Calvinist', interpretation of history.

For all he withstood such enemies, Frederick's religious uncertainties complicate his place in Carlyle's heroic pantheon. There is about the warrior-emperor something rather less than there is about the warrior-Lord Protector, and that something is religion, the religion marked out in Cromwell's Calvinist moment of conversion, and clarified by Carlyle as 'a grand epoch for a man: properly the one epoch; the turning-point which guides upwards, or guides downwards, him and his activity forevermore'. What is true of the individual believer is also true of a culture, as Carlyle immediately argues in the wake of describing Cromwell's conversion:

That the 'Sense of difference between Right and Wrong' had filled all Time and all Space for man, and bodies itself forth into a Heaven and Hell for him: this constitutes the grand feature of those Puritan, Old-Christian Ages; this is the element which stamps them as Heroic, and has rendered their works great, manlike, fruitful to all generations. It is by far the memorablest achievement of our Species; without that element, in some form or other, nothing of Heroic had ever been among us.[128]

The heroic in the age of Frederick was, therefore, necessarily transitory and elusive, but nonetheless heroic for all that: a 'Sceptico-Calvinist'

125 *FG*, ii. 62; iii. 330, 336, 342.

126 *FG*, iv. 85, 607; v. 163. Kaunitz was similarly depicted as the 'God-Brahma' and Burns as Thor, a peasant-god: *FG*, iv. 463; i. 473. On Carlyle's praise for Mohammed, see 'The hero as prophet', *OH*, 42–77.

127 *FG*, vi. 404. Hence also his recourse to images of the fantastic and the supernatural in his work on the French Revolution: *FR*, i. 132–3, ii. 335, 466–7.

128 *OC*, i. 45.

could be heroic in his own way as much as the resolute Calvinist had been in his more immediately and obviously eloquent manner. Was the age of Frederick fated, nevertheless, to be less heroic, or did the fact that it took place in a sceptical age render it equally heroic, facing as it did the need to overcome the morally compromised nature of the eighteenth century? Carlyle is silent on this matter, and it is an enigmatic silence, both in terms of his own religious understanding and in his very particular reading of history as a providential outpouring of human energy and spiritual potential.[129]

Something of the ambivalence Carlyle felt about the relationship between the eighteenth and nineteenth centuries is palpable in his remark regarding Franz Josias of Coburg: 'a GRANDSON'S GRANDSON of whom is, at this day, Prince of Wales among the English people, and to me a subject of intense reflection now and then!'[130] The postlapsarian dispensation of the eighteenth century necessarily affected the succeeding culture, and such a relationship was extremely unlikely to be a positive one in the estimate of so resolutely pessimistic a thinker as Carlyle. For Carlyle, the eighteenth century was a looking glass in which the Victorians could see a foreshadowing of their own reflections; it was this relationship between the two centuries that allowed Carlyle to indulge so much in prolepsis, and thereby trace the inseparable links between the two cultures. The unexpected could thus be found in such moments, and this could, on occasion, be positive, as in his later revealing, when berating a 'young foolish Herr', that he was the father of 'Old Queen Charlotte', whom Carlyle much respected, and hence 'a kind of Ancestor of ours, though we little guessed it!'[131] Prolepsis was a moralizing as much as a narrative device for Carlyle, a means of connecting cultures in a rich and suggestive manner, as was demonstrated in a definitive manner in his essay 'The Prinzenraub', published in 1855 as preparatory work in the history of Frederick. His evocation of the Prince Consort here as a member of a German princely dynasty is a consummate piece of Victorian self-awareness:

> Another individual of the Ernestine Line, surely notable to Englishmen, and much to be distinguished amid that imbroglio of little Dukes, is the '*Prinz* ALBRECHT *Franz August Karl Emanuel von Sachsen-Coburg-Gotha;*' whom we

[129] For a succinct and persuasive statement of Carlyle's religious commitments, see Ruth apRoberts, *The Ancient Dialect: Thomas Carlyle and Comparative Religion* (Berkeley, 1988).

[130] *FG*, i. 217.

[131] *FG*, ii. 612–13, 615.

call, in briefer English, Prince Albert of Saxe-Coburg; actual Prince Consort of these happy realms.[132]

II

What is certain is that it was the compromised and compromising modernity of the French Revolution that connected the eighteenth with the nineteenth centuries for Carlyle; the heroic achievements of Frederick were all effected before the events of 1789 had made any such displays of and opportunities for heroism increasingly unlikely. Carlyle was preoccupied by the eighteenth century precisely because he wanted a contrast between modernity, with its secularized morality, and those genuinely heroic ages from which the nineteenth century had been separated by the damaging legacy of the eighteenth century. The era of the long Reformation was the last of the heroic ages for Carlyle, and in the logic of his apocalyptic reckoning of history, it was impossible for his age to participate in such moral grandeur; indeed it could barely comprehend it. The repetitive rhetoric of his work on Cromwell declares this definitively for his nineteenth-century readers: 'But the thing we had to say and repeat was this, That Puritanism was not of the Nineteenth Century, but of the Seventeenth; that the grand unintelligibility for us lies *there*.'[133] Carlyle was happy to expand on the moment when two elderly figures from the seventeenth century had been present at Frederick's cradle, thus fleetingly linking the last heroic century with its all too unworthy successor; it is as if these elderly figures were to impart something of their heroic century to the one true hero of the decidedly unheroic eighteenth century.[134] Likewise, references to the Hanoverians in the work on Frederick serve to emphasize what had been lost, so that the arrival of the Hanoverians in England had coincided with the final loss of the faith that had been celebrated in Carlyle's work on Cromwell: 'The English nation, having flung its old Puritan, Sword-and-Bible Faith into the cesspool,—or rather having set its old Bible-Faith, *minus* any Sword, well up in the organ-loft, with plenty of revenue, there to preach and organ at discretion, on condition always of meddling with nobody's practice farther.'[135] Toleration was far from being a virtue in Carlyle's historical and political lexicon.

132 'The Prinzenraub', *HE*, 307–36, at p. 333.
133 *OC*, i. 7.
134 *FG*, i. 373.
135 *FG*, ii. 12.

Relations between Britain and Germany became increasingly important to Victorian historians following the publication of Carlyle's work on Frederick. This was to have not only historiographical, but also directly literary consequences. Within seven years of his review of Carlyle's *French Revolution*, Thackeray had anticipated Carlyle's impending move by working on eighteenth-century Germany in some telling passages in his novel, *The Memoirs of Barry Lyndon*, first published in 1844, and revised in 1856, a superb narrative feat in that his subject is one of the first and greatest unreliable narrators in British fiction. Although now overwhelmed by appreciations of *Vanity Fair*, at least one Victorian reader, James Fitzjames Stephen, thought *The Memoirs of Barry Lyndon* Thackeray's finest novel, not least because of the way in which he vividly brought the eighteenth century to life in its pages.[136]

No matter how unreliable a narrator he might formally be, Lyndon spoke for many of his nineteenth-century readers (as well as his supposed eighteenth-century contemporaries) when he declared that:

> It would require a greater philosopher and historian than I am to explain the causes of the famous Seven Years' War in which Europe was engaged; and, indeed, its origin has always appeared to me to be so complicated, and the books written about it so amazingly hard to understand, that I have seldom been much wiser at the end of a chapter than at the beginning, and so shall not trouble my reader with any personal disquisition regarding the matter.[137]

It was partly to remedy such shortcomings in the literature that Carlyle wrote his history, but it is debatable whether he ever put to rest among British readers the ambivalences regarding Frederick's character that recur in Lyndon's accounts of the monarch for whom he unexpectedly found himself fighting. As Lyndon warns his readers, 'I am not going to give any romantic narrative of the Seven Years' War.'[138]

Though he is first alluded to as a Protestant hero, and adored by Lyndon and his colleagues 'as a saint', Frederick's 'military genius' is seen to be grounded on the depraved appetites of 'starving brutes', the 'shocking instruments' of success in warfare.[139] Frederick's victories were dependent on the recruiting policies of his 'white slave-dealers'; he

[136] [James Fitzjames Stephen], 'Mr. Thackeray', *Fraser's Magazine*, 69 (1864), 401–18, at pp. 408–10. John Burrow has fruitfully suggested to me that there is also a parallel with an eighteenth-century Irish novel, Maria Edgeworth's *Castle Rackrent*, complete with its own unreliable narrator.

[137] William Makepeace Thackeray, *The Memoirs of Barry Lyndon*, ed. George Saintsbury and Andrew Sanders (Oxford, 1984), 67.

[138] Ibid. 101. [139] Ibid. 27, 67, 71.

killed thousands of Austrians 'because he took a fancy to Silesia', and 'the hero, sage, and philosopher' readily executed those soldiers who resisted 'his monstrous tyranny'.[140] He saw spies everywhere, and Lyndon's Catholic libertine uncle wonders in a letter to his nephew what Voltaire would have made of Frederick's tyrannous hold over his subjects and his suspicions of foreign nationals.[141] However ambivalent Lyndon shows himself to be about Frederick, he is altogether less so regarding the French Revolution, lamenting the 'cowardice of the French aristocracy (in the shameful Revolution, which served them right)', tones, in this particular, close to those of Carlyle.[142] Lyndon forever regrets the loss of the values of the eighteenth century—when 'Everybody was delightfully wicked'—writing in a Europe beset by the devastations wrought by another Frederick, Napoleon, with whom he draws strong parallels.[143] *The Memoirs of Barry Lyndon* thus set itself in a chronological relationship with the eighteenth century that allowed Thackeray both to collude with and to moralize against the eighteenth century, inviting his readers both to enjoy Lyndon's excesses and to condemn them, through the pious persona of Lyndon's fictitious editor, G. S. Fitz-Boodle, who, in language redolent of another creator of fictitious editors and of narratives within narratives—Carlyle—dismisses the 'sham' morality of Lyndon.[144] Thackeray's early notice of Carlyle was the beginning of a textual relationship between the two authors that was most apparent in Thackeray's fascination with the eighteenth century, nowhere more successfully sustained than in *The Memoirs of Barry Lyndon*, a sort of echo chamber of many of Carlyle's historical, moral, and stylistic preoccupations.

Carlyle laid the foundations for Victorian interpretations of the eighteenth century, foundations on which a variety of interpretative structures were to be formed. In assessing Carlyle's contribution to Victorian interpretations of the eighteenth century, it is well to bear in mind the acute analysis given by another Victorian historian of the period, Leslie Stephen, Thackeray's son-in-law, and like him a critical admirer of Carlyle, who wrote in 1900, at the close of the Victorian age, about the many paradoxes that surrounded Carlyle, the resonances of which have been apparent throughout this chapter:

140 Thackeray, *Barry Lyndon*, pp. 85, 100, 101–2.

141 Ibid. 116, 120, 123.

142 Ibid. 128–9.

143 Ibid. 229. On 'those good old days', see pp. 41, 48, 127, 129, 151, 184, 248, 285; on Frederick and Napoleon, see pp. 100, 134.

144 Ibid. 311.

With the imagination of a poet he yet cannot rise above the solid ground of prose; a sense of pervading mystery blends with his shrewd grasp of realities; he is religious yet sceptical; a radical and a worshipper of sheer force; and a denouncer of cant and yet the deviser of a jargon.

Stephen, the product of an Anglicized Scottish family, was quick to explain the roots of these paradoxes, discerning that Carlyle was 'a spiritual descendant of John Knox', possessed of a strong sense of duty which he combined with 'the hatred of priestcraft and the contempt for the aesthetic side of things which had been bred in or burned into the breed'.[145]

Carlyle, thus ably and persuasively identified as a decidedly late product of the Reformation, was not likely to prove a sympathetic chronicler of the age of Enlightenment, and in this he was very unlike Stephen, who, with other members of his family, provides the subject of the fourth chapter, and also very unlike John Morley, a supreme Liberal optimist and a disciple of John Stuart Mill, who countered Carlyle's narrative with a heroic recovery of his detested Voltaire and Rousseau, alongside praise, originally qualified but later more admiring, for Burke. Liberals such as Mill and Morley, who had made his name with a Millian text, *On Compromise* (1874), were determined to recover the French Revolution from Carlyle's excoriations: it was for them a progressive cause.[146] That Morley (who also, in common with Carlyle, wrote a work on Cromwell), had had to work so hard on this act of reclamation of the French Enlightenment and its leading participants is testimony to the strength of Carlyle's towering presence in Victorian interpretations of the eighteenth century.

145 Leslie Stephen, *The English Utilitarians* (3 vols., London, 1900), iii. 462.

146 John Morley, *On Compromise* (London, 1874); *Voltaire* (London, 1872); *Rousseau* (2 vols., London, 1873); *Diderot and the Encyclopaedists* (2 vols., London, 1978); *Edmund Burke: An Historical Study* (London, 1867); *Burke* (London, 1879); *Oliver Cromwell* (London, 1900). He was probably best known, in literary terms, as Gladstone's official biographer.

3

Gibbon, Newman, and the Religious Accuracy of the Historian

> Yet, upon the whole, the history of the decline and fall seems to have struck a root at home and abroad, and may, perhaps, an hundred years hence, still continue to be abused.
>
> Edward Gibbon, *Autobiographies*[1]

> The fathers wrote for contemporaries [. . .]. They did not foresee that evidence would become a science, that doubt would be thought a merit, and disbelief a privilege; that it would be in favour and condescension of them if they were credited, and in charity that they were accounted honest.
>
> John Henry Newman, *An Essay on Miracles*[2]

Writing in March 1823 to Jane Baillie Welsh, his future wife, about the historical reading he had assigned her, Thomas Carlyle characterized Gibbon and his work in terms that were to prove typical of many of the great historian's readers in the first half of the nineteenth century:

> You are right to keep by Gibbon since you have begun it: there is no other tolerable history of those times and nations, within the reach of such readers as we are; it is a kind of bridge that connects the antique with the modern ages. And how gorgeously does it swing across the gloomy and tumultuous chasms of those barbarous centuries! Gibbon is a man whom one never forgets—unless oneself deserving to be forgotten; the perusal of his work forms an epoch in the history of one's mind. I know you will admire Gibbon, yet I do not expect or wish that you should love him. He has but a coarse and vulgar heart, with all his keen logic and glowing imagination and lordly irony; he worships power and splendour; and suffering virtue, the most heroic devotedness if unsuccessful,

[1] *A*, 337–8. [2] John Henry Newman, *EM*, p. ciii.

unarrayed in the pomp and circumstance of outward glory, has little of his sympathy.[3]

Carlyle was writing in the wake of half a century of Christian responses to Gibbon.[4] In this chapter, the response of a prominent Christian reader of Gibbon, John Henry Newman—himself, in common with Carlyle, at least as much a product of Romanticism as an architect of Victorianism—will be used to explore how eighteenth-century unbelief was worried over, and occasionally accommodated, within the available framework of religious apologetic in nineteenth-century Britain. The example of the liberal Anglican historian Henry Hart Milman, Oxford's Professor of Poetry when Newman was a young fellow of Oriel, will similarly demonstrate that Gibbon's contribution to ecclesiastical history was capable of being accommodated within a variety of liberal Anglican theology strongly influenced by those developments in German historical thought of which Newman remained wilfully ignorant.[5]

I

The centenary of Gibbon's death in 1894 was celebrated with a markedly apologetic tone, as can be appreciated from the *Proceedings of the Gibbon Commemoration 1794–1894*, which met on 15 November that year. Sir Mountstuart Grant Duff, the President of the Royal Historical Society—under whose auspices the celebration took place—opined that Gibbon's attitude to Christianity was 'a most serious blemish' in *The Decline and Fall*, a judgement he ameliorated when he considered the supposedly sorry state of English Christianity in the eighteenth century.[6] This permitted him to make the somewhat contentious claim that 'if Gibbon had died in 1894 instead of 1794, although his conclusions as to many things might have been precisely the same, his

[3] Thomas Carlyle to Jane Baillie Welsh, 26 Mar. 1823, in Charles Richard Sanders and Kenneth J. Fielding (eds.), *The Collected Letters of Thomas and Jane Welsh Carlyle* (Durham, NC, 1970), ii. 314.

[4] On the initial forty or so years of which, see David Womersley, *Gibbon and the 'Watchmen of the Holy City': The Historian and his Reputation 1776–1815* (Oxford, 2002).

[5] On the nature of Newman's variety of Romantic sensibility, see John Beer, *Romantic Influences—Contemporary—Victorian—Modern* (Basingstoke, 1993), 110–46.

[6] See the entries for 5 Sept. and 15 Nov. 1894 in Sir Mountstuart E. Grant Duff, *Notes from a Diary 1892–1894* (London, 1904), ii. 109–10, 133.

tone would have been absolutely different'.[7] Even the guiding spirit behind the meeting, Frederic Harrison, an advanced apostle of the Comtean 'Religion of Humanity', regretted the interpretative faults of 'the incorrigible sceptic': 'No-one now thinks of defending Gibbon's treatment of the rise of Christianity, or the foundation of the medieval Church, of the work of the Catholic apostles, saints and statesmen. To myself all this is peculiarly offensive as well as misleading, as is much of his constitutional persiflage about enthusiasts, his sub-cynical humour, and his taste for scandal.'[8] Nevertheless, Duff undercut such judgements by invoking the name of a man whose death in 1890 had prevented him from adding his contribution to a reconsideration of an 'infidel' historian. 'Cardinal Newman,' Duff declared, 'as I know from one who conversed with him on the subject near the end of his life, retained to the last the profoundest respect for the author of the "Decline and Fall".'[9]

Similarly, in a study marking another centenary, that of the origins of the Oxford Movement in 1933, Geoffrey Faber (publisher, historian, and amateur Freudian) chose to demonstrate the distance between eighteenth- and nineteenth-century thought by noting that 'Gibbon was scarcely six years dead when Newman was born.' Extending the significance of his remark, Faber also emphasized the links between 'the leader of the Oxford movement and the infidel historian upon whom he modelled his youthful style': 'Both were men of enormous and incredible industry. Both were superb stylists. Both had the rare genius which casts its spell equally upon contemporaries and posterity.

[7] Carlyle to Jane Baillie Welsh, in *Collected Letters*, ii. 314.

[8] *Proceedings of the Gibbon Commemoration 1794–1894* (London, 1895), 22 and 30. On Harrison's leading role in the commemoration see his *Autobiographic Memoirs* (London, 1911), ii. 93–6, and Martha S. Vogeler, *Frederic Harrison: The Vocations of a Positivist* (Oxford, 1984), 345–7. One hears here an echo of Carlyle's conviction, voiced some seventy years earlier, that 'To the Christians he is frequently very unfair: if he had lived now, he would have written differently on those points' (*Collected Letters*, ii. 314). The author of the English Men of Letters Series biography of Gibbon was also a Positivist: James Cotter Morison, *Gibbon* (London, 1878).

[9] *Proceedings of the Gibbon Commemoration*, 16. Shelby T. McCloy, *Gibbon's Antagonism to Christianity* (Chapel Hill, NC, 1933), 167–75, discusses Newman, but much of this disappointing tally takes the form of a bland recital of Newman's career. Newman's Oriel colleague and future brother-in-law, Tom Mozley, noted that Newman was one of the few people who could be considered to have been 'thoroughly acquainted with Gibbon's great work': *Reminiscences chiefly of Oriel College and the Oxford Movement*, 2nd edn. (London, 1882), 40. There is a useful, if all too brief, discussion of Gibbon's scholarly influence on Newman by Curtis Adler, 'John Henry Newman on Edward Gibbon: indebted to the infidel', *Classical Bulletin*, 69 (1993), 17–20.

Both bent their minds to the study of the past, and of the same past. To each, standing on different sides of the watershed between the two centuries, the prospect was strangely different.'[10] While it suited Faber's purposes to play Gibbon off against Newman, it is equally revealing to consider in more detail what the two men had in common.

Both men were converts to Roman Catholicism, albeit of notably varying duration and levels of commitment. Both felt the attractions of religious scepticism, though once again the commitment of the one was markedly stronger than that of the other.[11] Both were disappointed early by their undergraduate experiences of Oxford. Both men also wrote autobiographies, defending their religious and intellectual preoccupations. It is perhaps these writings which are most familiar to modern readers; Gibbon's *Memoirs*, however reconstituted, are conventionally judged to be his second masterpiece, and Newman's *Apologia* is a frequent source for students of the nineteenth century, more especially pillaged by those fashionably concerned with the 'construction of the self'.[12] As a consequence of such contemporary fascination with privacy and selfhood, the sexuality of both men has been subject to scholarly scrutiny, both having had homosexual inclinations imputed to them, with varying degrees of conviction.[13] More significantly, and infinitely more demonstrably, Newman's style owed a good deal to Gibbon, as he confessed

[10] Geoffrey Faber, *The Oxford Apostles: A Character Study of the Oxford Movement* (London, 1933), 1–2.

[11] As Newman stated it: 'When I was fourteen, I read Paine's Tracts against the Old Testament, and found pleasure in thinking of the objections which were contained in them. Also, I read some of Hume's Essays; and perhaps that on Miracles. So at least I gave my Father to understand; but perhaps it was a brag. Also, I recollect copying out some French verses, perhaps Voltaire's in denial of the immortality of the soul, saying to myself something like "How dreadful, but how plausible!"' (*Apol.*, 17). Leslie Stephen claimed that Newman's philosophy of religion was at least congruent with scepticism: 'Cardinal Newman's scepticism', *Nineteenth Century*, 29 (1891), 179–201, and 'Newman's theory of belief', in *An Agnostic's Apology and Other Essays* (London, 1893), 168–241. Cf. Mozley, *Reminiscences*, 40.

[12] J. W. Burrow, *Gibbon* (Oxford, 1985), 4. For an early example of such readings of Newman, see James Olney, *Metaphors of Self: The Meaning of Autobiography* (Princeton, 1972), 202–32.

[13] See Lionel Gossman's psychoanalytic study, *The Empire Unpossess'd: An Essay on Gibbon's 'Decline and Fall'* (Cambridge, 1981), 14–16, and for a denial of such imputations, Patricia B. Craddock, *Young Edward Gibbon: Gentleman of Letters* (Baltimore, 1982), 106. More generally, see Brian Young, 'Gibbon and sex', *Textual Practice*, 11 (1997), 517–37. On Newman, see *inter alia*, Faber, *The Oxford Apostles*, 25–35, 215–32; Oliver S. Buckton, '"An unnatural state": gender, "perversion" and Newman's *Apologia pro vita sua*', *Victorian Studies*, 35 (1992), 359–83; David Newsome, *The Convert Cardinals: John Henry Newman and Henry Edward Manning* (London, 1993),

when, addressing the students of his new foundation at Dublin, he detailed with his usual deftness and ever-present sense of critical caution—especially marked before a Catholic audience—the quality of Gibbon's style as this was indissolubly connected with Gibbon's scholarly purposes: 'You must not suppose I am going to recommend his style for imitation, any more than his principles; but I refer to him as the example of a writer feeling the task which lay before him, feeling that he had to bring into words for the comprehension of his readers a great and complicated scene, and wishing that those words should be adequate to his understanding.'[14]

Since he reached maturity towards the end of the 'long' eighteenth century—and as his reaction to the closing events of that period help to mark the beginnings of a distinctively Victorian temper—all Newman's early stylistic influences were drawn from an 'Augustan' canon, although he dismissed his early models as 'mannerists'; 'For myself when I was fourteen or fifteen I imitated Addison; when I was seventeen, I wrote in the style of Johnson; about the same time I fell in with the twelfth volume of Gibbon, and my ears rang with the cadences of his sentences, and I dreamed of it for a night or two. Then I began to make an analysis of Thucydides in Gibbon's style.' Nor was Newman alone in the following this trajectory; as he observed of Gibbon, 'I seem to trace his vigorous condensation and peculiar rhythm at every turn in the literature of the present day.'[15] In his first long vacation from Oxford, Newman's rereading of Gibbon confirmed his earlier estimate of him as a historian:

> With all his faults, his want of simplicity, his affection, and his monotony, few can be put in comparison with him; and sometimes, when I reflect on his happy choice of expressions, his vigorous compression of ideas, and the life and significance of his every work, I am prompted indignantly to exclaim that no style is left for historians of an after day. O who is worthy to succeed our Gibbon![16]

It was not only how and what they wrote that demonstrate a kinship between Newman and Gibbon, but also what they read. Both had been early and avid readers of the *Arabian Nights*, a work which was defended by an evangelical character in a novel by Hannah More in

122–4; Frank M. Turner, *John Henry Newman: The Challenge to Evangelical Religion* (New Haven, 2002), 425–36.

[14] *Idea*, 214. [15] Ibid. 240–1.

[16] Letter to John William Bowden (Oct. 1819), *LD*, i. 67.

decidedly religious terms, since it, 'and other oriental books of fable, though loose and faulty in many respects, yet have always a reference to the religion of the country. Nothing is introduced against the Law of Mahomet: nothing subversive of the opinions of a Mussulman. I do not quarrel with books for having no religion, but for having a *false* religion.'[17] Gibbon and Newman were not, then, such unlikely enthusiasts for these tales, not least since both became historians of religion with a particular interest in the worldly shaping of faiths.[18] Indeed, both had something to say about Islam itself, not all of which—despite Gibbon's portrayal of Muhammad as an enlightened proto-unitarian—was particularly complimentary, leaving both men subject to the inevitable censures of Edward Said.[19] In his polemical history of the Turks, Newman frequently had recourse to Gibbon, referred to obliquely as 'an historian', 'a celebrated historian', 'an English historian', 'a well-known historian', acknowledging his authority only in cursory footnotes, the single name 'Gibbon' littering the bottom of many pages.[20] It was probably diplomatic tact on Newman's part, when addressing the Catholic Institute of Liverpool in 1853, to disguise Gibbon's authoritative presence before his pious auditors.

Newman's *Lectures on the History of the Turks* contain many references to eighteenth-century works of history, both in their 'conjectural' and purely factual modes. He cites (with amendment) Gibbon's favourite modern, Montesquieu, on the despotism attendant on hot climates, and a work much admired by Gibbon, Robertson's *History of America*, on the laws of the Incas and the nature of the 'savage'.[21] Elsewhere

[17] *A*, 49, 118, 296, 393–4; *Apol.*, 15; Hannah More, *Coelebs in Search of a Wife* (London, 1808), i. 384 (italic original). For more general comments on this taste, see Frances Mannsaker, 'Elegancy and wildness: reflections of the East in the eighteenth-century imagination', in G. S. Rousseau and Roy Porter (eds.), *Exoticism in the Enlightenment* (Manchester, 1990), 175–95.

[18] For perceptive comments on the significance of Gibbon's reading of the *Arabian Nights*, see G. M. Young, *Gibbon* (London, 1932), 7–8.

[19] Edward W. Said, *Orientalism: Western Conceptions of the Orient* (London, 1978), 59, 74, 117, 120, 153, 228. Said concedes, however, that Gibbon wrote as an ambivalent admirer of Muhammad, on which see Bernard Lewis, 'Gibbon on Muhammad', in G. W. Bowersock, J. Clive, and S. Graubard (eds.), *Edward Gibbon and the Decline and Fall of the Roman Empire* (Cambridge, Mass., 1977), 61–74; W. B. Carnochan, *Gibbon's Solitude: the Inward World of the Historian* (Stanford, Calif. 1987), 118–19. More generally, see Ian Richard Netton, 'The mysteries of Islam', in Rousseau and Porter, *Exoticism in the Enlightenment*, 23–45.

[20] *Lectures*, 6, 81, 121, 212.

[21] Ibid. 61, 197–8. Gibbon has been called the most successful and brilliant of Montesquieu's disciples: David P. Jordan, *Gibbon and his Roman Empire* (Urbana, Ill.,

he happily uses Hume's *History of England* alongside Ranke's *History of the Popes,* as well as supporting the observations of contemporaries such as Guizot (himself an annotator of *The Decline and Fall*) before advertising to Schlegel's study of China.[22] This is, then, an eclectic text, and one full of such characteristic features as a comparison of Islam with Protestantism, and an observation that the tribes of Tartary were only marginally evangelized, and that even this was regrettably undertaken by Nestorian heretics. Following other authorities, Newman also identified these tribes as the Gog and Magog of the sacred texts, the instruments of Antichrist against the faithful.[23] Although it is hard to make ready comparisons with Gibbon on these latter points, Newman, in common with Gibbon, whose 'cold heart, impure mind, and scoffing spirit' had led to his being dismissed by Newman in an 1832 sermon as a modern Antichrist, drew moral lessons from the decline of Rome, 'a drama of sustained interest and equable and majestic evolution [which] has given scope to the most ingenious researches into its internal history'.[24]

In his review of the opening stages of Henry Hart Milman's *History of Latin Christianity*, published in 1841, Newman noted the ironic prominence of Gibbon in English historiography, lamenting, 'It is notorious that the English Church is destitute of an Ecclesiastical History; Gibbon is almost our sole authority for subjects, as near the heart of a Christian as any can well be.' He went on to remark even more trenchantly that 'we consider it to be impossible even for a Gibbon to write an uninstructive history of the Evangelical Dispensation; and much less can Mr. Milman, who is not a Gibbon, but a clergyman, fail to be useful to those who are in search of facts, and have better principles to read them by.'[25] Milman, the only liberal Anglican historian to have admired Gibbon, was berated for writing a worldly history; ignoring the vital place of God acting providentially in ecclesiastical history led to the sanctioning of heresy, 'For the fact is undeniable, little as Mr. Milman may be aware of it, that this external contemplation of Christianity necessarily leads a man to write as a

1971), 71. For a perceptive appreciation of Robertson's influence on Gibbon, especially as mediated through the history of America, see Young, *Gibbon,* 79–82, and, more generally, J. G. A. Pocock, 'Between Machiavelli and Hume: Gibbon as civic humanist and philosophic historian', in Bowersock, *et al., Edward Gibbon,* 103–19.

[22] *Lectures*, 167, 177. [23] Ibid. 35, 72–3.

[24] Ibid. 174–5; 'Contest between faith and sight', in *Fifteen Sermons Preached before the University of Oxford,* 3rd edn. (London, 1872), 126.

[25] 'Milman's view of Christianity', *ECH,* ii. 186, 187.

Socinian or Unitarian *would* write, whether he will or not [. . .] He has unintentionally both given scandal to his brethren and cause of triumph to the enemy.'[26] Despite Newman's censures, Milman continued to enjoy the approbation of many distinguished scholars, notably another strong admirer of Gibbon, Macaulay, who recommended the last three volumes of Milman's *History* to Lord Lansdowne in 1855 as an 'excellent' work. To Milman himself, Macaulay wrote, 'I think this quite your best work; and that is saying a great deal. That the History of Latin Christianity will have a high and permanent place in literature I have not the slightest doubt.' Within a month of writing that letter, he was rereading the *History* 'with great interest'.[27] Of Newman and his works, Macaulay was predictably suspicious. He wrote to a friend in 1843 with palpably Gibbonian relish: 'I hear much of a defence of the miracles of the third and fourth centuries by Newman. I have not yet read it. I think that I could treat that subject without giving any scandal to any rational person; and I should like it much. The times require a Middleton.'[28] Without having to assume the mask of Conyers Middleton, whose essay on miracles had so affected Gibbon, Macaulay broached a review of Newman's *Lives of the Saints*: 'Newman announces an English hagiology in numbers, which is to contain the lives of such blessed saints as Thomas a Becket and Dunstan. I should not dislike to be the Avvocato del Diavolo on such an occasion.'[29] After Newman turned Catholic, Macaulay savoured his discomfiture when the convert was assaulted by a former co-religionist: 'Brave Achilli! And bravo Newman! Two apostate priests were well matched.'[30] Macaulay's rather self-conscious historico-religious raffishness had reached its high point in 1849 when he ventured a critique of *The Decline and Fall*

[26] Ibid. 202 (italic original). On Milman's admiration for Gibbon, as contrasted with Thomas Arnold's disavowal of his influence, see Duncan Forbes, *The Liberal Anglican Idea of History* (Cambridge, 1952), 2 and 116, and McCloy, *Gibbon's Antagonism to Christianity*, 316–23.

[27] Thomas Babington Macaulay, letters to Lord Landsdowne (24 Dec. 1855) and Henry Hart Milman (29 Dec. 1855, 22 Jan. 1856), in Thomas Pinney (ed.), *The Letters of Thomas Babington Macaulay* (Cambridge, 1974–81), v. 418, 483–4, vi. 10.

[28] Letter to Macvey Napier (27 Feb. 1843), *Letters of Macaulay*, iv. 107–8.

[29] Nor was Gibbon unique, for as Gloucester Ridley remarked concerning Middleton's influence, 'I never heard of one man who became a protestant, or who was kept from becoming a papist, by reading what he had wrote on the subject; but I have heard of more than one, whom it perverted to infidelity or confirmed in it': *Three Letters to the Author of the 'Confessional'* (London, 1768), letter III, pp. 140–1. Letter to Napier (20 Oct. 1843), *Letters of Macaulay*, iv. 158–9.

[30] Letter to Thomas Flower Ellis (21 Sept. 1851), *Letters of Macaulay*, iv. 195–6.

which reversed the purely theological reservations recently embodied in Thomas Bowdler's version of the text: 'I have always thought the indelicacy of Gibbon's great work a more serious blemish than even his uncandid hostility to the Christian religion.'[31]

Milman outlived Macaulay, about whom he wrote a dignified commemorative essay, displaying his deep respect and regard for Macaulay, both as a man and as a historian.[32] Milman was a churchman Macaulay could and did respect; it was quite otherwise with Newman. Milman and Newman represented successive intellectual generations and rather different traditions within the Church of England; they held notably different perspectives on the status and standing of the Roman Catholic Church. Henry Hart Milman (1791–1868) flourished in pre-Tractarian Oxford, becoming a fellow of Brasenose College (then ahead of Oriel as a leading scholarly society in the university), on the eve of Waterloo. John Henry Newman grew up intellectually in the Oxford that Milman (who was to be succeeded as Professor of Poetry at Oxford by John Keble) had only recently vacated in order to take up the important living of St Mary's, Reading, a former centre of Simeonite Evangelicalism.[33] Milman's appointment to St Mary's marked a symbolic moment in the internal economy of the Church of England: his more intellectually committed and consciously worldly style of churchmanship offered a liberal Anglican alternative to the emotionally engaged Evangelicalism that had shaped the young Newman and so many of his contemporaries. It was an alternative that Newman and his fellow Tractarians totally repudiated; Milman, on his part, was to continue to take an interest in Newman that culminated in a typically perceptive and influential review of the *Essay on the Development of Christian Doctrine* contributed to the *Quarterly Review* in 1846.

Tractarianism continues to dominate study of nineteenth-century religious history, and the personality and presence of Newman is especially prominent in such work. The consequent sense that Milman and his fellow liberal Anglicans had not had the intellectual recognition

[31] Letter to an unknown recipient (31 Mar. 1849), Ibid. p. v. 41–2.

[32] H. H. Milman, *Lord Macaulay* (London, 1859).

[33] Two of Milman's dramatic poems had their origins in chapters of the *Decline and Fall: Samor, Lord of the Bright City* (London, 1818), derived some of its inspiration from chapter 31, whilst *The Martyr of Antioch* (London, 1822) drew on Gibbon's account of the martyrdom of St Margaret. On the Evangelical roots of St Mary's, Reading, see Charles Smyth, *Simeon and Church Order: A Study of the Origins of the Evangelical Revival in Cambridge in the Eighteenth Century* (Cambridge, 1940), 202–47.

they deserved was felt quite early by historians, and W. E. H. Lecky's essay on Milman, published in a posthumous collection in 1908, is particularly suggestive of a change in attitudes towards their elders as this was experienced over the closing decades of the Victorian era. Lecky ranked Milman far higher than he did Newman as a religious and historical thinker. Detailing the impact of the Oxford movement, Lecky delivered a devastating broadside on Newman's shortcomings that was not untypical of the estimates of the recently deceased cardinal made by many of Lecky's mid-Victorian generation of scholars:

He was not a great scholar, or an original and independent thinker. Dealing with questions inseparably connected with historical evidence, he had neither the judicial spirit nor the firm grasp of a real historian, and he had very little skill in measuring probabilities and degrees of evidence. He had a manifest incapacity, which was quite as much moral as intellectual, for looking facts in the face and pursuing trains of thought to unwelcome conclusions. He often took refuge from them in clouds of casuistry. The scepticism which was a marked feature of his intellect allied itself with credulity, for it was directed against reason itself; and though he has expressed in admirable language many true and beautiful thoughts, the glamour of his style too often concealed much weakness and uncertainty of judgment and much sophistry in argument.[34]

That Newman was naturally a sceptic who took refuge in casuistry was something of a commonplace among his critics, Milman included, who referred to Newman's 'doubts' in the opening paragraph of his judicious review of the *Essay on the Development of Christian Doctrine* in 1846.[35] Newman was usually considered by such critics to be an evasive philosopher and a casuitical theologian, but only rarely was he thought of by them as a historian, and it was as a historian that Lecky preferred the work of Milman. Lecky's estimate of Milman's *History of Latin Christianity* (1854–5) is worth recalling when considering his current standing among historians of historiography: 'it gave its author indisputably the first place among the ecclesiastical historians of England and a high place among the historians of the nineteenth century.'[36]

Lecky rightly noted the centrality of Gibbon to Milman's evolution as a historian, and it is in their contrasting engagements with the historian

[34] W. E. H. Lecky, 'Henry Hart Milman, D.D., Dean of St. Paul's', in *Historical and Political Essays* (London, 1908), 249–74, at pp. 249–50.

[35] H. H. Milman, 'Newman on the Development of Christian Doctrine', *Quarterly Review*, 77 (1846), 404–65, at p. 404.

[36] Lecky, 'Milman', 264.

of the Roman empire that defining differences between Newman and Milman can be most effectively made. In doing so, it is important to consider that Milman's relations with the century during the last decade of which he had been born were complicated. It is not quite true to say, however, as Charles Smyth did in a 1949 lecture, that Milman 'belonged rather to the eighteenth than to the nineteenth century', although Smyth's subsequent claim is rather more convincing: 'he was a survivor from the Age of Reason, a kind of Christian Gibbon, without the indecency and without the fun.'[37] The so-called Age of Reason had led, however, to the French Revolution, or so thought many nineteenth-century historians, most prominently Carlyle, and it was the principles promoted by the revolutionary assault on Christianity for which Milman indicted the eighteenth century; in doing so, however, he contrasted the living inheritance of the Reformation with the unreal edifice of what he lamented as Newman's defence of 'Mediaeval Christianity'. Stating the problem, in his review of the *Essay on the Development of Christian Doctrine*, that 'of all historical questions the gravest is, how far the infidelity or at least the religious indifference which was almost universally dominant throughout the highest and higher orders of Christian Europe during the last century, Roman Catholic or Protestant' was actually due to disputes between Catholics and Protestants, Milman concluded that it was due to the wilful and politically disastrous obscurantism of those who desired to 'maintain Mediaeval Christianity'.[38] In this respect, Milman was no nostalgic Burkean, but he was more critically Gibbonian in that the concerns Gibbon had had with the developments in revolutionary France were not at all unlike those he had voiced when analysing that other, greater revolution which had transformed late pagan Rome into the centre of Catholic Christianity. For Milman this earlier revolution—'equally unprecedented in earlier, and unparalleled in later ages'—had been an enormous boon, the greatest revolution in human history, and it was on this issue that he most disagreed with Gibbon.[39]

In the Bampton Lectures which he delivered at Oxford in 1827, Milman took as his theme the character and conduct of the Apostles as an evidence of the truth of Christianity, thereby undoing at source

37 Charles Smyth, *Dean Milman (1791–1868), The First Rector of St Margaret's, Westminster, afterwards Dean of St Paul's* (London, 1949), 19.

38 Milman, 'Newman on development', 447.

39 Milman, *The Character and Conduct of the Apostles Considered as an Evidence of Christianity* (Oxford, 1827), 1.

the purely natural explanation for the growth of Christianity laid out by Gibbon in the first volume of the *Decline and Fall*. Indeed, Gibbon had very deliberately not included the Apostolic age in his account of the Christianization of the empire; by emphasizing that period in his lectures, Milman was using history to affirm the truth of the Christian religion in a spirit directly contrary to Gibbon's historical enterprise. He sought to demonstrate how, due to their simplicity and lack of education, the Apostles had needed supernatural assistance in promoting faith in Christ; and he affirmed this perspective yet further by stressing that the circumstances, natural and social, of the world at that time were not in themselves anything like enough to account for their success.[40] Arguing against his otherwise favoured Erasmus, Milman insisted on the literal nature of the gift of tongues, rejecting Erasmus's suggestion that the Apostles probably spoke the Greek of Palestine: Christian humanism was insufficient for Milman's apologetic enterprise, which drew instead on Locke and Paley in a firmly Anglican philosophical tradition.[41] As for the state of the world at the coming of Christ as a secondary cause of the rapid growth of Christianity, Milman accepted its assistance but denied its sufficiency. Providence was absolutely central to Milman's account. Entering into some detail regarding Gibbon's purely naturalistic account of the rise of Christianity, Milman reversed their explanatory power, suggesting, for example, that, far from immediately benefiting the spread of the faith, 'The universal empire of the Romans endangered an universal persecution.'[42] He reserved one of his most self-consciously eloquent passages to a ringing reversal of the logic of Gibbon's purely natural explanations; it is worth quoting in full, demonstrating as it does how his diction is indebted to Gibbon's style. Observing how Gibbon saw every element of Roman life as having been pervaded by the ceremonies of heathenism, Milman averred that:

> This opportunity of displaying the luxuriance of his diction, and the copiousness of his knowledge, is fatal to the theory which the writer would insinuate—the propagation of Christianity by natural causes alone. For if the old religion, conjured up by the powers of the imagination, could so fascinate the congenial mind of the historian, what must have been its influence when incorporated with all the prejudices, inoculated with traditionary reverence, and addressed directly and perpetually to the ardent passions of a gay and dissolute people.

[40] Milman, *The Character and Conduct of the Apostles Considered as an Evidence of Christianity*, 7–9.

[41] Ibid. 171–234. [42] Ibid. 261.

No topic of Christian evidence has ever been urged with greater frequency or success, than the contrast between the mean, indigent, unpretending and self-denying religion of the cross, and the splendour, opulence, the festive and indulgent ritual of paganism.[43]

In common, however, with Gibbon, Milman the liberal Anglican historian was to prove a considerable critic of the forms of Christianity which developed in the wake of its transformation into a political religion, and his disapprobation for precisely those periods of Christian history that Newman idolized reads like a Christianized development of Gibbon's religiously sceptical critique. This is most readily apparent in the language in which he elaborated, in his 1846 review of Newman, on what he considered to be one of the several paradoxes that lay at the heart of Newman's apologetic failure:

This is another singular circumstance. Christianity is advancing towards its perfect development, while mankind is degenerating into the darkest barbarism and ignorance. From the beginning of the fifth to the opening, at the earliest, of the twelfth century (notwithstanding the premature apparition of Charlemagne and of our own Alfred), is the age of the most total barrenness of the human mind, of the most unbroken slumber of human thought, of the utmost cruelty, and, must we not add, licentiousness of manners.[44]

The Gibbonian cadences of that passage (and note how subtly effective a ghosting 'apparition' is in this passage, immediately undoing the celebration he otherwise seems to make of Charlemagne and Alfred), echo his earlier remarks, complete with characteristically Gibbonian sexual innuendo, on the doctrine of Papal Infallibility:

but if ancient records speak true, Infallibility on its highest throne has cowered with fear or wandered into error; Infallibility has Arianised, has Pelagianised, has Monothelestised. Infallibility has dwelt with youths under age. If it has issued from the lips of some of the best, so it has at least from some few of the worst of men.[45]

The haunting presence of Gibbon in Milman's prose and style of thought ought to come as no surprise. He had considered the historian at length in an article on Guizot's edition of the *Decline and Fall* contributed to the *Quarterly Review* in 1833, when crises in French liberal politics were of more interest to Milman than were noises

[43] Milman, *The Character and Conduct of the Apostles Considered as an Evidence of Christianity*, 268–9.

[44] Milman, 'Newman on development', 427. [45] Ibid. 424.

of ecclesiastical discontent emanating from Oxford. As with many nineteenth-century historians, he was fascinated by survivors from an earlier epoch, true remnants of the 'Age of Reason', as is charmingly evinced in a letter he sent to his family in 1834:

> Think of my not remembering before the other day that my friend Lady Maria Stanley was Gibbon's favourite Maria Holroyd. I fortunately found her at home. When I began to talk on the subject, and mentioned Guizot, she broke out on the admirable article in the *Quarterly*, with which she had been so much delighted, and said that the author must have known Gibbon to have appreciated him so justly. Of course I told her immediately the real author, and confess that I felt not a little flattered by the compliment, for she had not the remotest suspicion that it was mine . . . [46]

Within two years of this happy meeting, Milman was approached by the Society for the Promotion of Christian Knowledge to edit a new edition of the *Decline and Fall*, an offer to which he replied in judiciously sceptical tones:

> You may depend upon it that no edition of Gibbon, however neutralized by annotations, will be ventured upon by the S.P.C.K. Nothing but the most merciless castration will bring him within their notions of safety and propriety; and if I go on with my edition, not one word of Gibbon is to be omitted,—besides that, I intend it for a scholarlike as well as a Christianized work, and shall be at some pains to bring it up to the present state of research in all points.[47]

This letter was written within ten years of the appearance of Thomas Bowdler's edition of the *Decline and Fall* in 1826 and whilst that lamentable editor would have regretted the improprieties of such a phrase as 'merciless castration', it is an altogether apt description of a version which excluded chapters fifteen and sixteen, but which, unwittingly, retained rather more of Gibbon's innuendo than a modern reader would otherwise suppose.[48] Milman's edition, incorporating and elaborating on Guizot's notes, appeared from John Murray in 1839, and it held the field until J. B. Bury's edition appeared in the early 1900s.

[46] Cited in Arthur Milman, *Henry Hart Milman, D.D., Dean of St Paul's, a Biographical Sketch* (London, 1900), at p. 130. Lecky's essay on Milman originated as a review of this memoir by Milman's son.

[47] Cited ibid. 101.

[48] On Bowdler's Gibbon, see Norman Vance, *The Victorians and Ancient Rome* (Oxford, 1997), 203.

How exactly did the mind of a liberal Anglican divine chime more readily with that of an eighteenth-century religious sceptic than it did with contemporary Evangelical or Tractarian sensibilities? Largely because Milman was prepared to allow that different ages contained very different sensibilities and habits of mind, and, consequently, that humanity's continually improving knowledge of the world and its history would increasingly allow one to remove the filigree of superstition from the structures of knowledge and experience left to humanity by generation after generation of less enlightened ancestors. Both of these mutually informing elements are discernible in his intellectually disappointed reaction to Newman, as when he observed that:

> There are periods in human history when despotism, temporal or spiritual, seems necessary or inevitable for the maintenance of social order. In those times the spiritual was the best, the only counterpoise to temporal despotism. But as in other despotisms that time passes away. Christianity, as Mr. Newman admits, did without it for five centuries; it will not endure it now.[49]

Temporal and conceptual relativism separated Milman's conception of the task of the religious historian from that of Newman and such earlier Evangelical historians as Joseph Milner. The need to add to the improvement of the human mind, to play one's intellectual part in what Milman considered to be genuine development in contradistinction to Newman's notion of that process, required him both to undo the religious prejudices of Gibbon by annotating the *Decline and Fall*, and to write new appreciations of that history, both in the *History of Christianity* and the subsequent *History of Latin Christianity*, the latter of which closes with the end of Pope Nicholas V's pontificate in 1455, two years after the terminal date of the *Decline and Fall.* Milman took Gibbon's historical territory and Christianized it for the modern enlightened, if importantly post-Enlightenment, reader.

Milman sought to contain the problem of the miraculous by defining two forms of the phenomenon: the one, of the type recorded in the Gospels, was calm and momentary; the other, the unreliable type recorded in the early history of the Church, was terrifying, prolonged, and overly emotional. Expanding on the distinction in a note to his *History of Christianity*, Milman made an observation regarding Augustine of a nature one might expect to have found in Gibbon, replete with a sideswipe at a later ecclesiastical historian:

[49] Milman, 'Newman on development', 457.

Augustine denies the continuance of miracles with equal distinctness . . . Yet Fleury appeals, and not without ground, to the respected testimony of St. Augustine, as eye-witness of this miracle; and the reader of St Augustine's works, even his noblest . . . cannot but call to mind perpetual instances of miraculous observances related with unhesitating faith. It is singular how often we hear at one time the strong intellect of Augustine, at another the age of Augustine, speaking in his works.[50]

Combining his notes with those of Guizot, he sought to contain Gibbon's scepticism in his edition of the *Decline and Fall*, and his brand of liberal Anglicanism managed to do so without losing its temper or reverting to older ways of thinking about the relationship between the divine and the sublunary in the history of religion. In this he was decidedly antagonistic to the plan of campaign undertaken by Newman in seeing off Gibbon, with whose mind and writings he enjoyed a lifelong engagement.

II

At the root of Newman's anger with Milman's work was a conviction, *pace* Macaulay, that theology was the supreme science, and the 'historical method', narrowly concerned with 'the external view of Christianity', was vastly inferior. It was this assumption which allowed him to parody Milman's clerical apology for his stance: 'My own profession cannot be brought to take an external view of Christianity; but I write for the world, which does.'[51] Here, stated with the utmost economy, is Newman's attitude towards history as an academic practice. History, by its very nature, was a purely human activity; revelation and the authority of the Church could alone aid it to a glimpse of the Divine acting in the world, otherwise 'What tenet of Christianity will escape prescription, if the principle is once admitted, that a sufficient account is given of an opinion, and a sufficient ground for making light of it, as soon as it is historically referred to some human origin?'[52]

In a letter of 1830, filled with his anger at Milman's poorly received *History of the Jews*, Newman made a telling comparison: 'It seems to

[50] H. H. Milman, *The History of Christianity, from the Birth of Christ to the Abolition of Paganism in the Roman Empire*, new rev. edn. (3 vols., London, 1863), iii. 23 n., 160 and n.

[51] 'Milman's view of Christianity', *ECH*, 207, 211. [52] Ibid. 241.

me that the great evil of Milman's work lies, not in the *matter of the* history, but in the prophane *spirit* in which it is written. In most of his positions I agree with him but abhor the irreverent scoffing Gibbon-like tone of the composition.'[53] For Newman, dogmatic religion provided the benchmark by which to judge the origin and progress of Christian history, a position he shared with the juvenile Gibbon, whose readings of the Church Fathers and Bossuet had famously led to his brief conversion to Roman Catholicism. The experience of conversion, and of reconversion, is a sharp instance of Newman's closeness to a secular historian with whose mind and writings he enjoyed a lifelong relationship.[54]

In his still-pertinent essay on Gibbon, G. M. Young, describing the 16-year-old's process of reading himself into Catholicism, concluded that 'Newman was to take the same road.'[55] This just fails to be accurate, but it serves to show up the distance between the two men. Gibbon's conversion to Rome was effected through the reading of historical sources and the assessment of historical arguments; in the case of Newman's conversion, however, dogmatic considerations prevailed over the reading of history.[56] In his review of the 1896 edition of Gibbon's *Memoirs,* Leslie Stephen noted the role of history in his subject's conversion, rightly seeing it as a perversely devout reaction against Middleton's deistic deployment of history over metaphysics in the displacement of miracles from Christian apologetic. As Stephen put it, 'Of the logic of this argument I say nothing; but its power over Gibbon is one proof that he was a heaven-born historian.'[57] It was as a historian, the author of a standard life of Cicero, rather than as a religious controversialist, that Middleton had most influenced the

[53] Letter to Simeon Lloyd Pope (28 Oct. 1830), *LD*, ii. 299 (italic original); cf. *Idea*, 64.

[54] For a useful study of Gibbon's conversions, see D. J. Womersley, 'Gibbon's apostasy', *British Journal for Eighteenth-Century Studies*, 2 (1988), 51–70. Newman likewise experienced two conversions: the first, when an Ealing schoolboy, to evangelical Christianity, the second at his reception into Roman Catholicism. For a contemporary comparison of Gibbon's conversion with the Oxford conversions of Newman's day, see Walter Bagehot, 'Edward Gibbon', in *The Collected Essays of Walter Bagehot*, ed. Norman St John-Stevas (London, 1965), i. 362–3.

[55] Young, *Gibbon*, 11.

[56] Just as 'it was the Fathers who made him an historian', so it was his researches concerning the status of Anglican claims to antiquity which led Newman to Rome, on which see Thomas A. Bokenkotter, *Cardinal Newman as an Historian* (Leuven, 1959), ch. 2.

[57] Leslie Stephen, 'Gibbon's autobiography', in *Studies of a Biographer* (London, 1907), i. 148–9.

young Newman, whose own early essay on Cicero was strongly indebted to that work.[58]

Stephen was similarly perceptive in his characterization of Pascal, whose enigmatic character he resolved in terms that could very easily have extended to the young Gibbon: 'Was Pascal a sceptic or a sincere believer? The answer is surely obvious. He was a sincere, a humble, and even an abject believer precisely because he was a thorough-going sceptic.'[59] Appreciation of Pascal's influence on Gibbon has largely failed to follow the insights of G. M. Young, and this despite Gibbon's famously placing the *Lettres provinciales* amongst the three great books that affected his writing, noting that it was a work which he reread every year and from which he learned the central lesson that was to provide him with a famously high valuation of forensic irony.[60] Alongside the stylistic instruction of Pascal, the learned authority of his fellow Jansenist Tillemont girded much of the erudition in the *Decline and Fall.* If Gibbon was in any sense a *philosophe*, he was also an erudite and an ironist, scholarly stances for which he was much indebted to what have been called his 'Jansenist mentors'.[61]

French influence on Newman is rather more difficult to detect. In his still-instructive biography of Newman, Wilfrid Ward noted how comparisons had frequently been drawn between his subject and Pascal, Bossuet, and Fénelon, and he adverted to a stylistic affinity between the *Sermons for Mixed Congregations* and Bossuet's pulpit oratory.[62] However, Ward also emphasized the disparity between Fénelon's ultramontanism and Newman's near-liberal Catholicism, along with that between Bossuet's Gallicanism and Newman's suspicion of Gallicanism.[63] Towards the end of his years as an Anglican, Newman had both regretted Pascal's association with a Church which habitually told lies, and berated 'Ultra-Protestants' for associating Pascal, Tillemont,

[58] 'Personal and literary character of Cicero' (1824), in *Historical Sketches* (London, 1894), i. 239–300. This piece also draws on Warburton's *Divine Legation* and Montesquieu's *Considérations sur les causes de la grandeur des Romains et de leur décadence.*

[59] Leslie Stephen, 'Pascal', in *Studies of a Biographer*, ii. 259. See now the work-in-progress by J. G. A. Pocock concerning Gibbon and his intellectual context, *Barbarism and Religion* (4 vols. so far, Cambridge, 1999–).

[60] *A*, 143; Young, *Gibbon*, 20–1, 112; Jordan, *Gibbon and his Roman Empire*, 145–7, 151, 158.

[61] Jordan, *Gibbon and his Roman Empire*, 125–41, 157–8.

[62] Wilfrid Ward, *The Life of John Henry Cardinal Newman* (London, 1912). i. 2–4, 228.

[63] Ibid. ii. 420

and Fleury with the Antichrist in their blanket condemnations of Catholicism.[64] As a Catholic, Newman was critical of the style of apologetic which Pascal developed in the *Pensées* and was dismissive of the Jansenist import of the *Lettres provinciales*.[65] Interestingly, despite his notably qualified approval of French theologians, Newman criticized Gibbon for being, intellectually, 'half a Frenchman'.[66] Newman's antagonism, therefore, was directed towards Gibbon the *philosophe* rather than the *érudit*. A critique of Protestantism in Bossuet's *History of the Variations of the Protestants* strongly influenced the young Gibbon, who 'surely fell by a noble hand'.[67] This critique also played its part in the development of Newman's religious sensibility, at least as regards his own formulation of the problems which it addresses. In Bossuet, dogma absorbs history; it also, necessarily, includes heresy, a point whose significance is lost neither in *The Decline and Fall* nor in Newman's writings on ecclesiastical history.

In his preface to the *History of the Variations*, Bossuet stated that variations were seen to have been a 'mark of falsehood' by the early Christians; the true faith spoke clearly and simply, so that 'this was one of the grounds, on which the ancient Doctors so much condemn'd the Arians, who, unable to fix themselves, were constantly setting forth new Confessions of Faith'. It was Bossuet's intention to demonstrate that, among Protestant denominations, 'no Change hath happen'd [. . .] which doth not mark out an *inconsistency* in their Doctrine, and is not the *necessary* result from it: their *Variations*, like those of the Arians, will discover, what they would fain have excused, have supplied, have disguised in their belief.'[68] In doing so, he had once persuaded the young Gibbon of the veracity of Catholicism: his own analysis of Arianism in *The Decline and Fall* is a reversal of Bossuet's reading, and of his own earlier acceptance of that reading.[69]

In order to appreciate what this meant for Newman, it is necessary to trace in detail what the history of heresy meant for Gibbon. Arianism was plainly a matter of some moment for Gibbon, despite his attempts at distancing himself from it in the *Memoirs*, where he claimed that

64 'The Catholicity of the Anglican church', in *ECH*, ii. 72, and 'The Protestant idea of Antichrist', in *ECH*, ii. 149.

65 *GA*, 199–202; *Idea*, 236.

66 Letter to Canon Walker (5 Aug. 1864), *LD*, xxi. 185.

67 *A*, 86.

68 J. B. Bossuet, *The History of the Variations of the Protestants*, trans. from the sixth edition of 1708 (Antwerp, 1742), pp. i. iv–v, xxviii–xxix (italic original).

69 *A*, 86.

'I dived perhaps too deeply into the mud of the Arian controversy; and many days of reading, thinking, and writing were consumed in the pursuit of a phantom.'[70] There are indeed good scholarly reasons for dismissing Arianism as a 'phantom', not least because of the paucity of extant materials for analysis, but it is clear that study of the movement served a very particular purpose in Gibbon's mordant appraisal of the intellectual enthusiasm of the early Church.[71] Such criticism of the early Church was a supremely sensitive matter in eighteenth-century England, a fact that was not lost on a historian whose family had once employed William Law, whose nonjuring defences of the early Church in influential devotional writings acted as an explicit critique of the declension of belief and morals in Walpolean England.[72] To undermine the early Church was, then, for many, to undermine modern Christianity, not least when many champions of the Church of England continued to appeal to it as the uncorrupted source of much of their non-Roman Catholic 'orthodoxy'. By placing so much energy in an examination of the sheer precariousness of the emergence of supposed orthodoxy, Gibbon subtly undercut the orthodox apologetic whose chief proponent, Bishop Bull, is quietly satirized in many of the footnotes to chapter 21 of the *Decline and Fall*.[73]

In his sceptical appraisal of the tragicomic scenario, Gibbon introduced the problem of the Trinity in worldly, historical terms, noting how imperial patronage dictated the fortunes of theology. As so often, Gibbon relied on antithesis to reinforce his argument:

The schism of the Donatists was confined to Africa: the more diffusive mischief of the Trinitarian controversy successively penetrated into every part of the Christian world. The former was an accidental quarrel, occasioned by the abuse of freedom; the latter was a high and mysterious argument, derived from the abuse of philosophy. From the age of Constantine to that of Clovis and Theodoric, the temporal interests both of the Romans and Barbarians were deeply involved in the theological disputes of Arianism.

[70] *A*, 315.

[71] For modern appraisals see Robert C. Gregg (ed.), *Arianism: Historical and Theological Reassessments* (Philadelphia, 1985), and Rowan Williams, *Arius: Heresy and Tradition* (London, 1987). On its eighteenth-century revival, see Maurice Wiles, *Archetypal Heresy: Arianism through the Centuries* (Oxford, 1996).

[72] For discussion, see B. W. Young, 'William Law and the Christian economy of salvation', *English Historical Review*, 109 (1994), 308–22.

[73] *DF*, i. 774, n. 23; i. i. 778, n. 39; i. 778, n. 40; i. 783, n. 57; i. 783–4, n. 60; i. 786, n. 69.

From this perspective Gibbon could claim a necessarily distanced role for himself, so that 'The historian may therefore be permitted respectfully to withdraw the veil of the sanctuary; and to deduce the progress of reason and faith, of error and passion, from the school of Plato to the decline and fall of the empire.'[74] Accordingly, irony was allowed to suspend religious commitment between the claims of rationality and revealed faith, as the enthusiasm of Plato was placed beside that of John in a theological dispute of no small moment:

> The eloquence of Plato, the name of Solomon, the authority of the school of Alexandria, and the consent of the Jews and Greeks, were insufficient to establish the truth of a mysterious doctrine which might please, but could not satisfy, a rational mind. A prophet or apostle, inspired by the Deity, can alone exercise a lawful dominion over the faith of mankind; and the theology of Plato might have been forever confounded with the philosophical visions of the Academy, the Porch, and the Lyceum, if the name and divine attributes of the *Logos* had not been confined by the celestial pen of the last and most sublime of the Evangelists.[75]

The patristic synthesis between Athens and Jerusalem was punctured by a sceptical suspicion that insoluble contradictions had been masked by an intellectual compromise redolent of religious enthusiasm. Again, Gibbon utilizes antithesis to telling effect:

> The divine sanction which the Apostle had bestowed on the fundamental principle of the theology of Plato encouraged the learned proselytes of the second and third centuries to admire and study the writings of the Athenian sage, who had thus marvellously anticipated one of the most surprising discoveries of the Christian revelation. The reputable name of Plato was used by the orthodox, and abused by the heretics, as the common support of truth and error: the authority of his skilful commentators, and the science of dialectics, were employed to justify the remote consequences of his opinions, and to supply the discreet silence of the inspired writers [. . .] An eager spirit of curiosity urged them to explore the secrets of the abyss; and the pride of the professors and their disciples was satisfied with the science of words.[76]

Even 'the great Athanasius himself' admitted to failure in this regard; Gibbon seized his sceptical advantage by noting how

> In every step of the enquiry, we are compelled to feel and acknowledge the immeasurable disproportion between the size of the subject and the capacity of the human mind. We may strive to abstract the notions of time, of space, and

[74] *DF*, i. 770–1. [75] *DF*, i. 773. [76] *DF*, i. 775.

of matter, which so closely adhere to all the perceptions of our experimental knowledge. But, as soon as we presume to reason of infinite substance, of spiritual generation; as often as we deduce any positive conclusions from a negative idea, we are involved in darkness, perplexity, and inevitable contradiction.[77]

If policy, history, and philosophy could be shown to have connived at the maintenance of such intricacies, then gentlemanly condescension could be brought into play on Gibbon's part, as he observed that

Those persons who, from their age, or sex, or occupations, were the least qualified to judge, who were the least exercised in the habits of abstract reasoning, aspired to contemplate the economy of the Divine Nature; and it is the boast of Tertullian that a Christian mechanic could readily answer such questions as had perplexed the wisest of the Grecian sages.[78]

Within the space of seven pages, Gibbon has used most of his familiar weaponry against the pretensions of metaphysics, and he had severely compromised Christian theology in the process.[79]

Nonetheless, it was at least as much Platonism, and more especially Neoplatonism, which was subject to Gibbon's criticism, as is apparent in his claim that 'the theological system of Plato was taught with less reserve, and perhaps with some improvements, in the celebrated school of Alexandria'.[80] Similarly, he observed that 'The Platonists admired the beginning of the Gospel of St John, as containing an exact transcript of their own principles [. . .] But in the third and fourth centuries, the Platonists of Alexandria might improve the Trinity by the secret study of the Christian theology.'[81] Nor was it only the early Church which suffered from Gibbon's analysis of this movement, as can be appreciated in his almost Sarpian note regarding a Platonist text: 'The book of the Wisdom of Solomon was received by many of the fathers as the work of that monarch; and although rejected by the Protestants for want of a Hebrew original, it has obtained, with the rest of the Vulgate, the sanction of the council of Trent.'[82] Again, antithesis revealed Gibbon's double approach to undoing the apparent purity of the early Church. In intellectual terms, he derided the Greek-inspired elements of its

[77] *DF*, i. 776. [78] *DF*, i. 776.

[79] On his dislike of metaphysics, see Jordan, *Gibbon and his Roman Empire*, 76.

[80] *DF*, i. 772. [81] *DF*, i. 773, n. 20.

[82] *DF*, i. 772, n. 16. He regretted that no observations on the Council of Nicaea on the part of a fourth-century 'Fra Paolo' had survived: DF, i. 782, n. 55. On Sarpi and his influence, see David Wootton, *Paolo Sarpi: Between Renaissance and Enlightenment* (Cambridge, 1983).

thought, so that its eastern portion was found guilty of Platonism and heresy:

The provinces of Egypt and Asia, which cultivated the language and manners of the Greeks, had deeply imbibed the venom of the Arian controversy. The familiar story of the Platonic system, a vain and argumentative disposition, a copious and flexible idiom, supplied the clergy and people of the East with an inexhaustible flow of words and distinctions; and, in the midst of their fierce contentions, they easily forgot the doubt which is recommended by philosophy, and the submission which is enjoined by religion.

The Latin portion was contrasted in almost bovinely docile terms, Gibbon sketching a strongly satirical group portrait of the orthodox party:

The inhabitants of the West were of a less inquisitive spirit; their passions were not so forcibly moved by invisible objects; their minds were less frequently exercised by the habits of dispute, and such was the happy ignorance of the Gallican church that Hilary himself, above thirty years after the first general council, was still a stranger to the Nicene creed. The Latins had received the rays of divine knowledge through the dark and doubtful medium of a translation.[83]

It was, then, Platonism which lay at the root of the Trinitarian controversy. Hence the rise of Arianism in 'the ancient seat of Platonism, the learned, the opulent, the tumultuous city of Alexandria', where resided Arius himself, interestingly portrayed by Gibbon as a blameless and learned priest.[84] It was not he but the city and its commitment to Platonism which turned Arianism into an intolerant, dogmatizing creed. A strong sense of the ridiculous is never far away in Gibbon's analysis of the Trinitarian controversy, as in his celebrated observation regarding the Arian formulation of Christ's likeness to God: 'The Greek word which was chosen to express his mysterious resemblance bears so close an affinity to the orthodox symbol, that the profane of every age have derided the furious contests which the difference of a single diphthong excited between the Homoousians and the Homoiosians.'[85] Ridicule turns into despair as Trinitarian debate developed into the politics of intolerance, as when, having detailed the hatred of orthodox clergy for Arian leaders, he noted, 'I cannot forebear reminding the reader that the difference between the *Homoousion* and *Homoiousion* is almost invisible to the nicest theological eye.'[86]

[83] *DF*, i. 787–8; cf. ii. 28. [84] *DF*, i. 779.
[85] *DF*, i. 787. [86] *DF*, i. 820, n. 154.

Having noted tellingly that 'The most ancient creeds were drawn up with the greatest latitude,' Gibbon instanced Constantine's 'moderation' towards his pagan subjects as the means by which 'the artful monarch advanced, by slow and cautious steps, to undermine the irregular and decayed fabric of polytheism'. Constantine's acts were significantly compared with the suppression of the Bacchanals and the demolition of the temple of Isis undertaken by the Roman magistrates, whose civic religion Gibbon had already celebrated in his evocation of the 'peace of the Augustans' in volume one.[87] It was the revival of theological divisions over the Trinity which had destroyed the peace and leisure which an edict of toleration had earlier guaranteed, just as it was the new identification of Church and state (instituted by the sons of Constantine as 'the prerogatives of the King of heaven were settled, or changed, or modified in the cabinet of an earthly monarch') which ultimately led to the inquisition founded during Theodosius's reign and to his rival Maximus's being the first monarch to spill the blood of fellow Christians 'on account of their religious opinions'.[88] The Arian condemnation of Athanasius provided Gibbon with the cue to descant on a wistful identification with an older way of ordering things:

The abuse of Christianity introduced into the Roman government new causes of tyranny and sedition; the bonds of civil society were torn asunder by the fury of religious factions; and the obscure citizen, who might earlier have surveyed the elevation and fall of successive emperors, imagined and experienced that his own life and future were connected with the interests of a popular ecclesiastic.[89]

Indeed, despite his celebratedly heroic portrayal of Athanasius and his struggle with the Arian emperors, it is possible to discern in Gibbon

[87] *DF*, i. 778, n. 40; i. 825, n. 166. Cf. his letter to Lord Sheffield, February 1791: 'The primitive Church, which I have treated with some freedom, was itself at that time, an innovation, and was attached to the old Pagan establishment' (J. E. Norton (ed.), *The Letters of Edward Gibbon* (3 vols. London, 1956), iii. 212–17; quotation at p. 216).

[88] *DF*, i. 789; ii. 37–8. Cf. i. 359: 'The ecclesiastical writers of the fourth or fifth centuries attributed to the magistrates of Rome the same degree of implacable and unrelenting zeal which filled their own breasts against the heretics or the idolaters of their own times.'

[89] *DF*, i. 816. Gibbon adverted to the fact that religious persecutions by Anthanasians and Arians were as bad as the massacres of Marius and the prescriptions of Sylla in Rome, and that Constantinople fell prey to similarly intense religious persecution: *DF*, i. 817, 819.

something of a *tendresse*, not only for the religious principles of a tolerant paganism, but also for Arianism itself.[90]

Even when condemning the religious cruelty of the Arian clergy under Genseric and the Vandals, Gibbon accepted that 'the partial acts of severity or injustice which had been recommended by the *Arian* clergy were exaggerated by the orthodox writers'.[91] It is important to note that, in this respect at least, Gibbon makes a tacit distinction between Arianism as a speculative doctrine and Arianism as an established faith. Hence his implicit support for Arius's claim that 'faith might humbly receive what reason could not be presumed to deny, that the Supreme God might communicate his infinite perfections, and create a being similar only to himself';[92] or again, his opinion, congruent with his deep antagonism towards religious enthusiasm, that, rationally speaking, 'The opinion of Arianism might satisfy a cold and speculative mind; but the doctrine of the Nicene Creed, most peacefully recommended by the merits of faith and devotion, was much better adapted to become popular and successful in a believing age.'[93] Whilst he was critical of the metaphysics of the most celebrated of eighteenth-century Arians, Samuel Clarke, he plainly identified himself to some extent with William Chillingworth, another Oxford-educated ex-convert to Catholicism, who, Gibbon noted, probably died an Arian or a Socinian.[94] Gibbon's religious opinions will probably never be fully deciphered, but his interest in the doctrine of the Trinity, as exemplified in his dismissal of 1 John 5:7, is typical of many of his contemporaries.[95]

Where Gibbon's analysis of Arianism was primarily historical, and only obliquely (if tellingly) a comment on the religious controversies of his own times, Newman's approach to heresy was patently bound up with the perceived crisis in the relations between Church and state which gave rise to the Oxford Movement and its assault on religious and political liberalism.[96] His pivotal work, *The Arians of the Fourth Century* (1833), was in part an attempt at defending the Church of England

90 Jordan, *Gibbon and his Roman Empire*, 105.

91 *DF*, ii. 435 (my italic). For some qualification of this remark, see ii. 440.

92 *DF*, i. 786. 93 *DF*, ii. 33. 94 *DF*, i. 177, n. 36; i. 780, n. 49. *A*, 129.

95 Paul Turnbull, 'The "supposed infidelity" of Edward Gibbon', *Historical Journal*, 25 (1982), 23–41; David Dillon Smith, 'Gibbon in church', *Journal of Ecclesiastical History*, 35 (1984), 452–63; B. W. Young, '"Scepticism in excess": Gibbon and eighteenth-century Christianity', *Historical Journal*, 41 (1998), 179–99; *DF*, ii. 442.

96 Robert Pattison, *The Great Dissent: John Henry Newman and the Liberal Heresy* (Oxford, 1991), 100–3, 115–16, 129; Stephen Thomas, *Newman and Heresy: The Anglican Years* (Cambridge, 1991), ch. 2.

from the Bossuetian comparison, a defence to be abandoned when he discovered the Anglican establishment to be a 'semi-Arian' institution.[97] In the very last pages of the book, Newman made explicit the parallels between the Church of the fourth century and the plight of the Church in the 1830s, noting how the higher reality of religion determined the course of history in a manner which reverses the worldliness of Gibbon's history. Witness Newman's Bossuet-like dismissal of Arianism after the Council of Constantinople, when it was formed into

a sect exterior to the Catholic Church; and, taking refuge among the Barbarian Invaders of the Empire, it merged among these external enemies of Christianity, whose history cannot be regarded as strictly ecclesiastical. Such is the general course of religious error; which rises within the sacred precincts, but in vain endeavours to take root in a soil uncongenial to it. The domination of heresy, however prolonged, is but one stage of its existence; it ever hastens to an end, and that end is the triumph of the Truth.[98]

In common with Bossuet, the Newman of the 1830s, rather more than the Gibbon of the 1770s and 1780s, assumed a uniformitarian picture of the past, in which the detail of history was necessarily subsumed by theology, since, as with so much else, 'The heretical spirit is ever one and the same in its various forms.'[99] It was this perspective which initially allied Newman with the patristic studies of Bishop Bull, although this very Anglican orientation gave way in the course of the work to a notion of doctrinal development that was to reach its fulfilment in the *Essay on the Development of Christian Doctrine*.[100]

Theological considerations aside, the impact of Gibbon as a historian is very marked in Newman's *Arians*.[101] As a source of purely factual material, Gibbon is acknowledged as a major modern contributor to an understanding of the Council of Nicaea and to an appreciation of the political success of Arianism as a court faction. Newman's language and tone are redolent of Gibbon on this latter point, as religion impurely melds with politics:

The eunuchs and slaves of the palace strangely embraced the tenets of Arianism; and all the most light-minded and frivolous of mankind allowed themselves to

[97] *Apol.*, 130. [98] *Arians*, 421–2. [99] Ibid. 153.

[100] For discussion, see Rowan Williams, 'Newman's *Arians* and the question of method in doctrinal history', in I. T. Ker and Alan G. Hill (eds.). *Newman after a Hundred Years: Centenary Essays* (Oxford, 1990), 265–85; Owen Chadwick, *From Bossuet to Newman*, 2nd edn. (Cambridge, 1987).

[101] Thomas, *Newman and Heresy*, 36, 176, 250.

abuse the solemn subject in controversy, into matter for fashionable conversation or literary amusement.

The arts of flattery completed the triumph of the heretical party.[102]

In locating the philosophical roots of Arianism, however, Newman differed from Gibbon, discerning the inspiration for Christian heresy in Aristotelianism rather than in Platonism. Whilst accepting that Arius had been educated in the principles of the New Platonic or Eclectic school, Newman, though himself an Aristotelian, minimized Plato's direct influence on doctrine, concluding rather that Platonism and Origenism 'became the *excuse* and *refuge* of the heresy when it was condemned by the Church'.[103] Indeed, rather than worry (however satirically) over the alleged Platonism of St John's Gospel, Newman opined that it stated the nature of Christ's divinity and His distinctiveness from God the Father 'as distinctly as any ecclesiastical comment can propound it'.[104] Where Newman did agree with Gibbon in the history of doctrinal corruption was in the role supposedly played by Jews, discerning 'the latent connexion between judaizing discipline and heresy in doctrine'.[105] Significantly, the only deep slight on Platonism in Newman's text concerns the Hellenized Jew Philo, whose separation of the Logos from God contributed 'perhaps to prepare the way for Arianism'.[106]

Newman's theological understanding of history did not lack in worldly insight, although he happily reversed the cynicism of Gibbon in his portrayal of the duties and privileges of the Church, acknowledging that 'Strictly speaking, the Christian Church, as being a visible society, is necessarily a political power or party. It may be a party triumphant, or a party under persecution; but a party it always must be, prior in existence to the civil institutions with which it is surrounded, and from its latent dignity formidable and influential, even to the end of time.'[107] In an effort to pre-empt a Gibbonian reading, he affirmed his certainty that the Church 'was framed for the express purpose of interfering, or (as irreligious men will say,) meddling with the world.'[108] It was from this positive perspective that he cited Gibbon's ironically expressed view that in Constantine's reign 'The Gospel seemed to be the fit instrument for

[102] *Arians*, 284.

[103] Ibid., 32, 43, 101, 111 (italic original). On Newman's Aristotelianism, see David Newsome, *Two Classes of Men: Platonism and English Romantic Thought* (London, 1974), ch. 4.

[104] *Arians*, 171.

[105] Ibid., 23. Cf. *DF*, i. 447, 449, 515–16.

[106] Ibid., 103.

[107] Ibid., 276–7.

[108] Ibid., 278.

a civil reformation.'[109] Similarly, the truthfulness of this belief allowed him to enjoy the observation that it was a heretical party, the Arians, 'who were the first among Christians to employ force in the cause of religion'.[110]

Newman's *Arians* represents his first *fully* considered public engagement with Gibbon's mind, and a passing remark in its attests to the source of his major disagreement with the historian: the question of the miraculous.[111] Before detailing this controversy, it is worth bearing in mind that whereas for Gibbon the problem of the 'miracle' of the transubstantiation bore a part in his conversion to and from Catholicism, for Newman it was airily dealt with in the *Apologia:*

> People say that the doctrine of Transubstantiation is difficult to believe; I did not believe the doctrine till I was a Catholic. I had no difficulty in believing it, as soon as I believed that the Catholic Roman Church was the oracle of God, and that she had declared this doctrine to be part of the original revelation. It is difficult, impossible, to imagine, I grant;—but how is it difficult to believe?[112]

Such, minimally stated, was Newman's acceptance of the reality of the miraculous, itself the 'characteristic' of sacred history, as 'distinguished from Profane' experience.[113] Gibbon, who seems to have learned to suspect miracles from his reading of Hume, took a rather different view.[114]

Gibbon's remarks on the death of Arius are unequivocal, as in his observation that 'the strange and horrid circumstances of his death might excite a suspicion that the orthodox saints had contributed more efficaciously than by their prayers to deliver the church from the most formidable of her enemies'. His footnoted elucidation is yet more pointedly satirical: 'Those who press the literal narrative of the death of Arius (his bowels suddenly burst out in a privy) must take their option

[109] *Arians*, 262 and n. [110] Ibid., 322.

[111] As Algernon Cecil later noted, the ecclesiastical historian could not ignore the issue of the miraculous, a question which was to make Gibbon a sceptic and Newman a Roman Catholic *Six Oxford Thinkers* (London, 1909), 66, 68.

[112] *Apol.*, 215. On Gibbon and the doctrine of transubstantiation, see Womersley, 'Gibbon's apostasy'.

[113] *EM*, p. xi.

[114] J. G. A. Pocock, 'Superstition and enthusiasm in Gibbon's history of religion', *Eighteenth-Century Life*, 8 (1982), 83–94; 'Gibbon's *Decline and Fall* and the world-view of the late Enlightenment', in *Virtue, Commerce, and History: Essays on Political Thought and History, Chiefly in the Eighteenth Century* (Cambridge, 1985), 143–56. For useful discussion of the wider eighteenth-century debate, see R. M. Burns, *The Great Debate on Miracles: From Joseph Glanvill to David Hume* (Lewisburg, Penn., 1981).

between *poison* and *miracle*.'[115] Newman entertained no such doubts: for him Arius's demise was a supreme example of divine judgement and the interposition of providences.[116] Intriguingly, in his controversial *Essay on the Miracles Recorded in the Ecclesiastical History of the Early Church* (1843), Newman developed Gibbon's elaboration into a *defence* of the miraculous nature of the event, arguing that the orthodox would not have dared attempt so public an action as a poisoning in an Arian city and court, leaving him to conclude that 'those who do not deny the moral governance of God and the heretical and ungodly character of Arianism, will have no difficulty in referring the catastrophe to miracle'.[117]

Almost all of the early miracles whose veracity Newman aimed to justify are mentioned, with a good deal more scepticism, in *The Decline and Fall*. Where Newman accepts the story of the Thundering Legion, Gibbon adverted to its undoubtedly pagan provenance; where Gibbon undercut pious belief in the appearance of the celestial cross before Constantine's victory at the Milvian bridge, chiefly through the silence of the Fathers on the matter, Newman rejected such a sceptical appraisal of the evidence.[118] Gibbon's repudiation of the supposedly miraculous fire which thwarted Julian's attempts to rebuild the Temple at Jerusalem was likewise reversed by Newman, appealing to the learned authority of another eighteenth-century witness, William Warburton, himself an early victim of Gibbon's caustic wit.[119] Newman introduced his observations on the miraculous return of the powers of speech to those African confessors whose tongues had been ripped out on Hunneric's orders with an appeal to Gibbon's authority as 'one who in such a case cannot be called a too favourable witness.'[120] This is itself a near-miracle of understatement when one considers Gibbon's judiciously partisan conclusion to his account:

> This supernatural gift of the African confessors, who spoke without tongues, will command the assent of those, and of those only, who already believe that their language was pure and orthodox. But the stubborn mind of an infidel is guarded by secret incurable suspicion; and the Arian, or Socinian, who has

115 *DF*, i. 791 and n. 83 (italic original).

116 *Arians*, 289–90.

117 *EM*, p. clxxiii.

118 *EM*, pp. cxxii, cxxiii–cxliii; *DF*, i. 551, 738–42.

119 *DF*, i. 888–91; *EM*, pp. clxxv–clxxxv. On Gibbon's altercation with Warburton, see *Critical Observations on the Design of the Sixth Book of the Aeneid*, in *The English Essays of Edward Gibbon*, ed. P. Craddock (Oxford, 1972), 131–62, and *A*, 281–3, 410–11.

120 *EM*, pp. cc–ccxiii.

seriously rejected the doctrine of the Trinity, will not be shaken by the most plausible evidence of the Athanasian miracle.[121]

Newman's detailed and committed defence of post-apostolic miracles marked him out from a great many of his Protestant contemporaries and predecessors. John Jortin, whom Newman dismissed as 'flippant' but whom Gibbon respected, gave voice to the Protestant view in his *Remarks on Ecclesiastical History*, affirming miracles and 'I would not engage for the truth of any of them, after A.D. 107, and that I desire to be ranked, as to this point, not amongst the *Denyers* and *Rejectors*, but amongst the *Doubters*'.[122] It was the apostolic miracles which mattered to *all* Christians, and it was Gibbon's notorious ironies regarding them in chapter fifteen which continued to trouble Newman.[123] In this particular, at least, Newman was almost at one with Milman, whose annotations to his edition of *The Decline and Fall* reveal his unease with Gibbon's deployment of the third of the five causes of early Christian triumphalism.

Milman's praise for Gibbon led him to conclude that Gibbon's work had left the period he discussed 'an unapproachable subject to the future historian'.[124] Having praised its literary and argumentative supremacy, Milman sketched its theological shortcomings, noting that while Gibbon's philosophical bigotry is not more unjust than the theological partialities of those ecclesiastical writers who were before in undisputed possession of this province of history, it was still unjust.[125] The 'great misrepresentations' pervading the history were 'his false estimate of the nature and influence of Christianity', a confounding together 'in one indistinguishable mass, the *origin* and *apostolic* propagation of the new religion, and its *later progress*'. It was only through the 'dark colouring with which he brought out the failings and the follies of the succeeding

121 *DF*, ii. 444.

122 *Arians*, 242; *DF*, i. 783, n. 58. John Jortin, *Remarks on Ecclesiastical History* (London, 1751–73), ii. 70–1. Milman was an admirer of Jortin, whose influence on Gibbon he approved: 'Life of Erasmus' in *Savanarola, Erasmus, and Other Essays* (London, 1878), 76–148, at p. 79.

123 *DF*, i. 446–7, 473–4, 497–8.

124 *The History of the Decline and Fall of the Roman Empire*, ed. H. H. Milman (London, 1838–19), i. iv. Such a perspective was shortly to be undermined by Milman's own *History of Latin Christianity*, the object of Newman's severe censure. It would be worth seeking an analogue in ecclesiastical history to the political biases apparent in work on the history of the Roman Republic, as evinced in Frank M. Turner, 'British politics and the demise of the Roman Republic: 1700–1939', *Historical Journal*, 29 (1986), 577–99.

125 *Decline and Fall*, ed. Milman, i. xiv.

ages, that a shadow of doubt was thrown back upon the primitive period of Christianity'.[126] Milman, the assured practitioner of a Protestant critique of Catholicism, allowed that Gibbon 'might have annihilated the whole fabric of post-apostolic miracles, if he had left uninjured by sarcastic insinuation those of the New Testament'. Hence also the centrality of the notes of Guizot, which Milman incorporated into his text, acting on the unfortunate conviction that 'on such a subject, to many, the authority of a French statesman, a Protestant, and a rational and sincere Christian, would appear more independent and unbiased, and therefore be more commanding, than that of an English clergyman'.[127] In Milman's estimates of those who had answered Gibbon, only Richard Watson emerged with honour, while one of his most influential critics was dismissed with all the *hauteur* available to a liberal Anglican: 'The name of Milner stands higher with a certain class of readers, but will not carry much weight with the severe investigator of history.'[128]

Joseph Milner, however, was much admired by the young Newman. It was from this source that Newman later claimed largely to have drawn his arguments against Hume and Gibbon on the nature and status of miracles.[129] In his posthumously published philosophical notebooks, Newman affirmed that some miracles are but a 'continuation or augmentation of natural powers', concluding that 'It is a confirmation of this to look at Gibbon's five causes of Xtianity. We do not deny them—but only say that they are not *sufficient*; i.e. the [. . .] spread of Xtianity was something *more* than natural.'[130] This was the staple of the argument which he developed in the *Essay towards a Grammar of Assent*, a critique whose language is reminiscent of Smart and Blake berating Newton, and which echoes Newman's own early dismissal of Gibbon's misleading prose in an essay on poetics: 'Does Gibbon think to sound the depths of the external ocean with the tape and measuring-rod of his merely literary philosophy?'[131] It was the coldness of those rationalistic impulses of eighteenth-century thought which Newman so disliked

126 *Decline and Fall*, ed. Milman, i. xiv–xvi. 127 Ibid. pp. i. xix, xxi.

128 Ibid. pp. i. xxii. See Joseph Milner, *Gibbon's Account of Christianity Considered: Together with some Strictures on Hume's 'Dialogue concerning Natural Religion'* (York, 1781). On Milner, see J. D. Walsh, 'Joseph Milner's evangelical church history', *Journal of Ecclesiastical History*, 10 (1959), 174–87. For his influence on Newman, see *EM*, p. iv, and *Apol.*, 32–3. For Milman's doubts concerning post-apostolic miracles, see *Decline and Fall*, ed. Milman, ii. 308 n.; ii. 310; ii. 311 n.; ii. 313 n.; iv. 100 n.

129 *Apol.*, 32–3. 130 *PN*, ii. 151 (italic original).

131 *GA*, 294–7, 310. Cf. 'Poetry, with reference to Aristotle's *Poetics*', in *ECH*, i. 22–3.

and which led him, after quoting Gibbon's admiring description of the philosophically resigned death of Julian the Apostate, to observe to his Dublin students: 'Such, Gentlemen, is the final exhibition of the Religion of reason: in the insensibility of conscience, in the ignorance of the very idea of sin, in the contemplation of his own moral consistency, in the simple absence of fear, in the cloudless self-confidence, in the serene self-possession, in the cold-self-satisfaction, we recognize the mere Philosopher.'[132] Newman's was, then, as much an emotional reaction, albeit one governed by philosophical reasoning, as it was an intellectual or even a religious one. It was part of a general Victorian reaction to the eighteenth century which found much of its predecessor culture unsatisfactory.[133] Leslie Stephen, the most professional of Victorian agnostics, and who shared with Newman pronounced evangelical origins, similarly berated Gibbon for lacking the seriousness which he deemed essential among effective critics of religion, while C. J. Abbey, a high-church chronicler of eighteenth-century Anglicanism, lamented the offensively deadening influence of *The Decline and Fall.*[134] Acton, Newman's fellow Catholic (whose kinship to the Gibbons Newman bore in mind), took a predictably loftier approach, pronouncing in a letter to his colleague J. R. Simpson, in language redolent of his early training at the feet of Döllinger (whose house he had first approached clutching a copy of *The Decline and Fall*), that

The science of history and the science of language, and the philosophical study of jurisprudence, are new discoveries of this century. Before this, historical controversy was nonsense, for the materials were imperfect and the method did not exist. There is a great difference between history now and in Gibbon's time as between the astronomy before Copernicus and after him.[135]

[132] *Idea*, 149.

[133] B. W. Young, 'Knock-kneed giants: Victorian representations of eighteenth-century thought', in Jane Garnett and Colin Matthew (ed.), *Revival and Religion since 1700: Essays for John Walsh* (London, 1993), 79–93. On the religious presuppositions of major Victorian historians, see Michael Bentley, 'Victorian historians and the larger hope', in M. Bentley (ed.), *Public and Private Doctrine: Essays in British History Presented to Maurice Cowling* (Cambridge, 1993), 127–48.

[134] Leslie Stephen, *History of English Thought in the Eighteenth Century* (London, 1876), i. 272; C. J. Abbey, *The English Church and its Bishops, 1700–1800* (London, 1887), ii. 257.

[135] Newman to Acton (20 June 1861), *LD*, xxi. 184–5. Herbert Butterfield, *Lord Acton*, (London, 1948), 3. Acton to Simpson (3 Sept. 1861), in *Correspondence of Acton and Simpson,*, ed. Josef L. Altholz and Damian McElrath (Cambridge, 1971–5), ii. 161. Acton, along with other historians (including Lecky, Maitland, Mommsen,

Accordingly, *The Decline and Fall* could do no harm to revealed religion, a conclusion which Newman, who had no sympathy with the claims of the new German-inspired history and who had grown up reading and debating with the style of reasoning represented in *The Decline and Fall*, could not have reached.[136] This sort of history which Gibbon represented, moralizing, epigrammatic, philosophically engaged, was closer to the strictly ecclesiastical history which Newman wrote than it was to any other variety of historical writing which developed over the course of the nineteenth century.

In a gossipy business letter written in 1792, Gibbon claimed that 'I speak with the religious accuracy of the historian,' an ironic observation acting as a subtle defence of a sense of vocation that effectively undermines the supposedly superior claims of the realms of devotion.[137] Had Newman known this letter it would have confirmed his suspicions. From Gibbon's parenthetical remark it is possible to appreciate the similarities and differences between the two historians. Whereas the philosophical and moralizing character of his ecclesiastical history drew Newman closer to his respected antagonist, it was Gibbon's continued deployment of mordant irony which would prove antithetical to the tone and purpose of Newman's devotionally driven conception of the writing of history. Nonetheless, it was to Gibbon that Newman's thought constantly recurred when engaged in consideration of ecclesiastical history; he maintained a relationship with eighteenth-century historical writing that he shared with Milman, although Milman knew much more about modern German scholarship than Newman ever did.

Seeley, Stephen, and Tout), was a member of the Gibbon centenary commemoration: *Proceedings of the Gibbon Commemorations*, 10–12.

[136] Cf. Josef L. Altholz, 'Newman and history', *Victorian Studies*, 7 (1964), 285–94.

[137] Gibbon to Lady Elizabeth Foster (Aug. 1792), in Carnochan, *Gibbon's Solitude*, appendix *A*, 181–2.

4

The Stephen Family and the Eighteenth Century

> The paternal is not usually an agreeable relation to the child, especially to sons; and though 'father' may be entitled to receive all reverence, duty, love, and so on, yet it is for the most part a mere parchment title, acknowledged in theory, and only in theory. And how can one blame the children that it is so?
>
> James Stephen, 18 January 1846[1]

> The man or woman can really mould the character of a little circle, and determine the whole life of one little section of the next generation; when it may be very difficult to say whether the influence which they can bring to bear upon a class or a nation is really perceptible at all, or does not even operate in the direction opposite to that directed.
>
> Leslie Stephen, 'Forgotten benefactors'[2]

> If we fall back, as we must perpetually do, upon our Lord's own leading principle of using the human relation of parent and child as the highest and most instructive type of the relation between God and the human spirit, we shall surely feel that the child, in learning to speak to its father and to understand his voice, has far other and larger hopes and purposes than that of getting things from him.
>
> Caroline Emelia Stephen, *Quaker Strongholds*[3]

Freud argued in his celebrated essay on the theme that 'the family romance' had a direct social consequence, since 'the progress of society in general rests upon the opposition between the generations'. Leslie

[1] *Letters*, 98. [2] *SRD*, ii. 225–67, at pp. 250–1. [3] (London, 1890), 74.

Stephen, who died in 1904, five years before the first appearance in print of *Der Familienroman der Neurotiker* (*Family Romances*), would certainly have assented to this portion of Freud's argument, as would his daughter, Virginia Woolf; both would also probably have dissented from the claim which immediately follows, though later readers of their work might have found it equally telling: 'there is a class of neurotics whose condition is recognizably determined by their having failed in this task'.[4] As this chapter will show, father and daughter effectively demonstrate the connection between Freud's contentions, and this is especially clear in their relations with the eighteenth century. The Stephen family emerged as a social, religious, and intellectual force at the very close of the eighteenth century, a period with which later members of the family, from Sir James Stephen (1789–1859), to his sons James Fitzjames (1829–94) and Leslie (1832–1904), and thence Virginia, became notably preoccupied. It is this Stephen family romance with the eighteenth century that will be used in this chapter to explore a very particular dimension of the Victorians' preoccupation with their immediate predecessor generations. Above all other members of the family, it was Leslie Stephen who was most immediately concerned in this romance, and it is surely not insignificant that he should have claimed that the eighteenth century as a period of speculation did not end until 1832. This was, after all, not just conventionally to be considered as the year of the Great Reform Act, the original of the political reforms to which the young Stephen would direct his considerable energies during the agitation over the Second Reform Act in 1867.[5] More intriguingly, 1832 was also the year of Leslie Stephen's birth.

Central to this family romance is a rebellion against Christianity, from Leslie Stephen's open advocacy of agnosticism to Virginia Woolf's uncompromising atheism. The Stephens had been firm Evangelicals in the closing decades of the eighteenth and opening decades of the

[4] Sigmund Freud, 'Family Romances', trans. David McLintock, in *The Uncanny: The New Penguin Freud* (Harmondsworth, 2003), 35–41, at p. 35.

[5] Leslie Stephen, 'On the choice of representatives by popular constituencies', in *Essays on Reform* (London, 1867), 85–125; writing eighteen years later, Stephen declared of the Second Reform Act of 1867 that 'the nation proceeded, as Carlyle put it, to "shoot Niagra", with consequences which will some day have to be summed up by the impartial historian of the future': *Life of Henry Fawcett* (London, 1885), 220. For Stephen's place in the mid-Victorian Liberal generation, see Christopher Harvie, *The Lights of Liberalism: University Liberals and the Challenge of Democracy, 1860–86* (London, 1976) and Christopher Kent, *Brains and Numbers: Elitism, Comtism, and Democracy in Mod-Victorian England* (Toronto, 1978).

nineteenth centuries, and the religion they practised was familial not only in context but also most firmly in content, as can be readily appreciated from Sir James Stephen's insistence, in a summa of his liberal restatement of his Evangelical inheritance, that God 'is still ever one and ever the same,—ever yearning over our fallen race with more than parental tenderness, and ever resisting our suicidal self-will with the wholesome, though reluctant, severity of a Father'.[6] Consider further his affirmation of one of the central claims of that creed, the doctrine of Original Sin. This had taken a deeply familial form in his thought, and one that could not but have laid the foundations for a family romance which his sons eventually composed around the tacit—and then explicit—repudiation of their father's firm persuasion:

> of a real, though wholly incomprehensible, intimacy (amounting almost to unity) of life, and nature between parents and their children, and their more remote posterity—the persuasion thence resulting of an ancestral corruption of our whole race—and the persuasion that, by the adoption of our nature, Jesus Christ has broken the otherwise indissoluble bonds which link us all to sin, and to sorrow, the child of sin.[7]

The Stephens were never strong on metaphors, and such a literal reading of Original Sin was pregnant with the possibilities of revolt by later members of the family against a morbid conviction of exactly the sort that this notably thin-skinned dynasty were apt to worry over incessantly.

Leslie Stephen, in his turn, was particularly appalled by the idea of the Atonement and expiatory sacrifice generally, decrying the alleged justice of a loving Father who wins the salvation of the world by ordaining the willing sacrifice, through a painful and humiliating death, of his sinless, trusting, and loving Son.[8] Unlike many of his contemporaries, however, he could not find any consolation from the unacceptable doctrine of Atonement by emphasizing in its stead the doctrine of the Incarnation, the dogma which affirms the humanity of Christ, a dogma to which, as Boyd Hilton has demonstrated, the post-Evangelical generations increasingly turned in the mid- and later nineteenth century.[9] The

[6] 'The Epilogue', *Essays*, ii. 460–501, at p. 498.

[7] *Letters*, 182.

[8] 'The Scepticism of Believers', *AA*, 42–85.

[9] Stephen plainly sympathized with Joseph Priestley's Unitarian attack on the doctrine of the Incarnation: *History*, i. 372. On the transition from Evangelical devotion to the doctrine of the Atonement to post-Evangelical commitment to the doctrine of the Incarnation, see Boyd Hilton, *The Age of Atonement: The Influence of Evangelicalism on Social and Economic Thought, 1785–1865* (Oxford, 1988).

familial language of Christianity lent itself to rapid dissolution over three generations of the Stephen family romance with its intellectual inheritance, and the Stephens were nothing if not intellectual.

I

The Stephens were at least as much the representatives of a literary aristocracy as they were of an intellectual aristocracy, a phrase originally made famous in a celebrated essay by Noel Annan in 1955, but used by Sir James Stephen in his *Lectures on the History of France* as early as 1851 to describe the French political classes from the fifteenth century onwards, itself a recurrence of a phrase concerning the 'political or intellectual aristocracy' he had earlier used in a private letter in November 1835.[10] Annan himself had attributed the first use of the phrase to James Kenneth Stephen, the son of James Fitzjames Stephen; that the phrase actually originated in the work of that short-lived writer's grandfather is even more indicative of the self-consciousness of the Stephen family's claims to membership of the intellectual aristocracy, itself a largely self-constituted elite.[11] This aristocratic ethos also informed their political views, as James Fitzjames Stephen approvingly noticed that 'Liberalism is in many respects an aristocratic creed, inasmuch as the essence of it is to produce a condition of things in which every individual will

[10] Noel Annan, 'The intellectual aristocracy', in J. H. Plumb (ed.), *Studies in Social History: A Tribute to G. M. Trevelyan* (London, 1955), 243–87, and in revised form in *The Dons: Mentors, Eccentrics and Geniuses* (London, 1999), 304–41. On Sir James Stephen's pioneering use of the phrase, see *Lectures*, i. 422, and his letter to Henry Taylor, 16 Nov. 1835 in *Letters*, 43.

[11] Noel Annan, *Leslie Stephen: The Godless Victorian* (London, 1984), 5. Leslie Stephen had used the phrase much more critically of J. G. Lockhart, Walter Scott's biographer and son-in-law: 'He was an intellectual aristocrat, fastidious and over-sensitive, with very fine perceptions, but endowed with rather too hearty a scorn of fools as well as of folly' ('The Story of Scott's Ruin', *SB*, i. 1–37, at p. 1). There has been some criticism of such readings of the Stephen family, as in remarks made by Margaret M. Jensen regarding the familial legacy in interpretations of Sir Leslie Stephen: 'Being a "Stephen", they hint, was all Sir Leslie needed to achieve canonical status.' Likewise, criticizing Noel Annan's original 1951 biography of Stephen, she concluded that: 'This view of Stephen as a pedigreed specimen carrying greatness as his birthright appears in virtually all biographies of him.' (*The Open Book: Creative Misreading in the Works of Selected Modern Writers* (Basingstoke, 2002), 35, 36). One might sympathize with elements of this criticism, but, equally, reading his work in terms of his familial legacy might make for a more just appraisal than those of the sort she criticizes, and also than the one she herself goes on to make in the course of her study.

have the fullest scope, and produce the most permanent results.' This was a perfect description of his own creed, and there was something of proleptic autobiography in his further claim that, 'The vigorous man will, under this system, get a maximum of advantage from his superior strength, and will transmit to his descendants the advantages which he has acquired.'[12] The intellectual aristocracy would, in this way, seek to claim its place in the political world; hence, perhaps, something of Virginia Woolf's marked disdain for the active politicians of her own generation.[13]

Their manifestly confident status as members of an intellectual aristocracy informed Stephen family perspectives on so much more than the making and endless reviewing of books. This was a family that read people as much as its individual members read and wrote books; indeed, in much of their work, people and books become impossible to disentangle: for Stephen the phrase 'Man of Letters' is a more than usually accurate description, and this identification of a writer with what he or she had written informed the way he himself wrote about Thomas Hobbes, Jonathan Swift, Alexander Pope, Samuel Johnson, and George Eliot in the *English Men of Letters* series.[14] Likewise, it is significant that the publication of a book, no matter how undistinguished, should have proved, during Stephen's founding editorship, to have been a determining criterion for the inclusion of many of the minor figures who featured in the *Dictionary of National Biography*.

There is a revealing moment in an essay on Johnson when this heuristic interpretative method was defended from apparent collapse:

> The whole art of criticism consists in learning to know the human being who is partially revealed to us in his spoken or written words. The two methods of inquiry may supplement each other; but their substantial agreement is the test of their accuracy. If Johnson, as a writer, appears to us to be a mere windbag and manufacturer of sesquipedalian verbiage, whilst, as a talker, he appears to be one of the most genuine and deeply feeling of men, we may be sure that our analysis has been somewhat defective.

[12] 'Cobbett's Political Works', *HS*, iii. 245. His father had described himself in 1838 as 'a kind of philosophical Whig' (*Letters*, 53).

[13] This is most marked in *Three Guineas* (1938), but can be readily found elsewhere. On the aristocratic flavour of much of Woolf's generation's politics, see the discussion of the politics of Bertrand Russell, an aristocrat *and* an intellectual, in Philip Ironside, *The Social and Political Thought of Bertrand Russell: The Development of an Aristocratic Liberalism* (Cambridge, 1996).

[14] *Hobbes* (London, 1904); *Swift* (London, 1882); *Alexander Pope* (1880); *Samuel Johnson* (London, 1878); *George Eliot* (London, 1902).

How then did Stephen rescue his analysis? He did so by observing that Johnson, a poor imitator of the prose style of Thomas Browne and John Milton, had 'the misfortune not so rare as it may sound, to be born in the wrong century; and is, therefore, a giant in fetters; the amplitude of style is still there, but it is checked into mechanical regularity.' In closing his essay, Stephen significantly extended this claim, writing that 'A century earlier or later he might have succeeded in expressing himself through books as well as through his talk; but it is not given us to choose the time of our birth, and some very awkward consequences follow.'[15]

In thus saving the appearances, Stephen met the problem he had himself raised in identifying a writer so completely with his or her work, but he did so by rendering problematic the historical method which he also described in the same essay as threatening 'to become a part of our contemporary cant'.[16] For Stephen, literary history dictated the way one thought about history as a totality, and books were not only identifiable with their writers, but also with the periods in which they were written. Quite how this worked remained a problem to him, and one which recurs in his work to the end of his life.[17] The statement he made in his major contribution to English intellectual history (and which J. W. Burrow sees as the founding text of the discipline in England), his *History of English Thought in the Eighteenth Century* (1876), remained true for him to the end of his writing life: 'We have not yet learnt the secret of the periodicity of intellectual life.' It was a combination of 'external circumstances' and the 'logical position of the thinkers' of a particular time that allowed such a problem to be addressed; thus it was that literary history of a peculiarly personalized kind was absolutely central to Stephen's conception of intellectual

[15] Stephen, 'Dr. Johnson's Writings', *HL*, ii. 1–31, at pp. 3, 13, and 29. The same fate was noted in the case of Thomas Hollis, the eighteenth-century revivalist of seventeenth-century political radicalism; likewise, the philosopher Richard Price was held to have revived outmoded seventeenth-century Platonism in the eighteenth century (*History*, i. 358, 363–4). He also used to enjoy speculating what people would have been in earlier periods from those in which they flourished: Robert Burns would, in the seventeenth century, have been a Covenanter (*History*, ii. 386). Biography was always considered by Leslie Stephen to be a vital component of broader intellectual understanding, as in the claim made in his last book, seen through the press by Maitland, that in the case of Hobbes 'as decidedly in that of any philosopher, a knowledge of the man is very important to a fair appreciation of the work' (*Hobbes*, 3).

[16] *HL*, ii. 25.

[17] For his pithy final statement, justifying the use of literature as a historical source in the Ford Lectures in English History at Oxford in 1903, see *ELS*, 1–3.

history.[18] Epochs, as well as men and women, were identified with the books they produced. It was, after all, from books that they would be remembered, a fact he drove home in his defence of Horace Walpole's mania for a strict delineation of the apparently trivial in his letters and histories:

Walpole's writings belong to a good old-fashioned type of history, which aspires to be nothing more than a quintessence of contemporary gossip. If the opinion be pardonable in these days, history of that kind has not only its charm, but its serious value. If not very profound or comprehensive, it impresses upon us the fact—so often forgotten—that our grandfathers were human beings.[19]

Humanity, paradoxically perhaps, could best be recovered from books.

It ought to come as no surprise, then, that Woolf, having been reared in such a pervasively bookish environment, was to observe in 'The Leaning Tower', an essay composed the year before her suicide, that, 'Books descend from books as families descend from families. Some descend from Jane Austen; others from Dickens. They resemble their parents, as human children resemble their parents; yet they differ as children differ, and revolt as children revolt.'[20] Woolf's first contribution to a published book was to *The Life and Letters of Leslie Stephen* (1906), compiled and written by F. W. Maitland. Was she alluding to a passage in this book when thinking about descent from books? It is a passage worth quoting at length, as it affirms the deep bookishness of the Stephen family, confirming the literary nature of its family romance, and of the interconnections of the various imaginative strands at work in a dynasty dating back to the days of James Stephen (*c.*1733–1779):

On many a page in the catalogue at the British Museum his progeny have left their mark, for whatever else a true Stephen might do, he would at all events publish some book or at least some pamphlet for the instruction of his fellow men. Solid and sober, for the more part, were the works of the Stephens: grave legal treatises—for theirs was pre-eminently a family of the long robe—or else pamphlets dealing argumentatively with some matter of public importance. We might amuse ourselves for a moment by suppressing the names of authors, and supposing that books begat books without human aid. Then taking one of Leslie's books, for instance, the 'History of English Thought in the Eighteenth Century,' and ascending the direct male line, we might say

[18] *History*, i. 26, 31. [19] 'Horace Walpole,' *HL*, i. 327–54, at p. 328.

[20] Virginia Woolf, 'The Leaning Tower', in *The Moment and Other Essays* (London, 1947), 105–25, at p. 106.

that it was the son of 'Essays in Ecclesiastical Biography,' which was the son of 'War in Disguise,' which was the son of 'Considerations on Imprisonment for Debt.' We might say that it was the brother of 'Liberty, Equality and Fraternity,' and of the 'History of Criminal Law'; the brother also of 'Quaker Strongholds.' We might say that it was the nephew of a classical treatise on Pleading: the nephew also of a very miscellaneous batch of books, including a novel, 'The Jesuit at Cambridge': the uncle of 'Lapsus Calami,' and—but the law books are too numerous to mention. Then, if we desert the agnatic lines, we observe that the 'Science of Ethics' is the grandchild of many sermons, the great-grand-child of the 'Complete Duty of Man,' the great-great-grandchild of 'The Eternity of Hell Torments asserted,' the first cousin of the 'Logic of Chance,' the first cousin also of the 'Law of the Constitution,' and while we are about it, we may add—for affinity also is important- that the 'Playground of Europe' is the brother-in-law of 'Old Kensington' and the son-in-law of 'Vanity Fair.'[21]

To this world of descent from Evangelical Stephens and Venns, out of which agnosticism emerged, and of cousinages with academic Diceys, and a first marriage into the Thackeray family, one ought also to add Maitland himself, since he married into Leslie Stephen's second wife's family; *The Life and Letters of Leslie Stephen* is thus itself deeply entangled in this family romance of books.[22]

The Stephens, whether they were believers, agnostics, or atheists, were Protestants to the core, firm believers in the teaching of the word, and critics of ambiguity whenever they located its unsettling presence. There was an unflinching dogmatism in their tone, from the certainties of the Clapham Sect Evangelicalism of the elder James Stephen (1758–1832),

[21] Frederic William Maitland, *The Life and Letters of Leslie Stephen* (London, 1906), 7–8.

[22] On Maitland's affinity with the Stephens, see Annan, *The Dons*, 339. Leslie Stephen's gratitude to his nephew, H. A. L. Fisher, for having delivered his Ford lectures for him led him to declare in their published form that: 'I would adopt the good old form of dedicating them to you, were it not that I can find no precedent for a dedication by an uncle to a nephew—uncles having, I fancy, certain opinions as to the light in which they are generally regarded by nephews' (*ELS*, p. vi). The Venns similarly moved away from pious Evangelicalism, and the Cambridge don John Venn, the historian of the family, was as respectful of the Clapham Sect as Leslie Stephen latterly proved to be. Venn celebrated his ancestor John Venn of Clapham by alluding to the familial connections in which Venns and Stephens lived: 'In his *Essays in Ecclesiastical Biography*, the late Sir James Stephen—drawing from the stores of his own early recollections—has described, with rare delicacy of touch and tenderness of sympathy, the strong and the weak points of the men amongst whom he had been brought up.' John Venn, *Annals of a Clerical Family: Being some Account of the Family and Descendants of William Venn, Vicar of Otterton, Devon, 1600–1621* (London, 1904), 145.

the religious liberalism of his son Sir James Stephen, the rugged agnosticism of his two surviving sons, James Fitzjames and Leslie, the semi-mystical Quakerism of their sister Caroline Emelia (1834–1909), and the Bloomsburian creed of Leslie's daughter, Virginia. As with the Clapham Sect, so with these representatives of Victorian agnosticism: their religious position became a family affair. James Fitzjames, though himself an unbeliever, would drive his wife and daughter to church, and await their return at the church doors; Thoby Stephen, Leslie's son, would write a tract in the year of his father's death against compulsory chapel at Cambridge, as befitted the issue of a sometime clergyman who had returned to a lay state after his loss of belief had obliged him to resign his clerical fellowship at Trinity Hall in 1864.[23] The logic of the family was firmly identified with the logic of their religious positions. This had its conventionally Protestant origins.

Sir James Stephen, who had desired a clerical career for both of his sons, was an emphatic critic of clerical celibacy.[24] He regretted that the religiously estimable and socially concerned nuns and recluses of Port Royal all died childless, insisting that celibacy counteracted the laws of nature and of providence, as he argued that 'filial affection, cheerfully, temperately, bountifully, and thankfully using the gifts of heaven, is the best tribute which man can render to Him who claims for himself the name and the character of a Father'.[25] He reserved particular praise for Luther as a husband and a father, celebrating the adroitness with which he 'continued to gratify at once his tenderness as a father, and his taste as a theologian'. For Stephen, 'the most important of all human duties' were those of 'parental and conjugal life'; such a conviction could take a stern turn, as in his remarks on William Wilberforce, the very type of the Clapham Sect father:

His parental tenderness had not, even in their early years, degenerated into fondness, or expressed itself by caresses, or by a blind and partial admiration. On the contrary, it was with an almost morbid acuteness that he detected the

[23] On Fitzjames Stephen's gradual loss of faith, see his 'Autobiographic fragment' in the Stephen family papers, Cambridge University Library, and, for discussion, see James A. Colaiaco, *James Fitzjames Stephen and the Crisis of Victorian Thought* (London, 1983), 167–90, and K. J. M. Smith, *James Fitzjames Stephen: Portrait of a Victorian Rationalist* (Cambridge, 1988), 215–18, 235–8, 241–4. On the reasons for his nephew's religious revolt at Cambridge, see Thoby Stephen, *Compulsory Chapel* (Cambridge, 1904).

[24] *Letters*, 138.

[25] 'Port Royal', *Essays*, i. 431–520, at pp. 520, 504.

germ of evil, moral or intellectual, in his children, and watched the growth, or the decline, of any wayward humour or dangerous prosperity in them.[26]

In these telling words, alive with inner conflict, Stephen betrayed his own sense of distance from the familial atmosphere in which he was raised, whilst simultaneously trying to do his historical duty by it in thus memorializing and apostrophizing Wilberforce, whose ultimate influence over his own sons was to lead to religious conversions a long way either from his own accustomed Evangelicalism or the pioneering agnosticism into which the Stephen sons would eventually retreat. Nor yet was it only Clapham which Stephen celebrated as a familial inheritance; he also praised the Venns, into which family he had himself married, and whose shaping of much of the eighteenth-century Evangelical Revival he traced in his *Essays in Ecclesiastical Biography* (1849), a collection comprising earlier contributions to the *Edinburgh Review*, thereby cementing familial Evangelicalism with the final journalistic product of the Scottish Enlightenment, an intellectual movement whose legacy was to prove far more fertile to the intellectual purposes of his sons than was their father's Clapham-derived theology.[27]

Leslie Stephen was to enjoy playing with such piously Protestant family ideology. He inverted the principles of asceticism when he referred to the life of the retiring eighteenth-century clergyman William Wollaston as having 'approached the life of a monastic student as nearly as it is possible to a man who begets eleven children'. Similarly, Bishop Wilson of Sodor and Man (an eighteenth-century hero in Matthew Arnold's *Culture and Anarchy*), whilst otherwise held to be very like Thomas à Kempis in his thinking, was less ascetic than his theological predecessor 'inasmuch as Wilson had the good fortune to be a married man instead of a monk'. Stephen also mildly satirized the more secular claims of nineteenth-century philosophy by instancing the life of Thomas Chubb, the artisanal deist who eked out his controversial career in Salisbury in the 1730s and 1740s: 'He deserves the praise of Malthusians; for he tells us that he never married, thinking it wrong

26 'Martin Luther', 'The "Evangelical" Succession', 'William Wilberforce', *Essays*, i. 291–359, at pp. 298, 300–1, and ii. 65–202, at p. 149, and 203–86, at p. 273. This latter was a review of the materials to a life of their father published by Wilberforce's sons, on their religious odysseys, see David Newsome, *The Parting of Friends: A Study of the Wilberforces and Henry Manning* (London, 1966).

27 'The French Benedictines', 'The "Evangelical" Succession', in *Essays*, i. 36–430, at p. 429, and ii. 99.

to introduce a family into the world without a prospect of maintaining them.'[28] Likewise, in praising Parson Adams in *Tom Jones*, one of Henry Fielding's 'finest conceptions', he observed that: 'He scorns the unborn Malthus, and is outrageously impecunious in his habits.'[29] Such asides were indicative of the need he felt, against the individualist ethic of Utilitarianism, for a coherent theory of the family, since a 'full understanding . . . of the functions discharged by the family in the social organisation would probably reveal many ulterior and vitally important consequences of any change in its constitution to which the rough calculations of the utilitarian are necessarily insensible'.[30] Within six years of the publication of the *History of English Thought in the Eighteenth Century*, Stephen would himself secularize the ideology of the family by making family organization central to the Darwinian philosophy he sketched in his unsuccessful contribution to late Victorian moral theory, *The Science of Ethics* (1882).[31]

The Evangelical-cum-agnostic legacy of the Stephen family *as* a family has been productively explored by Christopher Tolley in *Domestic Biography* (1997), his suggestive study of the family dynamics of Evangelicalism.[32] Similarly, a recent study by Barbara Caine, *Bombay to Bloomsbury* (2005), has surveyed in the interlocked biographies of members of the Strachey dynasty the generational shifts and revolts in a family that moved from service in India to commitments to feminism, leading to an epochal revolt against Victorianism in Lytton Strachey's *Eminent Victorians* (1918), and whose intellectual and cultural contribution to English life climaxed in the career of James Strachey, the pre-eminent English translator of Freud.[33] The Strachey family romance could usefully be compared with the Stephen family romance at many points. Religion is, however, altogether less evident in the history of the Strachey family:[34] it is absolutely central to that of the Stephen family,

[28] *History*, i. 109, 138; ii. 327. For Arnold's appreciation of Thomas Wilson (1663–1755), see *Culture and Anarchy* (1869), ed. J. Dover Wilson (Cambridge, 1932), 3–6, 48, 114.

[29] *History*, ii. 321.

[30] *History*, ii. 86.

[31] *SE*, 131–6.

[32] Christopher Tolley, *Domestic Biography: The Legacy of Evangelicalism in Four Nineteenth-Century Families* (Oxford, 1997), esp. pp. 251–9.

[33] Barbara Caine, *Bombay to Bloomsbury: A Biography of the Strachey Family* (Oxford, 2005).

[34] The parents of the family, Sir Richard and Jane, Lady Strachey, seem to have been singularly untroubled Victorian agnostics. Their eldest son, Dick, faced initial problems in marrying, such was his future father-in-law's suspicion of his lack of belief: ibid. 82, 143, 149.

whether as a staple of belief or as a perpetually troubling source of intellectual rebellion.

II

The Stephen family had emerged from Scottish obscurity to English notability late in the eighteenth century, a process of social and intellectual betterment which Stephen traced through their commitments to authorship. These eighteenth-century generations were to become an obsession with Leslie Stephen, and it is noticeable that references to grandparents and great-grandparents abound in his literary and historical writings, particularly in relation to literary production. He was concerned to do justice to both, for as he wrote in the *History of English Thought in the Eighteenth Century*:

> It has become a common practice to denounce the frigidity and formality of the eighteenth century. We always think our grandfathers fools because we value inordinately the changes which have been effected in our own times. For our great-grandfathers we can make allowances, for they are at a distance which levels all petty jealousies.[35]

By so historicizing the world which had made (and been made by) his own immediate ancestors, Stephen was determined to place the views of his own generation in perspective, as well as judging those of his ancestors.[36] The results of such a process were equivocal, not least because of the internal dynamic of the Stephen family romance in which the demands of intellectual secularization were placed against the reactionary glare of the dying lights of Evangelical religion.

In the Stephen family romance the production of books and ideas was always coeval with that of the generations who read and produced them. Indeed, at one point in Stephen's reflections, when describing Samuel Richardson's production of *Clarissa* and *Sir Charles Grandison*, literary and familial production become metaphorically indistinguishable:

[35] *History*, ii. 326.

[36] On the contemporary resonances of Stephen's study, see the classic essay by John W. Bicknell, 'Leslie Stephen's *English Thought in the Eighteenth Century*: A tract for the times', *Victorian Studies*, 6 (1962), 103–20, and the excellent discussion in Jeffrey Paul von Arx, *Progress and Pessimism: Religion, Politics, and History in Late Nineteenth-Century Britain* (Cambridge, Mass., 1988), 34–50.

The greatest woman in France, according to Napoleon's brutal remark, was the woman who had the most children. In a different sense, the saying may pass for truth. The greatest writer is the one who has produced the largest family of immortal children. Those of whom it can be said that they have really added a new type to the fictitious world are indeed few in number. Cervantes is in the front rank of all imaginative creators, because he has given birth to Don Quixote and Sancho Panza. Richardson's literary representatives are far below these; but Richardson too may boast that, in his narrower sphere of thought, he has invented two characters that have still a strong vitality.[37]

Scott, one of Stephen's favourite novelists, was similarly praised for his evocative appreciation of this generational and familial imagery from a reader's perspective, at least as much as from that of a writer: 'His best stories might be all described as *Tales of a Grandfather*. They have the charm of anecdotes told to a narrator by some old man who had himself been part of what he describes.'[38] Defoe was identified as 'a great-grandfather of all modern journalism' (an advantage of such genealogies is that an abundance of ancestors can be located).[39] The influence of the *Tatler* and the *Spectator* meant that: 'All the best-known authors of this eighteenth century tried their hands at this form of composition, as our grandmothers and great-grandmothers had good cause to know.'[40] (Moralizing essayists presumed a following amongst women, and it is telling that Stephen should have so isolated their influence in this gendered manner, at once criticizing and colluding with this male literary tradition, which his own daughter, Virginia, would later seek to undo.)

The tracing of intellectual genealogies—as was only fitting for this major figure in the English intellectual aristocracy—quickly became an established feature of Leslie Stephen's thinking. The *History of English Thought in the Eighteenth Century* was populated by a large and permanently argumentative community of ancestors. He attributed to the eighteenth-century clerical economist Josiah Tucker the view that John Locke was the 'intellectual ancestor' of the theological radicals Richard Price and Joseph Priestley; 'Godwin's intellectual genealogy' was traced to Swift, Mandeville, and Hume; Adam Smith was 'rightly regarded as the intellectual ancestor of a race of theorists, whose influence, though not uniformly beneficial, has at least been of great importance towards constituting the still rudimentary science of sociology'. Pope, who, in

[37] 'Richardson's novels', *HL*, i. 64. [38] 'Sir Walter Scott', *HL*, i. 152.
[39] 'The evolution of editors', *SB*, i. 37–73, at p. 55. [40] Ibid. 45–6.

common with Locke and Smith was actually a bachelor, was nonetheless the founder of a 'poetical dynasty'.[41] Intellectual fertility was far more effective than biological reproduction in the metaphorical generations Stephen traced, as when he declared Locke to be the 'intellectual progenitor of the whole generation of eighteenth-century iconoclasts—the teacher of Toland and Collins, the legitimate precursor of Hume and of Condillac, the philosopher before whom Voltaire is never tired of prostrating himself with unwonted reverence'.[42] Locke's line of descent was an originally religious, but ultimately secularizing genealogy, and it had its purely pious parallel in James Stephen's remarks on John Newton, a leading eighteenth-century figure, in an essay he significantly entitled 'The "Evangelical" Succession':

> In the genealogy which connects the spiritual ancestry of his age with their spiritual progeny in our own, he holds an eminent place. Himself the child of Whitefield, he was one of the progenitors of Claudius Buchanan, to whom the Church in India owes so large a debt of gratitude—of William Wilberforce, to whom the Church Universal is still more largely indebted—of Joseph Milner, whom he induced to write the 'History of the Church' of ancient times—and of Thomas Scott, who has bequeathed to the Church, in ages yet to come, writings of unimpeachable value, and the memory of a life passed in no unsuccessful emulation of those of whom this unhallowed world was the least worthy.[43]

The Evangelical succession constituted a series of families with whom the Stephen family intersected at several points, both as Claphamites and, through marriage to the Evangelical Venns, as inheritors of a pristine role in the origins of the Evangelical Revival of which James Stephen was so proud, and to the effects of which Leslie Stephen devoted some of the more pointedly polemical passages in the second volume of his *History of English Thought in the Eighteenth Century*.[44]

Evangelicalism was a central, if not *the* central, component in the complexities of the Stephen family romance. Stephen's earlier remarks on the forgiving distance between great-grandfathers and great-grandchildren as opposed to the more critical distance between grandsons and grandchildren informed his guarded praise for the first generation of the Evangelical Revival: 'Energy exerted on behalf of a sincere conviction

[41] *History*, ii. 184, 225, 269, 297; *ELS*, 108.
[42] Ibid, i. 78. [43] 'The "Evangelical" succession', *Essays*, ii. 121.
[44] *History*, ii. 347–69; B. W. Young, '"Knocked-kneed giants": Victorian interpretations of the eighteenth century', in Colin Matthew and Jane Garnett (eds.), *Revival and Religion since 1700: Essays for John Walsh* (London, 1993), 79–93.

is commendable; and the early Evangelicals were, in their fashion, men of surprising vigour.' It also affirmed his rather more openly cutting praise for the second generation of Evangelicals, amongst whom 'the abler disciples revolted against the strict dogmatism of their fathers, and sought for some more liberal form of creed, or some more potent intellectual narcotic'.[45] It is impossible not to read here an evocation of the intellectual and emotional relationship between James and Sir James Stephen, and thence that between Sir James and Sir Leslie and Sir James Fitzjames Stephen.

James Fitzjames Stephen also favoured the familial taste for tracing genealogies, but he always did so in strictly secular terms. He identified Hobbes as both 'the father of modern English philosophy, and indeed as the father of that great school of thought which at present has possession of the greater part of the intelligence of Europe'. This Hobbesian line of descent contained Hume, himself identified as 'the progenitor of Kant' (all three philosophers having been, in reality, bachelors, and Kant having died a virgin).[46] Hobbes was, then, 'the great progenitor' of a school of thought which led, in one direction, to Bolingbroke and Voltaire, and, on the other, to Hume and John Stuart Mill. He was, in terms of law and morals, 'the progenitor of Bentham', and, in logic, 'he was practically, and to a very considerable degree theoretically, the ancestor of Mr. Mill'.[47] A positive logic of the development of political and social philosophy was thus quietly preferred over the internal genealogies of religious descent (and dissent).

Genealogies could also look forwards, and Leslie Stephen was always desirous that his readers consider themselves as potential ancestors, and to measure themselves accordingly. This often occurred when he was being most critical of the eighteenth century. When concerned to elaborate on the emptiness of English literature between the dying moments of neoclassicism and the Romantic reaction, he keenly observed that, 'I do not doubt that Englishmen a hundred years ago had as much imaginative power, as much good feeling, and at least as much love of truth as their descendants of to-day.'[48] When criticizing the prosaic literature of Pope and his generation, he exhorted his readers that: 'In showering down our epithets of artificial, sceptical, and utilitarian, we

[45] *History*, ii. 364, 366.

[46] 'Hobbes on Government', *HS*, ii. 1–18, at pp. 1–2. De Maistre was found to advocate a doctrine that was 'pure Hobbism without the excuses which may be made for Hobbes' ('De Maistre on the Pope', *HS*, iii. 306–24, at p. 316).

[47] 'Hobbes's Minor Works', *HS*, ii. 36–53, at pp. 50–1.

[48] *History*, ii. 370.

do not seldom forget what kind of figure we ourselves are likely to make in the eyes of our own descendants.' Considering the Gothic revivalism of Sir Walter Scott and Horace Walpole, he questioned the haughtiness of contemporary revivalists towards such work: 'They laugh at the carpenter's Gothic of Abbotsford or Strawberry Hill, and do not ask themselves how their own more elaborate blundering will look in the eyes of a future generation.'[49] There could be no doubt as to where Stephen's sympathies lay when he detailed the 'petty crotchets' of Gilbert Wakefield, a theological radical of the 1790s: 'He was a teetotaller and vegetarian in the good old days of port wine and roast beef, and had he lived a generation later would doubtless have been at the head of numerous societies for the regeneration of mankind. Our ancestors dealt him shorter and sharper measure.'[50] His grandfather James Stephen would have been one of the strongest advocates of that ancestral disapproval of Wakefield, whose ideological allies in the search for peace with revolutionary France quite simply appalled the elder Stephen, a loyal supporter of Pitt the Younger.

James Stephen the elder, in common with Leslie Stephen, wrote an autobiography for the immediate use of his family; it was finally published in 1954 by the Hogarth Press, the publishing venture set up by his great-granddaughter, Virginia.[51] Singularly unlike that produced over a century later by his grandson, James Stephen's autobiography is suffused with invocations of the part providence played in the fortunes of his life; and providence, usually invoked in judgemental terms, is what linked the elder James Stephen's world-view with that of his more liberal son. At the core of this providential interpretation of his life and times was the event which marked the eighteenth century as the immediate progenitor of modernity for so many Victorians: the French Revolution.

The elder James Stephen was, in common with his follow Clapham Sect adherents, a sternly moralizing critic of the slave trade. In his tract *The Dangers of the Country*, published in 1807, Stephen had argued that calamities would prove inevitable for the British as God would judge them severely for their participation in, and encouragement of, that activity which, 'opprobriously to the character of commerce, is

[49] 'Pope as a moralist', *HL*, i. 87–128, at p. 90; 'Sir Walter Scott', *HL*, i. 149.

[50] *History*, i. 373–4.

[51] *The Memoirs of James Stephen, Written by Himself for the Use of his Children*, ed. Merle N. Bevington (London, 1954).

known by the name of the slave trade'. Detailing the scriptural and providential nature of this threat, he instanced the case of Louis XVI, who had extended the French slave trade to encompass over 300,000 people; judgement was surely to come: 'But the eye of the Almighty was over them; and to avenge devoted Africa at least, if not to save her, he dropped down among them the French revolution.'[52] For the elder James Stephen the French Revolution was a living fact of contemporary politics; for the younger James Stephen, himself born in the year 1789, it would become the focal point of his understanding of the whole of French history. The event which vindicated his father's conservative, morally certain world-view haunted and disturbed that of his more liberal, if morally no less certain son.

The Revolution was, to the younger James Stephen, the grand climacteric to all that had gone before in French history; invoking the meteorological metaphors that abound in so much nineteenth-century apocalyptic thought, from the lightning storms of Carlyle's *French Revolution* (1837) to Ruskin's *The Storm-Cloud of the Nineteenth Century* (1884), he described 'the bursting of that great tempest which, on the close of the 18th century, prostrated all the powers and all the institutions of France'.[53] The year 1789 came to define all that had gone before, so that Stephen could continually refer to a past whose interpretation was to be forever after marked by that moment. Stephen felt emboldened by this reflection to make precise statements even when writing about the constitutional squabbles of the fourteenth century, concluding that 'The statesmen of 1789 must have studied to little purpose the history of 1356,' and confidently asserting in his published lectures as Regius Professor of Modern History at Cambridge, and originally delivered in the immediate wake of 1848, the year of European revolutions, that 'The obvious, though very imperfect, analogies between the constitutional struggles of that kingdom in the 14th and the 18th centuries, have of late given a peculiar interest and significance to these passages of history on which we have been dwelling'.[54] Such parallels were carried forward to the eve of the Revolution itself. Louis XVI was compared with Charles VI, and the troubled Paris of the 1400s was adduced as having foreshadowed events there in the 1790s: 'In this reign of terror of the 15th century, the Duke of Burgundy assumed the character

[52] James Stephen, *The Dangers of the Country* (London, 1807), 163–227; quotations at pp. 190 and 222.

[53] *Lectures*, i. 338.

[54] Ibid. 363, 377.

which Philippe Egalité was to enact nearly 400 years afterwards in the same city.' In proceedings of the Estates General during the sixteenth century, a 'singular parallelism' held between Le Coq, who was 'as arrant a socialist as Sièyes', and Marrel, who was 'as a great a blunderer as Danton'. A telling fear of such troubling fecundity marked the concluding pages of the first volume of his published lectures:

The history of the States General of Blois well pondered, and rightly understood, by the French people, might have arrested the monstrous progeny of revolution, of wretchedness, and of crimes, which, exactly two hundred years afterwards, sprang from the too prolific womb of the States General of 1789.[55]

A Carlylean comparison with the French Wars of Religion in the sixteenth century allowed Stephen to deploy the sort of Catholic/Revolutionary parallel beloved of some Protestant historians:

And thus, in the year 1560, were exactly anticipated the Noyades of the Revolution; except, indeed, that a Prince of the Church, Charles, Cardinal of Lorraine, took the place of the butcher Carrier; and except that Catherine of Medici, and the ladies of honour, assumed, in this dismal tragedy, characters to which, even in the frenzy of the reign of terror, the vilest of the Poissardes of Paris would scarcely have descended.[56]

Similarly, the Duc de Guise undertook personations that only the historian could confidently attribute: 'Proposing to become the Napoleon, he commenced by becoming the Mirabeau of his generation.' Mirabeau trotted back into history as Stephen's stalking horse for dictatorial ambition, so that even 'Richelieu was but a more successful Mirabeau.'[57] This economical and quietly shocking conjunction of a worldly cardinal and a revolutionary agitator was representative of Stephen's interpretation of the past, embedded as it was in a providential, and therefore more than occasionally proleptic, reading of history.

The whole history of France was implicated within the divinely grounded progress of culture in Stephen's reckoning, so that even study

[55] *Lectures*, i. 391, 393, 435–7, 471. The parallels had English as well as purely French resonances: 'There is indeed no new thing under the sun. When, in the year 1788, the Prince of Wales, by his friends in the House of Commons, claimed, as of right, the regency of Great Britain, the indignant and democratic protest of William Pitt might have passed for an imitation of that which, in the year 1484, had been made, in the States General of France, by Philip Pot, against the corresponding pretensions of the Duke of Orleans' (Ibid. i. 429).

[56] Ibid. ii. 97.

[57] Ibid. 135, 317. Leslie Stephen similarly observed that 'under other circumstances, Chatham might have developed into a Mirabeau' (*History*, ii. 174).

of the Merovingian kings—of whom he rather disapproved—was important, because, 'barbarous as they were, they were chosen by the Supreme Ruler of the nations to lay the basis of that great European commonwealth, to every pulse of which the whole civilised world has been so long accustomed to vibrate'. The tragedy of the Albigensian Crusade was likewise controlled by 'that divine agency which alone imparts to human affairs their true, though mysterious, significance'. Meditating on the guilt of Simon de Montfort for this outrage, he concluded in words entirely in accord with those uttered by his father in 1807: 'But the march of a retributive providence among men has not really been arrested.' The 'scroll of Providence' could be read in the sublunary history of nations and communities; the 'modern science of Sociology' (of which Leslie Stephen would become an enthusiastic advocate) neglected such an interpretation at its own great cost.[58] Sir James Stephen self-consciously and pointedly maintained a religious understanding of history at a moment when he feared historians were too readily colluding with purely secular means of necessarily abridged understanding.[59]

Such an interpretation allowed him to be, in common with his father, severely judgemental, as in his remarks on Henry IV's *politique* conversion to Catholicism:

What the future history of France would have been if Henry had clung to his integrity, is known only to the Omniscient; but, with the annals of France in our hands, we have no difficulty in perceiving that the day of his impious, because pretended, conversion was among the *dies nefasti* of his country.[60]

If Omniscience alone could interpret that particular event in the history of the French monarchy, a providential reading of a later period allowed the historian to trace the sublunary consequences of Louis XIV's ruinous and religiously intolerant wars in the most directly moralizing ways:

If the immutable laws of God had not decreed that such wars, however, successful, should be followed by a fearful rebound of misery against the aggressors, this earth would not be habitable. The French nation never recovered the waste of strength and treasure in the campaigns of their once idolised

[58] *Lectures*, i. 59, 214, 234, 236, 242, 243. Charles VIII's invasion of Italy was likewise 'a wanton and an audacious invocation of that retributive Providence which rules over the nations of the earth' (Ibid. ii. 281).

[59] The contemporary historian Stephen most admired was, predictably, the French Protestant François Guizot: Ibid. i. 474.

[60] Ibid. ii. 159.

monarch, until his dynasty and his institutions had been subverted in the same common ruin.[61]

Providence was the *leitmotif* of all Sir James Stephen's excursions into historical thought. It was there in reflections on the Hildebrandine Papacy, on Luther's unique role as a divine agent, and on the puritanical nature of England's Benedictine archbishops (from Lanfranc to Becket); the inner experience of human beings also provided an opportunity for him to meditate on God's direct presence in the continuing economy of spiritual improvement.[62] It was the ability to make, and the imputed desirability of making, such claims that drew Stephen, a theologically driven thinker, to the study of history, as he made clear to a lecture audience at Cambridge comprising Leslie Stephen's direct undergraduate contemporaries (the dons and what he called 'donnesses' had tended to disappear as the lectures progressed):[63]

> it is not only permitted us to trace the march of a retributive Providence in the history of mankind, but that reverently and humbly to interpret the laws by which the Divine government of the world is conducted, is the highest of the ends with a view to which any wise man engages in a review of that history.[64]

Such a statement was already contested by many of Sir James Stephen's contemporaries; and it was exactly the opposite point of view which led his son Leslie to the study of history.[65]

Some twenty-five years later, Leslie Stephen undermined the apparent certainties of his father's conception of the doctrine of providence in an aside in the *History of English Thought in the Eighteenth Century*. Commenting on the nature of God as He was conceived by the generality of eighteenth-century divines, Stephen cuttingly observed that: 'He appears, at most, under the colourless shape of Providence—a word which may be taken to imply a remote divine superintendence,

[61] *Lectures*, ii. 437.

[62] 'Hildebrand', 'Martin Luther', 'The French Benedictines', 'William Wilberforce', in *Essays*, i. 1–88, at p. 87, 291–359, at p. 357, 360–430, at p. 377, and ii. 203–86, at pp. 214–15.

[63] To Lady Stephen, 4 May 1852: *Letters*, 158.

[64] *Lectures*, ii. 411–12. He emphasized his providential reading of history in a letter to the Evangelical Bishop Wilson of Calcutta on 18 Apr. 1852, and, writing some eight years later to another correspondent, Mrs Russell Gurney, he read in the ruins of ancient Rome 'the retributive Providence of God' (*Letters*, 154, 260).

[65] For the classic statement on the secularizing role played by the study of history in this period, see Owen Chadwick, *The Secularization of the European Mind in the Nineteenth Century* (Cambridge, 1975), 189–228, and on the related fortunes of providence as an idea during the same period, 250–66.

without admitting an actual divine interference.'[66] The God of Stephen's father thus disappeared from His apparent centrality in the enterprise of gaining any true understanding of the world. In a historicized reading of the doctrine as a key component of the Evangelical Revival in which his own ancestor, Henry Venn, had been directly and unattractively involved, Stephen further undermined the viability, still more the desirability, of a belief which he dismissed as belonging to humanity's intellectual childhood (and which was part of his own direct childhood experience of the Stephen family romance):[67]

The hand of God was to be seen everywhere. Venn used to take his children to the window during a thunderstorm, and tell them that the lightning was directed by God's will. [John] Newton perhaps, more than any of the others, appears to be impressed by a constant sense of a superintending providence in the most minute events of life—a state of mind perhaps fostered by his early adventures as a slave-trader. Wesley's writings . . . are full of a doctrine which frequently leads to an unlovely superstition; and sometimes, as in the writings of Berridge, to a grotesque familiarity of address to a Being as constantly and tangibly present. As clearly it implies a vivid sentiment, never to be despised for its ugly clothing, and, as the example of the older Puritans showed, sometimes terribly efficacious.[68]

In an essay published in the 1860s, a decade after the publication of his father's Cambridge lectures and a decade before the appearance of his brother's *History of English Thought in the Eighteenth Century*, James Fitzjames Stephen had made an implicit challenge to the explicit reading of the nature of the French Revolution made by his father. It was a challenge which tacitly associated his father's liberal views with the mystical authoritarianism of Joseph de Maistre, the reactionary philosopher of St Petersburg, as he concluded that:

To look at the French Revolution, and the whole of that immense movement of which it was only a part, as one vast mad revolt against all that is holy and true, or as punishment providentially ordained for such a revolt, is utterly to

[66] *History*, ii. 286.

[67] The metaphor of childhood played an interestingly complex role in Stephen's conception of the social nature of the history of thought, which was: 'in great part a history of the gradual emancipation of the mind from the errors spontaneously generated by its first childlike attempts at speculation . . . Old conceptions are preserved to us in the very structure of language; the mass of mankind still preserves its childish imaginations; and every one of us has repeated on a small scale the history of the race . . . It is no wonder, then, if the belief, even of cultivated minds, is often a heterogeneous mixture of elements representing various stages of thought; whilst in different social strata we may find specimens of opinions derived from every age of mankind' (Ibid. i. 4).

[68] Ibid. ii. 367.

misunderstand it; and no genius, no shrewdness, no learning, will save those who permit themselves to take such a view, from being imperfect, one-sided, and radically sophistical.[69]

By turning his back on such a providential reading, James Fitzjames was rejecting the thought of his father and his grandfather, repudiating their religious interpretations for a more consciously worldly perspective. It was a crucial moment in the dialectic of the Stephen family romance with the legacy and the meaning of the eighteenth century.

In discarding the religious materials of that inheritance, the Stephen brothers looked increasingly to the purely secular understandings of politics and society for guidance in rescuing them from Evangelicalism. Indeed, whilst Evangelicalism had served to prevent the importation of revolution at the close of the eighteenth century, it itself could not and should not, the brothers Stephen believed, withstand the political transformations of the nineteenth century. Worldly explanations were increasingly deduced to be satisfactory alternatives to religious ones: hence Leslie Stephen's pleasure in concluding, in a throwaway remark—made long before Halévy became associated with the idea, and even longer before E. P. Thompson elaborated it yet further—that the 'religious reaction' overseen by John Wesley had been a large component in preserving England from the experience of anything like the convulsions of the French Revolution.[70] In the developing thought of James Fitzjames and Leslie, politics would continue to secularize religion, and religion, despite the attempts of the Tractarians and their allies, would necessarily fail to re-sacralize politics, a process James Fitzjames had approvingly discerned in the pioneering work of Hobbes, and whose early history Leslie Stephen had critically traced in the *History of English Thought in the Eighteenth Century*, and on which he would comment again in his own late study of Hobbes published in 1904, the year of his death.[71] It was a process which Leslie Stephen consciously promoted both as theorist and as historian.

[69] 'De Maistre's minor works', *HS*, iii. 279–80.

[70] *History*, ii. 367. He was fascinated by Wesley and Wesleyanism, which he considered, 'in many respects, by far the most important phenomenon of the century'. He declared of Wesley that: 'No such leader of men appeared in that century; and in a lower sphere he might have been a first-rate statesman or a general' (Ibid. ii. 330, 348). On the 'Halévy thesis' see John Walsh, 'The Halévy thesis', *Studies in Church History* (1975), 1–25.

[71] 'Hobbes on government', 'Hobbes's *Leviathan*', 'Hobbes's minor works', *HS*, ii. 1–18, 19–35, 36–53. Leslie Stephen made a tantalizing comment in his study of Hobbes that leads one to wonder what any study by him of the seventeenth century might have been like, when he observed that Hobbes 'shared the fate of all his contemporaries, as the eighteenth century came to think the seventeenth century hopelessly old-fashioned'

III

Leslie Stephen's last substantial work to be published during his lifetime, his three-volume study *The English Utilitarians* (1900), is littered with familial references, both literal and metaphorical. The Stephen family is present in its pages, both explicitly and implicitly, as he quietly cited his brother's *History of the Civil Law* and his father's essays in *Ecclesiastical Biography* as authoritative works in the first volume, where he also described Erasmus Darwin as an advocate of 'a theory of evolution eclipsed by the teaching of his more famous grandson'.[72] The life of the mind, whether described in political, religious, or scientific terms, was thus identified as a familial legacy. Familial language also operated metaphorically. Noting that the Radicals had called Major Cartwright of the Society for Constitutional Information the 'father', Stephen muted this appeal when he chose to refer to him as 'the rather tiresome[,] patriarch of the Radicals'. Patriarch was plainly an equivocal term for Stephen, since not only was Cartwright demeaned in this way, but Jeremy Bentham himself, evoked as 'the patriarch of the English Utilitarians', was subsequently burlesqued as the rather unsatisfactory would-be lover of Caroline Fox, the sister of Lord Holland, the great Whig patron:

> Miss Fox seems to have been the only woman who inspired Bentham with a sentiment approaching to passion. He wrote occasional letters to the ladies in the tone of elephantine pleasantry natural to one who was all his life both a philosopher and a child.[73]

As a lifelong philosopher-child, who was not only never in love, but who also seemed never even to have 'talked to any woman except his cook or housemaid', Bentham's patriarchal achievement was, therefore, entirely and necessarily intellectual (was Stephen aware of Bentham's probable homosexuality?). Mischievously citing Bentham's claim that we mostly learn only folly from our ancestors, Stephen called him an ancestor in his turn: Bentham was decidedly one who 'may teach us by his errors'.[74]

(*Hobbes*, 69). Was the dying Victorian making a tacit identification with the fate of an intellectual progenitor?

[72] Leslie Stephen, *EU*, i. 25 n., 114 n., 66. He refers likewise to a review of John Austin's *Jurisprudence* contributed to the *Edinburgh Review* by James Fitzjames Stephen: *EU*, iii. 333.

[73] *EU*, i. 125, 185.

[74] *EU*, i. 233, 296.

Of the three generational leaders who comprised the life of English Utilitarianism from Bentham to John Stuart Mill in Stephen's survey, the only true father was James Mill. Stephen subjected the elder Mill to a great deal of criticism, not least, as with Bentham, because the inadequacies of his social thought were held by Stephen to reflect the inadequacies of his own icy personality.[75] There is, however, surely a more positive echo of the Stephen family history when James Mill is evoked at the very beginning of volume two as 'one of the countless Scots who, having been trained at home in strict frugality and stern Puritanic principles, have fought their way to success in England'.[76] The Utilitarian inheritance, however, was to be interpreted altogether less positively than the Stephen dynasty had been elsewhere in his writings. The conventionally progressive portrayal of Utilitarianism was to be inverted, as the creed was seen to atrophy and collapse in John Stuart Mill's stewardship as the nineteenth century came of age intellectually, with historicism and evolution prevailing over older philosophies, Utilitarianism very much included.

In the economy of the trilogy's sequential narrative the progressive dynamic of the Mill inheritance has its internal contrast in Stephen's description of the relationship between Thomas Robert Malthus and his father, whose study of Rousseau's *Émile* 'probably led to the rather desultory education of his son'. In the Malthus family, 'The usual relations between junior and senior were inverted; the elder Malthus, as became a follower of Rousseau, was an enthusiast; and the younger took the part of suggesting doubts and difficulties.' The product of this inversion was, suggestively, Malthus's *Essay upon Population* (1798), a work whose method Stephen valued more highly than its argumentative content, no doubt because it fed into the methodological considerations informing Darwin's *Origin of Species*.[77] The peculiarities of the Malthus family romance called into question John Stuart Mill's explanation for reaction as a feature of intellectual progress, complete with its suggestively partriarchal metaphor. According to Mill, as paraphrased by Stephen, 'A "reaction" is a very convenient phrase. We are like our fathers; then the resemblance is only natural. We differ; then the phrase "reaction" makes the alteration explain itself.' For Stephen, then, the Millian explanation of intellectual progress was quite simply

[75] *EU*, i. 233–4; ii. 337. For a slightly more appreciative reading of the Mill father–son relationship, see 'Autobiography', *HL*, iii. 223–53, at pp. 243–4.

[76] *EU*, ii. 1.

[77] *EU*, ii. 139–40, 174.

inadequate, not least as it failed to do anything like justice to the motivation and interests of Tory thinkers, be they Edmund Burke, Samuel Taylor Coleridge, or Sir Walter Scott.[78] In this respect, John Stuart Mill merely repeated the error Stephen continually imputed to Bentham and James Mill: he failed either to understand or to respect history. History, interpreted as a study of the relations between different generations, acted as Stephen's means both to chronicle the logical developments within Utilitarianism and also to attack its original philosophical presuppositions. He echoed here his father's *Lectures on the History of France*, published just short of fifty years earlier, which contained a ringing critique of Comte, George Grote, and the younger Mill. Sir James considered this trio of thinkers to have been unworthy successors to the altogether more solidly historical reflections of Montesquieu and his intellectual allies.[79]

By tracing Utilitarianism through three generations of thought, Leslie Stephen successfully employed the language of familial inheritance to undo the a-historicity of Utilitarian doctrine, and in this sense the familial language of *The English Utilitarians* actively undid the abstractions of the philosophy it sought to interrogate. In Stephen's opinion, the Utilitarians, though committed to practical policies, were actually too committed to appeals to abstractions to be successful; and Stephen justified his use of biography to effect this critique at the very outset of the three volumes, noting tellingly that, 'One obvious principle of unity, or tacit bond of sympathy which holds a sect together depends upon the intellectual idiosyncrasy of the individuals.'[80] Writing in the same volume about the background to Thomas Reid's contest with Hume, Stephen claimed that 'we must trace the genealogy of "ideas"', thereby affirming a metaphorical imperative that informed so much of his work in intellectual history.[81] The organic metaphors of his own *System of Ethics*, the immediate predecessor as a major original work by Stephen before the composition of *The English Utilitarians*, were thus the implicit source of his historicized critique. The intellectual filiation between the philosophical and the historical in Stephen's own systematic thought was made explicit in the relationship between *The System of Ethics* and *The English Utilitarians*.

[78] *EU*, ii. 366.

[79] *Lectures*, i. 244, 248–9. For Leslie Stephen's remarks on Grote's shortcomings as a historian, see *EU*, iii. 336–44.

[80] *EU*, i. 1–2.

[81] *EU*, i. 145.

Intriguingly, it is possible to read the Stephen family history alongside the history of the Mills as it is offered in these volumes. Indeed, this is something that *The English Utilitarians* positively invites the reader to attempt. Consider, for example, the use of the word 'sect' (with its direct Claphamite echoes) in Stephen's description of the education of John Stuart Mill (note also the oddity of the imputed nature of the filiation between biological father and son in this context):

James Mill and Bentham looked upon him from early years as their spiritual heir . . . John lived his manhood almost exclusively in their little circle; and no child was ever more elaborately and strenuously indoctrinated with the views of a sect. Had James Mill adhered to his early creed his son would probably have become a fit subject for one of those edifying tracts which deal with infantile conversions.[82]

The reader of the third volume would, at this point, legitimately think back to the defence Stephen had made in the previous volume of the true motivations of the Evangelical reformers, a circle to which his own family had so signally belonged, and who occasionally act as rivals to the Utilitarians in these volumes:

it would be the height of injustice to assume that they tried to do good simply from fear of hell and hope of heaven, or that their belief in Christianity was due to a study of Paley's *Evidences*. Their real motives were far nobler: genuine hatred of injustice and sympathy for suffering, joined to the conviction that the sects to which they belonged were working on the side of justice and happiness; while the creeds which they accepted were somehow congenial to their best feelings, and enabled them to give utterance to their deepest emotions.[83]

An intellectual and moral genealogy which reached back to Wilberforce and the presence of the Stephens in the Clapham Sect was thus effectively deployed against the Utilitarian inheritance from Bentham and the Mills, father and son. Significantly, James Stephen, in a letter to James Fitzjames of 14 February 1858—replete with a confident reading of the family romance—had himself made a simultaneously playful and grandiloquent comparison between the two of them and James and John Stuart Mill:

[82] *EU*, iii. 3. The unnaturally intellectual nature of the father–son relationship between the two Mills was emphasized, and the lack of the happy charm in more natural filiations noted accordingly: *EU*, iii. 7. James Fitzjames Stephen was more direct about the character of this education: 'Mr. Mill's account of the education which he received from his father shows that Mr. James Mill, at events, did not shrink from the responsibility of deciding religious questions for his son. It leaves open, however, the question whether the son thanked his father for it' (*LEF*, 100 n.).

[83] *EU*, ii. 359.

> Time was when I enjoyed a repute as a writer of 'Edinburgh Reviews,' and from the bottom of my heart, I hope, as I very sincerely believe, that you will eclipse me even more than the elder Mill has been eclipsed by the younger. Perhaps the day will come when you may form the same wish about your own boy, and when what I now say will be more intelligible to you.[84]

Two years after receiving this letter, James Fitzjames repaid the compliment by remarking of the recently deceased Lord Macaulay, in an essay in the *Fortnightly Review*, that he 'was not the only remarkable man in the present generation who was brought up in his infancy at Clapham'.[85] Sir James Stephen had died in 1859, the same year as Macaulay, and it was this essay which acted as his son's quiet memorial to him, treating as it implicitly did his father's reputation with the same respect naturally accorded to the premier Whig historian of that generation.

A further insight into the familial placing of *The English Utilitarians* can be gained from reflecting on the notably dismissive language Stephen used in relation to Mill's feminism. Even his depiction of Mill's marriage to Harriet Taylor—otherwise so effective a contrast with Bentham's emotional singularities—moved from a positive to a negative assessment with quite remarkable speed, although Stephen's very introduction of the topic itself betokened caution:

> It is necessary to say something of the woman to whom Mill was thus devoted. Yet it is very difficult to speak without conveying some false impression. It is impossible, on the one hand, to speak too respectfully of so deep and enduring a passion. Mill's love of his wife is a conclusive answer to any one who can doubt the tenderness of his nature. A man who could love so deeply must have been lovable himself. On the other hand, it is necessary to point out plainly certain peculiarities which it reveals. Mill speaks of his wife's excellences in language so extravagant as almost to challenge antagonism.[86]

Stephen certainly met the standards demanded of such antagonism, and this quintessential 'manly fellow' quickly began to dispute Mill's claims to manliness in a manner reminiscent of his brother's attack on Mill a quarter of a century earlier in *Liberty, Equality, Fraternity* (1873).

In that controversial and confident work, James Fitzjames Stephen had stated that *On the Subjection of Women* was a book 'from which I dissent from the first sentence to the last'. He accused the essay of 'indecorum' in its description of the differences, and the nature of the relations, between the sexes, and he feared that teaching boys to sew,

[84] *Letters*, 267.

[85] 'Lord Macaulay', *EB*, 97–106, at p. 104.

[86] *EU*, iii. 56–7.

keep house, and cook, whilst teaching girls to play cricket, row, and drill, would destroy the true basis of education. Mill was found guilty of entertaining a 'complete misapprehension of the nature of family government'; as with his brother in 1900, so the elder Stephen writing in 1873 attributed Mill's views on the natural equality of the sexes to 'a mistaken view of history', the consequences of which were disastrous. The progress Mill desired had unfortunate consequences for manliness, as the deeply gendered nature of James Fitzjames Stephen's conception of the good society was sacrificed to Mill's ideal of futurity:

> I suspect that in many ways its has been a progress from strength to weakness; that people are more sensitive, less enterprising, and ambitious, less earnestly desirous to get what they want, and more afraid of pain, both for themselves and others, than they used to be. If this should be so, it appears to me that all other gains, whether in wealth, knowledge, or humanity, afford no equivalent. Strength, in all its forms, is life and manhood. To be less strong, is to be less of a man, whatever else you may be.

The 'humanity' that Mill identified as increasing its presence in nineteenth-century society was, to James Fitzjames Stephen, 'a mere increase of nervous sensibility in which I feel no satisfaction at all'.[87] Mill's liberalism was, then, for Stephen, a form of decadence, and the ideal of progress and the cult of 'humanity' were jointly identified as the dangerous diminution of the natural struggles for life that made the organic nature of existence so vital were individuals and societies properly to flourish.

Leslie Stephen followed the views of his brother when he insisted that Mill could not describe character and that he was a 'bad judge of men', thus placing him beyond one of the set standards of Victorian conceptions of masculine sociability.[88] Yet more compromisingly, Mill's feminism was identified with what Stephen asserted to be an uncertainly gendered personality:

> Mill could never admit any fundamental difference between the sexes. This is, I believe, a great but natural misconception for one who was in character as much feminine as masculine. He had some of the amiable weaknesses which we at present—perhaps on account of the debased state of society—regard as

[87] *LEF*, 188, 190, 194, 196, 199.

[88] *EU*, iii. 58. This intriguingly complicates Stefan Collini's account of the relationship between Stephen's critical support for Mill and the cult of the 'manly fellow' which Stephen incarnated and about which Collini has written perceptively: see Stefan Collini, *Public Moralists: Political Thought and Intellectual Life in Britain 1850–1950* (Oxford, 1991), 121–96.

especially feminine. The most eminent women, hitherto, at least, are remarkable rather for docility than originality. Mill was especially remarkable, as I have said, for his powers of assimilation. No more receptive pupil could ever be desired by a teacher. Like a woman, he took things—even philosophers—with excessive seriousness; and shows the complete want of humour often—unjustly perhaps—attributed to women.[89]

Uncertainty in gender roles had likewise troubled their father, albeit in relation to more openly unsettling sexual manifestations, as in his description of Henry III of France:

The next hour would find him bestowing the most costly and extravagant favours on the youths by whom he was surrounded, or outraging not only the dignity of his crown, but the decorous gravity of manhood, by the exaggeration, in his own person, of their debauched manners and effeminate appearance; or even descending so low as to amuse them by assuming female attire, and representing before them equivocal female characters.[90]

Here, albeit displayed in a yet stronger register, is much of the disapprobation of those men who lacked 'the decorous gravity of manhood' that would make his sons so critical of anyone who did not accord with their own resilient conceptions of manliness.

In Sir James Stephen this gendered language was usually more balanced than it was to become in the altogether fiercer writings of his sons. Whilst Sir James could readily discern masculinity in John Newton, the Evangelical leader, it was too marked a feature of the former sea captain's personality, leading to 'the strange predominance of the male above the female elements of his nature'. Only the 'most absolute *masculinity*' could have challenged Newton's manliness; similarly, when George Whitefield, the leader of the Evangelical Revival, fasted, he 'set about it like a man', unlike the 'fastidious' Tractarian Richard Hurrell Froude, who, in common with other leaders of the Oxford Movement, indulged in 'ecclesiastical fopperies'.[91] More typically, it was a spiritually productive balance of gendered characteristics that Stephen sought out in the religious characters of the people he admired. Angelique Arnauld of Port Royal had an understanding, a spirit, and a resolve that 'were all essentially masculine', but she and her sister Agnes gave of their best as substitute mothers to the children of their community.[92] It was as praise

89 *EU*, iii. 73. Allied claims are produced later in the volume: iii. 283–4.
90 *Lectures*, ii. 139.
91 'The Evangelical secession', in *Essays*, ii. 65–202, at pp. 107, 183, 194.
92 'The Port Royalists', *Essays*, i. 431–520, at pp. 436, 471.

that he pointed to the fact that William Wilberforce had possessed an 'almost feminine tenderness', and likewise that the Clapham Sect preacher Thomas Gisborne combined a 'masculine intellect' with a 'feminine soul'.[93] More peculiarly, he observed of Isaac Milner, a protector of the Evangelical creed in the Cambridge in which Stephen had been educated, that 'His muscular and his nervous structure seemed to belong to two different men, or rather to be of different sexes.' Granville Sharpe, the great opponent of the slave trade, gained the best from the otherwise occasionally suspect lineage of humanity, as Stephen attributed to him 'all the sternness which Adam has bequeathed to his sons, wedded to all the tenderness which Eve has transmitted to her daughters'. Such a judicious balance had its humorous element, as Stephen quietly reflected that Sharpe had also 'waged a less fortunate war against the theatrical practice of either sex appearing in the habiliments of the other'.[94] Sir James Stephen had a judiciously secular sense of the ridiculous as well as a suitably becoming taste for the religious sublime.

Manliness was more clearly an obsession with both James Fitzjames and Leslie Stephen. James Fitzjames approved of the 'manly logic' with which William Warburton undid the frequently 'disgusting' writings of Bernard de Mandeville, although he disapproved of his name-calling. Conyers Middleton was also firmly praised, since he 'always wrote both like a gentleman and like a good man'.[95] Manliness played a not unexpected part in politics, and he noted of Cobbett's Tory Radicalism that, 'The whole of the Young England theory of things is nothing more than an effeminate parody of one side of his views.' Manly politics melded into manly piety, and Bishop Berkeley's politico-economical tracts were lauded for inculcating 'a plain, manly, solid, courageous way of life'. The Paley on whom two generations of Stephens were reared at Cambridge was singled out for the 'vein of manly simple piety' that 'ran through his character'.[96] More significantly in terms of the Stephen family romance, manly piety had its religious contrasts, and James

93 'William Wilberforce' and 'The Clapham Sect', in *Essays*, ii. 203–86, at p. 250, 287–459, at p. 300.

94 'The Clapham Sect', *Essays*, ii. 364, 314, 315.

95 'Warburton's *Divine Legation*', 'Mandeville', and 'The miscellaneous works of Conyers Middleton', *HS*, ii. 315–32, at p. 324, 193–210, at p. 207, 349–66, at pp. 351–2. Leslie Stephen also disliked Mandeville's 'offensive coarseness' (*History*, ii. 32).

96 'Berkeley's occasional works', 'Paley's *Evidences*', *HS*, iii. 36–56, at p. 47, 75–92, at p. 78. 'Berkeley's occasional works', *HS*, ii. 51; 'Cobbett's political works', *HS*, iii. 230–49, at p. 240.

Fitzjames praised Berkeley's High and Dry Anglicanism against what he called 'the unmanly hysterics of more emotional schools' (and one assumes that Clapham Sect spirituality might have qualified as much as did Tractarianism for such derision).[97]

Leslie Stephen was yet more confidently explicit in his excursus on the polluting effects of late eighteenth-century 'sentimentalism', especially as it affected religion. Sentimentalism was 'a mood rightly despised by men of a masculine nature'; sensibility was 'petted' by the 'namby-pamby' school, and ultimately degraded itself into ritualism in nineteenth-century religion (and Stephen was as firm an opponent of the Oxford Movement as the most confirmed of Victorian Evangelicals). He consequently defined 'modern sentimentalism' as 'the effeminate element in Christianity'. Immediately affirming that the 'true sentimentalist accepts all that appears to be graceful, tender, and pretty in the Gospels', the sentimentalist so described was condemned for turning away from 'the sterner and more masculine teaching which enables a religion to rule the world, as well as to amuse our softer hours'. Berating this 'milk-and-water version of the old theories', he concluded that, 'To attempt to make a religion out of the most effeminate elements is necessarily futile.'[98] As if aware that he had left Wesley exposed to such charges in his *History of English Thought in the Eighteenth Century* in 1876, Stephen repaired any possible damage in his *English Literature and Society in the Eighteenth Century*, published in 1904, by declaring that 'Wesley was far too masculine and sensible to be a sentimentalist; his emotions impel him to vigorous action; and are much too serious to be cultivated for their own sakes or to be treated aesthetically.'[99]

Although sceptical that authors could ever properly represent members of the sex opposite to their own, Leslie Stephen was always ready to discern manliness or effeminacy in the authors he discussed.[100] Samuel Richardson promoted 'namby-pamby sentiment'; the 'feminine element' in this author, who plainly troubled Stephen, was 'a little in excess'. Likewise, Horace Walpole, 'a person of effeminate appearance', was a 'man of squeamish tastes and excessive sensibility' who 'jostled amongst' a 'thin-skinned, iron-nerved generation'; he was a 'mincing dandy', a lapdog amongst mastiffs.[101] Walpole's Eton and Cambridge contemporary Thomas Gray belonged to 'the class fop or

[97] 'Berkeley's occasional works', *HS*, iii. 51.

[98] *History*, ii. 371, 376.

[99] *ELS*, 161.

[100] 'Balzac's novels', *HL*, i. 189–222, at p. 213.

[101] *History*, ii. 314, 374; 'Richardson's novels' and 'Horace Walpole', in *HL*, i. 62, 333–4.

petit-maître, mincing, precise, affected', whilst Laurence Sterne's promotion of sentimentalism left him isolated in the sexually equivocal position of being a 'literary prostitute'.[102] On the other hand, and perhaps unexpectedly, Stephen declared that Pope, the 'little cripple, diseased in mind and body, had in him the spirit of a man'. Similarly unpredictable was his judgement on William Cowper, a man of 'nervous sensibility', whose jeremiads nevertheless contained a 'true masculine vigour'.[103] More predictably, whilst argumentatively suspect, Samuel Johnson's loyalist, anti-American pamphlets were 'at least' the 'sincere utterances of a thoroughly masculine nature'.[104] Johnson's critique of Lord Chesterfield met with particular approval. Chesterfield was associated by Stephen with 'triumphs of tailoring, and with an effete dandyism of the most artificial type. His very memory smells of rouge and false teeth and stays and the unsavoury apparatus of an ancient buck's dressing-room.' Confronted by Johnson, the 'fine gentleman was unlucky in coming into collision with that rough mass of genuine manhood'; the Whig aristocrat had been felled by the poor Tory journalist.[105] Masculine thought was not, however, the exclusive property of one political grouping. William Hazlitt's altogether more radical essays displayed 'masculine' thought, and Fielding's novels benefited from his gift for 'masculine observation' and 'masculine portraiture'; in much the same way, Macaulay's works and career were stamped with his 'manliness', and Stephen extolled Macaulay's own admiration of manliness.[106] The seventeenth-century theologian William Chillingworth, the eighteenth-century classicist Richard Bentley, and William Cobbett, whose politics long continued to intrigue both of the Stephen brothers, conveyed a 'masculine sense' in their writings. Similarly, the early eighteenth-century Christian apologist Thomas Sherlock had a style that was 'invariably clear and masculine'; he was, in argumentative terms, as suited this one-time Master of the Temple, 'a lawyer in a cassock, and a thoroughly masculine lawyer'.[107]

In a glancing critique of what he perceived to be the prime instance of the intellectual declension of the nineteenth century, Stephen

[102] 'Gray and his school', *HL*, iii. 95–129, at p. 107; *History*, ii. 375.

[103] 'Pope as a moralist', *HL*, i. 87–128, at p. 118; 'Cowper and Rousseau', *HL*, ii. 199–228, at p. 215;

[104] *History*, ii. 175.

[105] 'Lord Chesterfield', *Cornhill Magazine*, 24 (1871), 86–101, at pp. 87–8, 101.

[106] 'William Hazlitt', 'Fielding's novels', 'Macaulay', *HL*, iii. 65–98, at p. 66, 169–96, at pp. 174, 187, 331–60, at pp. 331, 358.

[107] *History*, i. 173, 204; ii. 290.

observed that whilst the eighteenth-century theologian Samuel Clarke was frequently mistaken in his logic, he was both 'more honest and more manly' than many of his Victorian successors.[108] Declension was much more evident in religion than it was in literature, and Stephen happily defended Sir Walter Scott's interest in the past against the antiquarianism of his direct eighteenth-century forebears, asserting that his interest in ballad literature was 'the interest of finding that our ancestors had been genuine human beings, capable of exploring manly emotions in a straightforward way'. Stephen insisted of Scott's novels that 'no work in our literature places us in communication with a manlier or more lovable nature'.[109] Robert Burns, a Scottish writer from the era when the Stephens were forging their new identities south of the Border, evidenced in his poems, 'the presentment of the truly vigorous peasant life, not stained by idyllic sentimentalisms, and with strong manly blood coursing through every vein'.[110] Allied to this strict identification of reliability with manliness was a suspicion of the sorts of moral critique urged by Matthew Arnold and John Ruskin, as Stephen observed that use of the word Philistine enabled 'intellectual coxcombs to brand men with an offensive epithet for being a degree more manly than themselves'.[111] Such an observation emphasized the strength of the fraternal bond between Leslie and James Fitzjames Stephen, both of whom were always happy to play the Philistine when occasion demanded it. Their own manliness was clearly suspect enough to them both—despite addictions to athleticism and Alpine mountaineering—for them to wish continually to emphasize it against their own internally policed predilections for poetry and spiritual insight.[112]

The agnostic manliness of the Stephen brothers ultimately made them stern critics of Millian liberalism, just as their father's Christian manliness had made him a critic of Henry III, an effeminate monarch:

[108] *History*, ii. 326.

[109] Ibid. 379; 'Sir Walter Scott', *HL*, i. 157.

[110] Ibid. ii. 386.

[111] 'Macaulay', *HL*, iii. 348. This provided an odd echo of his father's use of the phrase 'intellectual coxcombry' in a slighting reference to critics of the Clapham Sect: 'The Clapham Sect', *Essays*, ii. 308.

[112] Consider the language used by Stephen's contemporaries to describe his care for his Cambridge friend Henry Fawcett when his blindness was first diagnosed: 'I am told that when the blow had fallen, and Fawcett had returned to Cambridge, Stephen's tender care for him was beautiful to see. Men said it was almost womanly.' (Maitland, *Life and Letters of Leslie Stephen*, 105.) It is almost as though Stephen was so loath to acknowledge this side of his passionate nature that he continually denied its reality, both to himself and to others.

an Evangelical sense of the necessary and morally transforming struggle against sin had transmuted into a commitment to the socially effective principles of Darwinian natural selection.[113] The Stephen brothers had evolved from and then defended a different legacy from that of the Utilitarians; the allied dynasty they most respected was that traceable between Erasmus and Charles Darwin, an evolutionary analogue to their own Clapham Sect-derived connections with Calvinism, a Calvinism celebrated, against Mill's disapprobation of the 'Calvinistic theory', in *Liberty, Equality, Fraternity*.[114] It is important, however, when considering this to recall that their father had been altogether less forgiving of Calvin, as his own personal theology moved away from his own Clapham-dominated childhood.

Whilst recognizing Calvin's intellectual conquest of subsequent generations, Sir James Stephen had regretted the highly theoretical form it had developed in France; slighting Calvin's insistence that *his* reason should predominate over that of all others in religious matters, Stephen promised his readers that he would one day deduce how the religious rot of Socinianism had had 'its root in the despotic logic' of the founder of the Calvinism of New England, France, and Switzerland.[115] Leslie Stephen was also critical of full-blooded Calvinism, an antagonism displayed in his essay on 'Jonathan Edwards', the eighteenth-century New England theologian, in which the doctrine of eternal damnation (against which Sir James Stephen held fast, despite the condemnation of orthodox Cambridge clergy for so doing) was held up by him for particular excoriation.[116] Again, as with his father's critique, so also with his: Calvinism was seen as mutating into a suspect species of Christianity as it merged, eventually, with the transcendentalism of Emerson 'and other leaders of young America'. This unexpected development was related to his claim that Edwards himself advocated a theology which led to a form of pantheism, as his belief that God's absolute sovereignty logically extended over all nature as well as the individual human soul, a conclusion that led to his becoming a 'kind of Spinoza-Mather', combining metaphysics with superstition and a

113 For a classic statement on the fortunes of Christian manliness in the nineteenth century, see Norman Vance, *The Sinews of the Spirit: The Ideal of Christian Manliness in Victorian Literature and Religious Thought* (Cambridge, 1985).

114 *LEF*, 79, 81–3.

115 *Lectures*, ii. 86, 147, 235, 237. This did not prevent him from describing himself to Bishop Wilson of Calcutta as a Calvinist (Ibid. 154).

116 'Jonathan Edwards', *HL*, i. 325, at pp. 308–9, 310–11.

'degrading supernaturalism'.[117] Leslie Stephen paid minute attention to the several mutations and transformations affecting Calvinism in the eighteenth century, from Francis Hutcheson's rationalistic version of his inherited creed, to Joseph Priestley's transformation of theological predestination into philosophical determinism, and Augustus Toplady's simultaneous revival of what he saw as truly orthodox Calvinism.[118] The internal dynamism of Calvinism was, then, for Leslie Stephen a sign both of religious strength and of philosophical weakness. In this respect, as elsewhere, James Fitzjames Stephen, despite losing his own faith, had reverted to defending a stronger variant of his father's religion than his brother ever did.

If the religion of their family managed, somehow, to make its authoritative presence felt in these critiques of Utilitarianism and Millian liberalism, the religion of their sister, Caroline Emelia Stephen, fared rather less well in the work of her brothers. Quakerism was denounced in quite savage terms in *Liberty, Equality, Fraternity*, where James Fitzjames Stephen concluded that: 'Mr. Mill's doctrines about liberty of opinion and discussion seem to me to be a kind of Quakerism. They are like teaching that all revenge whatever, even in its mildest form, is wrong, because revenge carried to an extreme is destructive to society.'[119] To a critical admirer of de Maistre, such an attitude smacked of appalling weakness.[120] In an essay on Paine, James Fitzjames addressed the positive as well as the negative strains in Quakerism. The 'great merit of implicit obedience' to the dictates of conscience, the Quaker Inner Light, was to be found in Paine, but it combined with 'the Quaker contempt for external authority' in leading Paine, by an 'easy transition', to an unattractively dogmatic version of Deism and Republicanism; the 'Quaker broken loose from his creed' turned against English institutions, and a formerly religious creed mutated from a purely passive state into an 'active and dogmatic stage'.[121] As with Calvinism, so with Quakerism: variant strands spelled dogmatic trouble. The Stephen need to contain by definition was defeated by such troubling mutations.

117 'Jonathan Edwards', *HL*, i. 287, 311. James Fitzjames Stephen was to remark of American intellectual life that: 'Since the Declaration of Independence they have had no Franklin, no Hamilton, it might almost be said no Jonathan Edwards—though whether that is a loss is another question' ('The Federalist', *HS*, iii. 172–86, at p. 172).

118 *History*, ii. 47, 363.

119 *LEF*, 122.

120 'Joseph de Maistre', *EB*, 267–79; 'De Maistre—*Soirées de St. Pétersbourg*', 'De Maistre's minor works', 'De Maistre's *Principe générateur*', 'De Maistre on the Pope', *HS*, iii. 250–69, 270–86, 287–305, 306–24.

121 'Tom Paine', *HS*, iii. 186–209, at pp. 191–3.

More positive references to Quakerism are, however, to be found in *The English Utilitarians*, a study in which the consciously ageing Leslie Stephen found more constructive things to say about religion than he had in such polemical collections as *Essays on Freethinking and Plainspeaking* (1873) and *An Agnostic's Apology* (1893), or the religiously challenging *History of English Thought in the Eighteenth Century*. Noting the marked presence of Quakers in philanthropic activities throughout the eighteenth and nineteenth centuries, he explained this as their contribution to a society in which their political exclusion and anti-militarism would otherwise have marginalized them. The praise they gained from eighteenth-century Rationalists he attributed to an unexpected kinship, incarnated by such admirers of Quakerism as Franklin and Paine, the apostate Quaker: '"Rationalisation" and "Spiritualisation" are in some directions similar.' Quakers and freethinkers shared similar views on practical questions, and 'The fundamental differences of theological belief were not so productive of discord in dealing with the Quakers as with other sects; for it was the very essence of the old Quaker spirit to look rather to the spirit than to the letter.'[122]

Leslie Stephen's more generous assessment of the Quakers is not unrelated to his closeness to his sister, a relationship whose importance he significantly alluded to in *The Mausoleum Book*, which remained unpublished until 1977, the book he wrote for his children in order to explain himself and, more especially, his love for their dead mother. As with his dutiful work on his brother's biography in the 1890s—commissioned by his sister-in-law—so again with this book: Stephen had quite literally created a family romance.[123] What is striking in this instance is how this relationship with his sister (two years his junior, and who outlived him by five years) is immediately refracted through a reference to his biography of their brother:

It gives the best picture I could draw of the household in which I spent my days until I went to College. I will only add that living as I did at home, where my sister and I were close companions, we two formed an especially close intimacy which has lasted till now.[124]

This intimacy, not shared by them with their pugnacious elder brother, allowed the otherwise consistent agnostic to accept his sister's

[122] *EU*, i. 116–17, ii. 11.

[123] On familial indebtedness in the creation of this book, and of his belief that he was morally and intellectually like his brother, see *JFS*, pp. v–vii.

[124] *MB*, 5.

love for the Quakers; he quietly accepted that her initial meeting with members of the Society of Friends had been 'a very important event in her history'. Something of the strangely parallel nature of their relationship is strikingly conveyed as he described how she had found 'something sympathetic' in Quaker quietism and in their 'semi-mystical tendencies'; he alluded with quiet pride to her study, *Quaker Strongholds* (1890), although he regretted her concerted attempts to revive the spirit of Quakerism, as this led to 'exertions which have, I fear, injured her'. Caroline Emelia was typically seen as existing, in no small part, for Stephen's benefit, and it is plain that he regretted the distance between them that her Quakerism induced:

Now Milly has loved me all her life; she has been more like a twin than a younger sister . . . the society which would have suited me would have struck her as worldly; while her friends, though very worthy and some of them very clever people, struck me as intolerably dull.[125]

Caroline Emelia Stephen somehow contrived to live parenthetically in her brother's account of his life, an impression later and all too characteristically aided by her appearing merely as an addendum to his own entry in the *Dictionary of National Biography*.[126] Her removal from this parenthetical status has been one of the achievements of the *Oxford Dictionary of National Biography*; her place in the Stephen family romance, symbolically engorged by her brothers both during and immediately after her own lifetime, can now begin properly to be appreciated. As with any other member of her family, religion is central to any understanding of it.[127] In maintaining a religious commitment, Caroline Emelia was more obviously her father's child than were either of his surviving sons; she must have taken particular pleasure in transcribing a letter from 1877 written by one of her father's friends to another in which he insisted that James Stephen had been regarded by some as 'a transcendental Quaker with a tendency to Popery'.[128] Excluding the latter tendency, this Quaker affinity was plainly to Caroline Emelia's

[125] *MB*, 21, 54–5.

[126] Aspects of the *DNB* took on the nature of a family enterprise, as when, and very strikingly, Stephen commissioned his sister-in-law, Anne Isabella Ritchie, to write the entry on Elizabeth Barrett Browning, seemingly without giving thought to the fact that he had entrusted the life of a woman whose marriage was made notoriously against the wishes of her family to a woman whose marriage to a much younger man he and his family had also strongly opposed.

[127] The entry for Caroline Emelia Stephen in the *Oxford Dictionary of National Biography*, written by Margaret M. Jensen, describes her as a 'religious writer'.

[128] Aubrey de Vere to Henry Taylor, 5 Oct. 1877, in *Letters*, 81.

taste; and she must, similarly, have relished her father's insistence in a letter to Henry Taylor of January 1850 that, 'A better gift than a daughter seldom falls to the lot of those whom He most highly favours.'[129] She repaid this sentiment by editing her father's letters, publishing them privately, with binding material, into something very like a biography, yet another example of a literal Stephen family romance.

Caroline Emelia Stephen was preoccupied by many of the matters discussed by members of her family. In common with her father, she was an admirer of Madame de Guyon and other mystics; like him and her grandfather, she was resolutely opposed to slavery, and insisted on demonstrating that eighteenth-century Quakers in America had distanced themselves from that institution.[130] Unlike her father and grandfather, however, she grew suspicious of one of the defining elements of their theology, declaring in *Quaker Strongholds* that 'The glibness, the exasperating completeness, the unconscious blasphemy, of many "orthodox" vindications of Providence, are enough to disgust people with mere orthodoxy.'[131] She was closer to her brothers in her dissatisfaction with 'mere orthodoxy' than she was to her father and grandfather, something she noted as a generational concern:

> Few amongst us can have altogether escaped the paralyzing influence of the flood of unsolved, and apparently insoluble, moral problems, and at the same time of new and absorbingly interesting views of material things, into which this generation has been plunged.[132]

In a less expected echo of their preoccupations, she sought to affirm the 'manly independence' preached by Christ in language strikingly reminiscent of Leslie and James Fitzjames. Regretting the feminization of Catholicism, she found a correlation between female patterns of worship and a dominant clericalism, a tendency which alienated 'thinking men' from religion. The 'masculine mind' was to be saved for religion by emphasizing the masculinity of Christ:[133] in this way, Quakerism became for this committed teacher of women—through the agency of her niece, James Fitzjames Stephen's daughter Katherine, the Principal of Newnham College, Cambridge, she would regularly hold discussions on religion with young university women—an agent of Christian manliness. Likewise, it was the eighteenth century that she identified as pivotal in developments in Quakerism, but in entirely negative ways:

[129] Sir James Stephen to Henry Taylor, 15 Jan. 1850, in *Letters*, 141.
[130] *QS*, 24, 33–4, 121, 205–11.
[131] *QS*, 189. [132] *QS*, 69. [133] *QS*, 177–8.

the seventeenth century was the heroic founding period, the eighteenth century becoming instead hidebound and rule-ridden, and it was not until John Gurney and Elizabeth Fry broke out into social reform in the early decades of the nineteenth century that it rediscovered its reforming momentum.[134] Intriguingly, one of the features of eighteenth-century Quakerism she found least attractive was the practice of marrying-in: for this convert to Quakerism, the need for the movement to absorb outsiders was paramount, although it is interesting to note just how plangent are her references to the special Christian character formed over the generations (and generational growth is a major dynamic in her discussion of spirituality) by old Quaker families.[135] It is clear that a family romance in which Quakerism had supplanted Evangelicalism suffused Caroline Emelia Stephen's religious thinking.

IV

Leslie Stephen the disappointed philosopher saw in biography a means of narrating lives that would be of use to political and literary historians, reducing 'one bit of chaos into order', raising the standard of accurate research, and thereby conferring a benefit, 'if not a very important benefit', on mankind. The biographer laid bricks, where a philosopher might merely blow 'futile soap-bubbles'.[136] *The Science of Ethics* effectively disappeared into the *Dictionary of National Biography*. As with the argument of *The English Utilitarians*, however, it was not so much a complete disappearance as a process of absorption, since Stephen continually stressed in so much of his later writings, themselves increasingly biographical in character, that 'heredity and "environment" explain everything'.[137]

Such an explanation had one major familial difficulty for Stephen, and that concerned his eldest daughter Laura, the product of his marriage to Thackeray's daughter. There is an extraordinary and understated moment in a letter Stephen wrote to his second wife on 25 January 1883 relating his experience as the concerned father of a seriously ill daughter to his altogether longer-lived, if no less difficult progeny, the many lives which he composed for the *Dictionary of National Biography*.

[134] *QS*, 162–3, 168.
[135] *QS*, 35–6, 77–8, 120, 161.
[136] 'National biography', *SB*, ii. 1–36, at p. 7.
[137] 'Introduction' to James Payn, *The Backwater of Life, or, Essays of a Literary Veteran* (London, 1899), pp. ix–xliv, at p. xi.

Early in his editorial labours on the 'damned dictionary' he had spent a day of research in the British Museum, where, as he noted, 'I made a discovery about Addison, confuting all previous biographers on a point of no importance whatever.' He then asked Julia to enquire of her father, an old India hand, what the value of pagodas (a unit of currency in the India of Addison's day) was, having discovered that the writer's brother had left an estate worth 30,000 pagodas. Later that day, Stephen returned home to 13 Hyde Park Gate South, where he attempted to continue the thankless task of educating Laura, his daughter from his first marriage. All too shortly afterwards, Laura was to be diagnosed as being incurably backward, which shortly afterwards led to her long incarceration in an asylum run by J. L. H. Langham Down, the man who isolated the features of the illness named after him, Down's Syndrome. Stephen, a father *and* a scholar, was stung into a moment of recognition, which he haltingly and economically conveyed at the close of this Addisonian day:

> Then I came back & Laura read to me for a longish time. I am getting more to feel the mischief of losing one's temper with her & sorry to think that I have done it so much. We had one little stoppage but on the whole, she did well. Miss J made her write to Stella, I believe. I saw today some letters of Addison's only daughter, one when she came of age, in a kind of schoolgirl hand. She seems to have had something wrong; but he died when she was only a baby.[138]

How much could be unpacked by a sympathetic biographer from this typically understated short paragraph! Mr Ramsay, often identified with the author's father, famously found it impossible to get from 'P' to 'R' in his ordered philosophical musings in Woolf's *To the Lighthouse*; with a mind as sensitive to the echoes of suffering as was Stephen's, it is a great tribute to his emotional resilience that he ever got beyond 'A' in his biographical dictionary.[139] The entry on Addison was the one Stephen came to use as a model for other contributors; how many of them could possibly have known what a heavy reflection on personal suffering over two centuries that entry contained? Scholarship was not, ultimately, a means of escape for Stephen, nor could it have been; rather, it was a productive channel for the acute sensibility that can be discerned in all

[138] Stephen to Julia Prinsep Stephen, 25 Jan. 1883, in *Selected Letters of Leslie Stephen*, ed. John W. Bicknell (2 vols., Basingstoke, 1996), ii. 300–1.

[139] For sensitive readings of the relationship between Ramsay and Stephen, see Gillian Beer, 'Hume, Stephen, and elegy in *To the Lighthouse*', in *Essays in Criticism*, 34 (1984), 33–55, and John W. Bicknell, 'Mr Ramsay was young once', in Jane Marcus (ed.), *Virginia Woolf and Bloomsbury: A Centenary Celebration* (London, 1987), 52–67.

of Stephen's deceptively unemotional, rigorously disillusioned writings. His experience of old age, and the passing of one generation's passions, desires, and concerns into those of another was one such source of disillusion.

Stephen acknowledged the extraordinary pace of change through which he had lived, a transformation in intellectual life so total as almost to overwhelm this mid-Victorian Cambridge liberal. This was strongly voiced in *Some Early Impressions*, a work originating in essays contributed to the *National Review* in 1903 and which were originally designed to chronicle such change for Edwardian readers (as if Stephen were thus assenting to his becoming a 'Victorian'):

when I remember the thrill of indignation which ran through the respectable world, the clerical manifestoes which I was adjured to sign, the masses of polemical literature, the prosecutions for heresy and the vehement assertions that the very foundations of religion and morality were being assailed, and then remind myself that we are all now evolutionists, and that orthodox divines accept the most startling doctrines of *Essays and Reviews*, I feel as though I have lived through more than one generation.[140]

He might also fairly be said to have anticipated the rejection of that culture by the succeeding generation, as he had noted in an essay on Scott that, 'however far the taste for revivalism may be pushed, nobody will ever want to revive the nineteenth century'.[141]

This self-distancing from the nineteenth century marked Stephen out as a Victorian who chose to look both backwards to his ancestors and forwards to his descendants. There can be little doubt as to which direction proved more attractive to his occasionally gloomy, if always perceptive, gaze, as in an extended waking dream about the eighteenth century as a way out of the all-pervasive realities of the late Victorian age:

We are beginning to regard our ancestors with a strange mixture of contempt and envy. We despise them because they cared nothing for the thoughts which for the last century have been upheaving society into strange convulsions; we envy them because they enjoyed the delicious calm which was the product of that indifference. Wearied by the incessant tossing and boiling of the torrent which carried us away, we look back with fond regret to the little backwater so far above Niagara, where scarcely a ripple marks the approaching rapids. There is a charm in the great solid old eighteenth-century mansions, which London is so rapidly engulfing, and even about the old red-brick churches with 'sleep-compelling' pews. We take imaginary naps amongst our grandfathers

140 *SEI*, 54–5. 141 'Sir Walter Scott', *HL*, i. 150.

with no railways, no telegraphs, no mobs in Trafalgar Square, no discussions about ritualism or Dr Colenso, and no reports of parliamentary debates. It is to our fancies an 'island valley of Avilion', or, less magniloquently, a pleasant land of Cockaine, where we may sleep away the disturbance of battle, and even read through *Clarissa Harlowe*. We could put up with an occasional highwayman in Hyde Park, and perhaps do not think that our comfort would be seriously disturbed by a dozen executions in a morning at Tyburn.[142]

Typically, the idyll is both disturbed and supported by an image of violence and suppression; all societies operate at a cost in the Stephen family audit. Realism intrudes at all points, and Stephen reminded his readers that even in such 'visionary glances' we assume the advantage of selecting the correct position in the society so idealized. Significantly, this idyll comes at the close of an essay on Horace Walpole, and it reminds the reader that Walpole was able to lead the comfortable life he enjoyed through 'the warm folds of a sinecure of £6,000 a year bestowed because our father was a prime minister'.[143]

The Stephen family romance engaged with the romance of other families, other dynasties, and it was aware of just how much such romances curtailed as well as enabled lives, both those of their eighteenth-century ancestors and those of their putative twentieth-century descendants. It did so always through books, and in this sense the late essay by Woolf cited earlier in this chapter echoed the intellectual activity in which her father had engaged when she beckoned to her reader: 'let us glance at English writers as they were a hundred years ago—that they may help us to see what we ourselves look like.'[144] This remark echoes very strongly one of the last things her father wrote, as he had observed in his *English Literature and Society in the Eighteenth Century* (1904) that: 'Our descendants will be able to see the general character of the Victorian age better than we, who unconsciously accept our own peculiarities, like the air we breathe, as mere matters of course.'[145] In order to achieve this insight into the past and the present Woolf had to engage with the writers who had been at work when her father was a young man, including Thackeray, the man who would be his first (posthumous) father-in-law, and to whose writings Stephen himself had frequently and invariably approvingly referred throughout his writing

142 'Horace Walpole', *HL*, i. 336. For similar remarks written towards the very close of his life, see *ELS*, 98.

143 'Horace Walpole', *HL*, i. 337.

144 'The leaning tower', 106–7.

145 *ELS*, 9.

career. The study of literature, and the attempt to understand oneself through such study, were elements of what it was to be a Stephen, and to have undertaken either or both was, necessarily, to be part of its own family romance. For the Stephen family, as Maitland had recognized in 1906, books were the means by which they understood what it was to be a family, and this was especially true in the relationships that subsisted between fathers and sons. In the most signal instance in the Stephen family romance it involved the relationship between a father and a daughter.

Woolf's own writings intersected at so many points with those of her father. She parodied the conventions of the literary biography in her novel *Flush*, the biography of Elizabeth Barrett Browning's lapdog; many of her literary essays concerned authors who had preoccupied Stephen—the first volume of her 1925 collection *The Common Reader* contained a brilliant essay on Addison, as well as a response to the *Dictionary of National Biography* in an essay entitled 'Lives of the obscure'.[146] Most intriguingly, the issue of gender was prominently played out in the transsexual experiences of the hero/heroine of *Orlando*, whose foppish experience of the worlds of Pope and Addison owed not a little to the literary histories of the period created by her father. The Victorian pages of that novel repay even more attention, as the attenuated world of her own family is thrown into relief against the foreclosed experiences she described in that section of her novel. The creator of Shakespeare's sister was constantly interrogating the inheritance her father had left her; his ghost haunted the closing pages of *To the Lighthouse*, whose central image probably owes something to an essay by Caroline Emelia Stephen, and the Stephen family romance can be traced throughout Woolf's writings.

Leslie Stephen himself observed of that most psychoanalysed of sons that: 'Hamlet may have been morbid—an interview with one's father's ghost is rather upsetting—but at least he was not contemptible.'[147] From Freud's own occasional analyses of the play to rather more recent explorations of *Hamlet* as a drama in which an older generation's beliefs haunt those of its successor—in this instance through the afterlife of the doctrine of Purgatory in the uncertain years of Elizabethan Protestantism—the interview between Hamlet and his father has been a

[146] For essays on subjects also written about by her father, see *The Common Reader* (London, 1925).

[147] 'Life of Tennyson', *SB*, ii. 196–240, at p. 237.

central image of the dialectic between fathers and sons, and Stephen must have been aware of the power of that image within the particularities of the Stephen family romance.[148] The depth of his sense of the 'upsetting' nature of such a colloquy is confirmed rather than undermined by the casually throwaway nature of the observation. It was an image which plainly carried resonances for him, as in his playful variant of it when stating, in a letter of April 1877 to his Thackeray sister-in-law, that 'Mrs Huth asks me questions as though she were my g'mother's ghost.'[149]

Stephen the agnostic occasionally drew on the familiar Victorian resonance of the ghostly in his histories of thought and opinion. This is instanced strongly in his account of the confrontation between the deism which sought to undermine Christianity as a revealed faith in the first half of the eighteenth century, and the defenders of that older religion. The sarcasm of the deists was thus defended 'on the ground that ridicule is the most effective charm for laying the ghosts of dead opinions. When a phantom dogma persists in haunting the living world, a laugh will cause it to vanish more rapidly than the keenest logical slashing.' This was but a rehearsal of deeper problems that neither side had as yet discovered, so that there was about the encounter between the warring parties 'a strange sense of unreality. Theologians are striving to support the existence of a set of phantoms placed in an uncongenial atmosphere, where their ultimate doom is certain, and fancying that they have won a decisive victory, when they have shown that the fatal blow has not yet been struck.'[150] The logic of that sentence is interesting; how can one, after all, strike a *fatal* blow to a phantom? The phantom/spectre was a potent symbol of unease and anxiety in nineteenth-century England, and there can be no doubt that Stephen continued to feel a sense of dissatisfaction about the state of the religious question, the 'phantom' that he and his allies had sought to lay. If phantoms still haunted religion, they were altogether less tangible in the world of social investigation which Stephen was ever desirous of exploring, and even Utilitarianism had played its role in this particular exorcism, as in his declaration in the close of the section on moral philosophy in the second volume of the *History of English Thought in the Eighteenth Century*:

Bentham's influence on morality was destructive of many phantoms which were still going about in spite of Hume's more searching scepticism, and if its

148 Stephen Greenblatt, *Hamlet in Purgatory* (Princeton, 2001).

149 Stephen to Anne Isabella Thackeray, 12 Apr. 1877, in *Selected Letters*, ed. Bicknell, i. 200.

150 *History*, i. 157, 163.

constructive efficacy was not great in the sphere of speculation, it encouraged the adoption of profounder methods.[151]

Writing only some twenty-five years after the *Communist Manifesto* had first appeared, Stephen referred to the manner in which Burke, a great hero of his, had confronted with suitable horror the 'spectre' of the French Revolution.[152] It is to the Victorian obsession with the ghostly, from Marx's deployment of the 'spectre' of revolution against Burke's counter-revolutionary successors, to Freud's conception and exploration of the 'uncanny' ('unheimlich'), that the following and final chapter of the present study will be devoted.

151 *History*, ii. 108.

152 Ibid. 206. On the *locus classicus* of revolutionary spectrality, see Karl Marx and Freidrich Engels, *The Communist Manifesto.* For suggestive comment, see Jacques Derrida, *Specters of Marx: The State of the Debt, the Work of Mourning, and the New International*, trans. Peggy Kamuf (London, 1994).

5

Hanoverian Hauntings

> It's a very odd fact... that the only ghosts people ever see are the ghosts of a generation very close to them. One hears of lots of ghosts in eighteenth-century costume, because everybody has a clear idea of wigs and small-clothes from pictures and fancy-dresses. One hears of far fewer in Elizabethan dress, because the class most given to beholding ghosts are seldom acquainted with ruffs and farthingales; and one meets with none at all in Anglo-Saxon or Ancient British or Roman costumes, because those are only known to a comparatively small class of learned people; and ghosts, as a rule, avoid the learned...
>
> Grant Allen, 'Pallinghurst Barrow' (1893)[1]

Towards the close of *Studies in Eighteenth-Century Italy* (1880), the first of what would be her many books, the 24-year-old art historian Vernon Lee observed:

> In re-reading the foregoing pages there has come home to us an impression felt but vaguely while writing them; the impression that in our search for art we have been wandering through rooms long closed and darkened; that we have been brushing away, perhaps over roughly, cobwebs and dust which lay reverently on things long untouched, that we have been intruding into a close weird atmosphere filled with invisible ghosts.[2]

This impression would grow stronger in Lee's writings, and the pioneering studies in aesthetics she continued to produce during a long and fruitful writing career—including a late study on the language

[1] In *Ivan Greet's Masterpiece* (London, 1893), 68–89, at pp. 76–7.

[2] Vernon Lee, *Studies in Eighteenth-Century Italy* (1880), 291. On the relationship between such interests and her ghost stories, see Catherine Maxwell, 'Vernon Lee and the ghosts of Italy', in Alison Chapman and Jane Stabler (eds.), *Unfolding the South: Nineteenth-Century British Women Writers and Artists in Italy* (Manchester, 2003), 201–21.

of poetry published by Virginia and Leonard Woolf at the Hogarth Press—intersected increasingly with her collections of ghost stories, for which she is now probably better known.[3] Several of the figures haunted by the past in her stories are isolated scholars, whose ordered minds are initially disorientated and finally undermined by their experiences of the spectral. The distorting presence of the eighteenth-century in the nineteenth century is a central element of the uncanny in many of Lee's stories; in her staging of this confrontation with a seemingly undying predecessor culture, she is not untypical of many of her contemporaries. This chapter will examine her interest in this theme alongside that of another scholar and writer of ghost stories, M. R. James. As the examples of Lee and James will demonstrate, the ghost story is a vital source for the Victorian historian of thought, not least as it could and did act as both an agent of religious authority *and*, in different hands, as a consciously secular assault on that authority.

This chapter will strengthen the important claim made by the literary critic Terry Castle, who has argued for the need for modern scholars properly to appreciate a vitally important 'spectral' dimension in what she describes as Leslie Stephen's otherwise all too rational eighteenth century, and even though she respects the impetus behind W. E. H. Lecky's progressively rationalizing thesis in his *History of the Rise and Progress of Rationalism in Europe* (1865), she has offered her own richly suggestive series of discrete genealogies that account for the survival of the uncanny into the nineteenth century and rightly make much of its continuing power.[4] This chapter will, therefore, take the form of an archaeology of the haunting sense of the eighteenth-century past in the nineteenth-century present. Haunting is both a reality and a metaphor in Vernon Lee, and the eighteenth century was an important factor in this experience of haunting, as it was also to prove to be for M. R. James.

In an essay entitled 'Rococo' from her 1887 volume, *Juvenilia*, Lee recorded her early obsession with the experience and the legacy of the eighteenth century in the country in which she had largely grown up with her itinerant English family:

[3] Lee, *The Poet's Eye* (1926). For an argument that Lee's notion of empathy influenced aspects of Woolf's thought, see Dennis Dennisoff, 'The forest beyond the frame: picturing women's desires in Vernon Lee and Virginia Woolf', in Talia Schaffer and Kathy Alexis Psomiades (eds.), *Women and British Aestheticism* (Charlottesville, Va., 1999), 251–69.

[4] Terry Castle, 'Introduction' to *The Female Thermometer: Eighteenth-Century Culture and the Invention of the Uncanny* (Oxford, 1995), 3–20.

I found myself in the midst of the Italian eighteenth century. I have selected that form of words with the intention of your taking it literally. I really did find my way into that period, and really did live in it; for I began to see only the things belonging thereunto; and I had little or no connection with anything else. The eighteenth century existed for me as a reality, surrounded by faint and fluctuating shadows, which shadows were simply the present.

The essay continues to catalogue this obsession with ruthlessly self-critical precision. She notes how, through her intense reading programme, she became 'a remarkably well-educated young person of the eighteenth century, perfectly up to all the last new things of that time'; but she was not satisfied with merely reading her way back in time. Her desire became still more one for sensual stimulus, for bodily immersion in the eighteenth century, for immediate contact with those who had been *there*:

I should have liked to see, to hear; if not directly, at least through the mediumship of some one who had seen and heard the things of those days. There was in me a vague hope of being able to come nearer to that century, of finding, in some mystic way and hidden place, a hidden corner thereof. I was tremendously interested in very old people, hoping that they might bring me into contact with the days of their childhood; for I forgot all that immense sea of nineteenth century in which their few impressions of earlier times must have got drowned, or at least discoloured; and many disappointments did not quell my ardour in seeking out these precious half-living relics of my beloved period.[5]

Lee, who published this piece at the age of 31, demonstrated a mature and modern (almost a Modernist) sense of the porous nature of time, and of the myriad complications that beset any straightforward assessment of the relations between the generations. It was, then, through the eighteenth century that she both began to think historically, and also

[5] Lee, 'Rococo', in *Juvenilia: Being a Second Series of Essays on Sundry Aesthetical Questions* (2 vols., 1887), i. 131–47, at pp. 137, 139–41. Lee's aesthetic would come to acquire a bodily dimension; she noted that music had a bodily as much as a spiritual impact: 'The riddle of music,' *Quarterly Review*, 204 (1906), 207–27, at p. 211. On the physicality of her aesthetics, which also had, on occasion, a same-sex character, see Dinana Maltz, 'Engaging "delicate brains": from working-class enculturation to upper-class lesbian liberation in Vernon Lee and Kit Anstruther-Thomson's psychological aesthetics', in Schaffer and Psomiades, *Women and British Aestheticism*, 211–29, and Kathy Alexis Psomiades, ' "Still burning from this strangling embrace": Vernon Lee on desire and aesthetics', in Richard Dellamora (ed.), *Victorian Sexual Dissidence* (Chicago, 1999), 21–41.

to appreciate just how acutely limiting to the imagination, to the direct *experience* of the past, such thinking could be.[6]

At the close of 'Rococo', Lee noted how her younger self had gradually matured into deciding to write about the eighteenth century not because she was obsessed by it, but because it had been 'among the great artistic periods of the world's history, along with the times of Pericles and Leo X'. It was a process of intellectual maturation about which she was to grow decidedly self-critical, not least in regard to what it said about her attitude to history as having been something separable from the immediacy of lived, or even of merely imagined, experience:

> Pericles; Leo X; history of art; artistic periods! how little did I understand at that moment the meaning of all this sudden eruption of philosophical and Hegelian verbiage! I really imagined that I loved the eighteenth century as much as ever. Alas, all this phraseology of modern criticism signified that my much-loved century had ceased to be alive, that it had become, in my eyes, a mere corpse, and that I was preparing to dissect it! It signified that I looked at it no longer from within, but from without; that in issuing from the eighteenth century, I had emerged also out of childhood; that the days of great imaginative passions, of Joan of Arc and Marie Antoinette, of Sioux and Mohicans, were gone for ever.[7]

In a great many ways, Victorians, both believers and sceptics, were haunted by Hanoverians. This theme was strongly to the fore in Henry

[6] Lee's explorations of the eighteenth century, alongside those of Emilia Dilke, fashioned a new period in, and a new way of pursuing, art history, on which see also Hilary Fraser, 'Regarding the eighteenth century: Vernon Lee and Emilia Dilke construct a period' in Francis O'Gorman and Katherine Turner (eds.), *The Victorians and the Eighteenth Century: Reassessing the Tradition* (Aldershot, 2004), 223–49. Emilia Dilke, first married to Mark Pattison, whose essay on eighteenth-century religion so strongly affected Leslie Stephen's career as an intellectual historian, and then to the Liberal politician Sir Charles Dilke, wrote several volumes on the arts in eighteenth-century France, often of a rather technical kind, but always attractively written, and with none of the knowing idiosyncrasy of Lee's texts. These are: *French Painters of the Eighteenth Century* (London, 1899), *French Architects and Sculptors of the Eighteenth Century* (London, 1900), *French Furniture and Decoration in the Eighteenth Century* (London, 1901), and *French Engravers and Draughtsmen of the Eighteenth Century* (London, 1902). Like Lee, she also wrote about the Renaissance and the culture of Louis XIV's France, in her magisterial *Art in the Modern State* (London, 1888). Also like Lee, she wrote two collections of mystically inclined stories: *The Shrine of Death and Other Stories* (London, 1886), and *The Shrine of Love and Other Stories* (London, 1891). Unlike Lee, with her marked indebtedness to Pater, it was Ruskin, in many ways Lee's *bête-noire,* who first encouraged Dilke as a very young woman, and his presence is visible in her studies. On Dilke, see Kali Israel, *Names and Stories: Emilia Dilke and Victorian Culture* (Oxford, 1999). Emilia Dilke's life and writings can very interestingly be read alongside the experience and writings of Vernon Lee.

[7] *Juvenilia*, i. 146–7.

James's late unfinished novel, with its evocatively resonant title, *The Sense of the Past*, in which a modern man literally enters the world of a predecessor of 1820 as both live out this uncanny experience of doubling in an elegant eighteenth-century house:

What he wanted himself was the very smell of that simple mixture of things that had so long served; he wanted the very tick of the old stopped clocks. He wanted the hour of the day at which this and that had happened, and the temperature and the weather and the sound, and yet more the stillness, from the street, and the exact look-out, with the corresponding look-in, through the window and the slant on the walls of the light of the afternoons that had been. He wanted the unimaginable accidents, the little notes of truth for which the common lens of history, however the scowling muse might bury her nose, was not sufficiently fine. He wanted evidence of a sort for which there had never been documents enough, or for which documents mainly, however multiplied, would never *be* enough. That was indeed in any case the artist's method—to try for an ell in order to get an inch. The difficult, as at best it is, becomes under such conditions so dire that to face it with any prospect one had to propose the impossible. Recovering the past was at all events on this scale much like entering the enemy's line to get back one's dead for burial; and to that extent was he not, by his deepening penetration, contemporaneous and present? 'Present' was a word used by him in a sense of his own and meaning as regards most things about him markedly absent. It was for the old ghosts to take him for one of themselves.[8]

It was this powerful need to *experience* the past that linked James's late novel, strictly a supernatural rather than merely a ghost story, with the scholarly hauntings that abound in the fictions of Vernon Lee and M. R. James. This desire to transcend the division between the past and the present, to move from intellectual and historical empathy to direct sensual experience, is at the root of much of the horror in their supernatural tales. It is a scholarly and existential desire that made emphatic a dominant historical register in much Victorian scholarly life, the register of historicism.

In describing that sense of the shadowing of the present by the not so distant past, Vernon Lee and M. R. James deployed in the

[8] Henry James, *The Sense of the Past* (1917), 48–9. For a suggestive reading of the novel see Karl Miller, *Doubles: Studies in Literary History* (Oxford, 1981), 234–9. The best statement on James's deployment of the uncanny is T. J. Lustig, *Henry James and the Ghostly* (Cambridge, 1994). Early in his career James had written an atmospheric ghost story set in mid-eighteenth-century Massachusetts: 'The romance of certain old clothes', in Leon Edel (ed.), *The Complete Tales of Henry James* (12 vols., London, 1962–4), i. 297–319.

'ghost' story a uniquely problematic narrative structure in which the whole apparatus of rational assent—the reliability of witnesses, the coherence of the stories they told, and, above all, the probability of those narratives—was repeatedly challenged. The stern demands of a dominant historicism—M. R. James had, after all, been chosen to write the chapter on 'The Christian Renaissance' for the *Cambridge Modern History* by no less a practitioner than Lord Acton—occasionally proved too much for his deeply imaginative sensibility, and such tales thus provided something in the way of a busman's holiday for the exhausted scholarly mind.[9] The rules of historical explanation could be deployed in plotting a ghost story, but only for them to prove unworkable; M. R. James laid it down as a firm rule of the ghost story that it should provide space for a rational explanation of the events it describes, but that, ultimately, the rational explanation should be seen not to work.[10] The irrational had, then, always to evade rational explanation, and a subsidiary element in the argument of this chapter will be provided by an occasional appeal to the insights regarding the uncanny made by another Victorian, Sigmund Freud, who was born in 1856, making him Vernon Lee's exact contemporary. Freud will not be treated here as a privileged exegete, but in this instance as only as one of several narrators of the presence of the uncanny in Victorian culture. In so historicizing Freud, one can begin to make more sense of the centrality of haunting in nineteenth-century literature.[11]

[9] On the commission, see Richard William Pfaff, *Montague Rhodes James* (1980), 141. For the result, see M. R. James, 'The Christian Renaissance', in A. W. Ward, G. W. Prothero, and Stanley Leathes (eds.), *Cambridge Modern History*, i: *The Renaissance* (Cambridge, 1902), 585–619. James, all too aware, perhaps, of the Actonian spirit which was to pervade the *Cambridge Modern History*, almost parodies the nature of his scholarly enterprise in his essay. He notes, of an inventory of the books belonging to Pope Nicholas V, that 'A short survey of the collection, if dry, will at least afford some basis of solid fact.' Similarly, halfway through his essay, he declares: 'To most men the study of inventories and catalogues seems dry work; but the evidence derivable from it is of a kind not easily to be upset' (ibid. 594, 600). Such a strategy is almost reversed by the rather differently dry surprises awaiting the unlucky scholars in his ghost stories.

[10] M. R. James, 'Introduction' to V. H. Collins (ed.), *Ghosts and Marvels: A Selection of Uncanny Tales from Daniel Defoe to Algernon Blackwood* (1921), pp. v–xiii, at pp. vi–vii.

[11] For recent and suggestive attempts to historicize Freud's writings, see Michel de Certeau, 'What Freud makes of history: "a seventeenth-century demonological neurosis"' and 'The fiction of history: The writing of *Moses and Monotheism*', in *The Writing of History*, trans. Tom Conley (New York, 1988), 287–307, 308–54, and Carl E. Schorske, 'To the Egyptian dig: Freud's psycho-archaeology of culture', in *Thinking with History: Explorations in the Passage to Modernism* (Princeton, 1998), 191–215.

One has also to take very seriously the huge degree of speculation about the reality of ghost stories that preoccupied so many Victorians; at Cambridge in 1849 the young Leslie Stephen had discussed with other members of a debating society 'the old problem as to the truth of ghost-stories'.[12] The deep seriousness of such interests reached its apogee at Cambridge in the academic generation following Stephen's, when Edward White Benson, the future Archbishop of Canterbury (who later provided Henry James with the germ of what became *The Turn of the Screw*) had founded the 'Ghost Society' in the 1860s, which formalized discussion of such phenomena. Henry Sidgwick, the philosopher, who, like Stephen before him, had had to resign his fellowship due to his inability to sign his assent to the Thirty-Nine Articles, nonetheless also maintained a strong conviction regarding the very real possibility of life after death, devoting considerable scholarly labour to researching the problem. Alongside his wife Eleanor, the Principal of Newnham College, he presided over the Society for Psychical Research from 1882, many of whose members were themselves Cambridge dons.[13] Some years later, in a contest between differing conceptions of psychic phenomena, Eleanor Sidgwick would strongly criticize a celebrated narrative of an eighteenth-century haunting produced anonymously by two Oxford dons, Charlotte Anne Moberly and Eleanor Jourdain, the Principal and Vice-Principal of St Hugh's College. Moberly and Jourdain had claimed, in *An Adventure*, first published in 1911, when visiting Versailles in 1901, to have been caught up psychically in a peculiarly charged moment from the life of Marie-Antoinette.[14] The resonances of this strange tale have lasted for a very long time, and the most recent attempt at a solution to the peculiar enigma as to why two supremely well-educated women would have published such a potentially compromising account of haunting has been provided by Terry Castle, who has repudiated an explanation of it as a *folie à deux*, preferring to see it as a knowing challenge to sceptics laid down

[12] Leslie Stephen, 'Introduction' to James Payn, *The Backwater of Life, or, Essays of a Literary Veteran* (London, 1899), pp. ix–xliv, at p. xviii.

[13] For excellent discussion, see Bart Schultz, *Henry Sidgwick, Eye of the Universe: An Intellectual Biography* (Cambridge, 2004), 90, 275–334.

[14] [Charlotte Anne Moberly and Eleanor Jourdain], *An Adventure* (London, 1911); Eleanor Sidgwick, review from the *Proceedings of the Society for Psychical Research* (London, 1911), reproduced in Lucille Iremonger, *The Ghosts of Versailles: Miss Moberly and Miss Jourdain and their Adventure: A Critical Study* (London, 1957), 146–55. She dismissed the book as not adding 'anything of interest on the positive side of Psychical Research' (p. 155).

by Moberly and Jourdain.[15] However explained, the story provides a striking instance of the cultural authority of haunting in Victorian Britain. The Victorian ghost story, then, whether ostensibly real or totally imagined, and whatever its undoubted limitations as a literary genre, had developed in an ethos of extreme scholarly seriousness. It was in this atmosphere at Cambridge that the young M. R. James had been educated.

I

As a historian, and one who edited and published a collection of medieval ghost stories, dating from around 1400, in the *English Historical Review* in 1922, James was deeply aware of their great importance in opening up the worlds of the past to imaginative modern scholarship.[16] Ghosts have played a large part in the myriad narratives that constitute what we know of European history, and the student of the Victorian ghost story can learn much by considering that long history. Recently, Keith Hopkins demonstrated how ghosts had strategically intervened in the uncertain belief systems of ancient Rome; later, between the eleventh and thirteenth centuries, their appearances in England aided clarifications of theological doctrines concerning penance and purgatory, as religious uncertainties were replaced by ever more concrete dogmas.[17] Jean-Claude Schmitt has likewise shown how apparitions of the dead to the living played a large part in the evolution of 'the imaginary of Western society'. Instancing an important parallel with his own acts of cultural decoding, Schmitt observed that the success of haunting narratives in medieval Europe depended on a complex of contemporaneous interpretations, leading him to conclude that 'some of the clerics who passed on these tales of "apparitions" were "intellectuals" whose theological and philosophical reasoning and relentlessness in distinguishing

[15] Terry Castle, 'Contagious folly: *An Adventure* and its skeptics', *Critical Inquiry*, 17 (1991), 741–72; Castle, *The Apparitional Lesbian: Female Homosexuality and Modern Culture* (New York, 1993), 112–25, 149.

[16] M. R. James, 'Twelve medieval ghost stories', *English Historical Review*, 37 (1922), 413–22.

[17] Keith Hopkins, *Death and Renewal: Sociological Studies in Roman History* (Cambridge, 1983), 226–35; C. S. Watkins, 'Sin, penance, and Purgatory in the Anglo-Norman realm: The evidence of visions and ghost stories', *Past and Present*, 175 (2002), 3–33.

the "true" from the "false" were not, in their logical approach, all that different from our own'.[18] Indeed, Schmitt emphasized just how integral the medieval intellectual was to the promotion and exposition of ghost stories; judging the credibility of the storyteller was, therefore, very much part of this legitimization process. The authority accorded these stories by clerics and monks placed them beyond suspicion; and it was in the interest of ecclesiastics, who often used such visions as moral *exempla* through which they could further their much desired reform of lay society, that they should be believed to be true. The ghost story, then, has to be considered an important source for the historian of medieval society, especially since it vitally informed an inherently religious interpretation of everyday life.[19] It performs an analogous role for the historian of Victorian thought, as it was a genre that contested intellectual authority, and one that attracted secular as well as religious practitioners. What is more, and contrary to Grant Allen's assertion in his secular ghost story 'In Pallinghurst Barrow' (a portion of which acts as the epigraph to this chapter), ghosts might well have avoided the learned in the nineteenth century, but the learned did not themselves avoid ghosts.

In Schmitt's richly suggestive study, the learned, both past and present, are fused in a mutually rewarding interest in ghosts. As interpreters of the interpenetration of the celestial and terrestrial worlds, intellectuals in medieval society had pored over ghostly tales, and 'the maniacal concern with detail' which resulted from their involvement 'enabled the clerics to become masters of the supernatural and to reduce the ambivalence of its meanings'. Likewise, modern historians have to move beyond the Enlightenment-sponsored disapprobation so long engineered against such tales, and 'without giving up anything of their own reason', they must, Schmitt continues, recognize in these hitherto suspect narratives a unique source in writing 'a social history of the imaginary'.[20] Schmitt has signally contributed to the study of the ways in which societies imagine themselves, and of how these constructions ultimately contribute to a culture's critical self-understanding. When concluding his study, Schmitt observes that he could easily have taken his study forward to the end of the nineteenth century.[21] His concerns, therefore, offer a powerful parallel to those that provide the dynamic of

[18] Jean-Claude Schmitt, *Ghosts in the Middle Ages: The Living and the Dead in Medieval Society*, trans. Teresa Lavender Fagan (Chicago, 1998), 2, 8, 9–10.

[19] Ibid. 77–8, 141. [20] Ibid. 158, 9–10. [21] Ibid. 224.

this study: eighteenth-century ghosts hovering over the Victorian psyche reveal a great deal about how the nineteenth century saw its relations with the undead of its predecessor culture.

A study of the status of ghosts in another self-consciously rationalizing culture—in this instance, sixteenth-century England—also assists in the attempt to understand the status of the supernatural in nineteenth-century England. In *Hamlet in Purgatory*, Stephen Greenblatt considered the afterlife of medieval Catholicism in a society that had, supposedly, repudiated its central dogmatic contention, namely that the living and the dead were indissolubly linked through the charitable endeavours that depended on a belief in the purgatorial middle state which subsisted between the death of the individual and God's final judgement of humanity. Greenblatt insisted that the principal power of priests, against which Protestant reformers contended, had resided in 'their hold upon the imagination of their flock'. There was, he notes, an important conviction amongst reformers that Purgatory was exactly what Tyndale had called it, 'a poet's fable'. In examining 'the poetics of Purgatory', Greenblatt emphasized the centrality of narrative as a means of creating and maintaining belief. It was not so much the creation of a doctrine but, rather, a means of 'shaping and colonizing the imagination' that priests and allied intellectuals had promoted in their deployment of haunting narratives.[22]

Greenblatt recognized that the Protestant reformers had to take on a vast imaginative matrix when they began to undo Purgatory, but undo it they did. Naturally, the uncanny continued to survive in a few well-chosen spaces, but what had previously been a central part of religiously directed cultural poetics underwent a significant displacement to a new locus: the stage. Ghosts took to the stage in the closing decades of the sixteenth century, and with no greater success

[22] Stephen Greenblatt, *Hamlet in Purgatory* (Princeton, 2001), 33, 35, 40–1, 61, 85. Intriguingly, Purgatory was treated by many of its believing proponents, especially in the work of Thomas More, as the centre of intergenerational activity: see p. 144 for Greenblatt's reading of this claim. For a reading of the same phenomenon by a social historian, see Peter Marshall, 'Deceptive appearances: Ghosts and reformers in Elizabethan and Jacobean England', in Helen Parish and William G. Naphy (eds.), *Religion and Superstition in Reformation Europe* (Manchester, 2002), 188–208. On the survival of supposedly accredited ghostly tales into the late seventeenth century, and its place in religious apologetic, Dissenting and Anglican, see Sasha Handley, 'Reclaiming ghosts in 1690s England', in Kate Cooper and Jeremy Gregory (eds.), *Signs, Wonders, Miracles: Representations of Divine Power in the Life of the Church* (Studies in Church History 41) (London, 2005), 345–55.

than in the plays of Shakespeare.[23] Greenblatt's bravura engagement with the cultural politics of *Hamlet* is an important display of the ways in which the imaginative inheritance of one generation is reimagined by its successors. In addressing the proposition that the playwright's father had been a recusant who had asked in his secret last testament that his son see to it that prayers were said for his departed soul, Greenblatt demonstrated that the son's encounter with Catholic theology was actually played out in a new cultural key, that of a Protestantism which was still finding its distinctive voice, and which necessarily owed more than it could then acknowledge to what it had formally repudiated.[24] Stage-plays are, therefore, central sites for the deep play of cultural transformation. The tensions in *Hamlet* are those attendant on intergenerational cultural shifts, and something of an allied kind can be felt in the way that nineteenth-century writers imagined the survival into their own very specific world of frequently troubling eighteenth-century cultural memories.

As both Schmitt and Greenblatt argue, the dead are the centre of both cultural memory and cultural forgetting; as the ghost in *Hamlet* disastrously pleads, 'remember me'.[25] Encounters with ghosts in nineteenth-century fiction are an important aspect of this constantly repeated act of cultural memory; when they are laid to rest, as they often are, they can also be seen as an aspect of the act of forgetting that matters so much in the Freudian encounter with the imagined dead. As Freud wrote in *Little Hans*, regarding therapeutic intervention, 'What remains in the understanding, however, will come again; like an unredeemed ghost it will not be at peace until it is laid to rest and redeemed.'[26] As Schmitt observed in this connection, what Freud said of individuals can be said of nations;[27] it can also be said of generations, in particular of those generations whose neuroses were so influentially unpicked in Freud's own narratives, the generations whose narratives form the core of the present study.[28]

At the beginning of his chapter on 'The Rights of Memory', Greenblatt observed that: 'Reports of hauntings were going to recur from time

23 Greenblatt, *Hamlet*, 151–204. 24 Ibid. 229–57.

25 Schmitt, *Ghosts*, 5–6, 33, 35, 53, 66, and *passim*; Greenblatt, *Hamlet*, 143, 205–8, 214–29.

26 Freud, 'Analysis of a phobia in a five-year-old boy: Little Hans', in *The 'Wolfman' and Other Cases*, trans. Louise Adey Huish (Harmondsworth, 2002), 1–122, at p. 100.

27 Schmitt, *Ghosts*, 227, referring to the essay by Freud in the preceding note.

28 For a sustained argument relating Freud to his own Victorian generation, see Peter Gay, *The Bourgeois Experience: From Victoria to Freud* (5 vols., New York, 1985– 98).

to time, no matter what churchmen soberly declared. (They continue to recur, for that matter, no matter what intellectuals declare.)'[29] This terse statement could be equally strongly applied to Victorian culture; it could also be said to apply to the age of Enlightenment itself. Whilst both Schmitt and Greenblatt make much of the Enlightenment as the age that permanently undid the uncanny power of the dead, something persisted beyond the 'Age of Reason' that would cause disquiet even amongst its self-conscious heirs.[30] Vernon Lee would have seen herself as just such a rationalist, whilst M. R. James was the heir to the Evangelicalism that had arisen in reaction to it. Lee and James, in both their upbringings and their personal commitments, personify that persistent struggle between rationality and religious revival that provides the dynamic of much of the argument of Stephen's *History of English Thought in the Eighteenth Century*.

II

Violet Paget, who wrote as Vernon Lee, was brought up in Italy by a consciously Voltairean, freethinking mother, herself the child of a father whose eighteenth-century rationalism had put him at odds with an England which he thought altogether too rigidly given over to piously driven politics. Born in 1856, six years before M. R. James, Lee died in 1935, a year before him, but, aside from writing ghost stories and a shared preoccupation with the monuments of the past, they had little in common, save that both were born, and largely lived, as Victorians, and, what is more, as Victorians of a firmly homosocial cast of mind and spirit. Most importantly, Lee was brought up as a legatee of the very brands of eighteenth-century rationalism against which the Evangelicalism imbibed by M. R. James's father had so violently reacted.[31] What religion would have been for the generality of mid-nineteenth-century women, the progressive evolutionism of Henry Thomas Buckle, as developed in his enormously influential *History of Civilization in England* (1857 to 1861) (which contained much reflection on eighteenth-century England, Scotland, and France), was to become to Lee's mother. Mrs Paget saw in Buckle's writings the

[29] Greenblatt, *Hamlet*, 102.

[30] Schmitt, *Ghosts*, 224–7; Greenblatt, *Hamlet*, 46–9, 229.

[31] Peter Gunn, *Vernon Lee: Violet Paget, 1856–1935* (London, 1964), 1, 14, 16–17.

inspiration for a life lived as part of a progressive process, and she saw in it a spirit that would foster in the coming generations the same liberating faith in the future. The eighteenth and the nineteenth centuries were thus richly combined in the secular education of the young Violet Paget, just as they would be in the imagination of Vernon Lee, the androgynous writer and critic who this predominantly self-taught and independently minded young woman would quickly become.

For Lee, the supernatural was always to take a very different form from that evoked by most of her contemporaries; for her, ghosts are frequently the products of scholarship and the attendant dangers of a life only half-lived in the present: M. R. James's and Lee's protagonists usually suffer as a result of their having too great a love of the past, which comes dangerously to haunt them as a result of their inattention to the vital importance of the present.[32] The 'ghostly' took a fictional form in Lee's short stories, but was itself firmly based in a psychologically aware notion of aesthetics consciously independent of—indeed, often directly antithetical to—the supernatural components of Christianity, a system of ideas which she had only ever known as a relic of the 'past' that constantly fascinated her.[33] Writing in 1893 in the introduction to *Althea*, a collection of dialogues, she emphasized that 'some of us, professed unbelievers, have traversed sloughs of despond by no means inferior to those of the orthodox'. One has to remind oneself that this text pre-dates Freud's *Totem and Taboo* by some twenty years when she goes on to declare that, by not following some of her friends 'back into unsatisfactory orthodoxy', into 'the darkness revealed by reason', she preferred to demonstrate how 'increased thoughtfulness and experience ought to make such intellectual apostasy more difficult, by showing the unreasonableness, the exaggerated personality, the childish expectation that all things should be arranged to suit our likings, which is always at the back of it'. This escape from the childlike and the 'barbarously odious' was a consciously generational undertaking, as she observed that 'we have all of us, however unorthodox, been nourished on theological

[32] Christa Zorn has argued that the narrative uncertainties deployed by Lee in her fantastic stories allowed her to develop a critique of conventional history writing, particularly as it applied to the growing fields of art and cultural history: *Vernon Lee: Aesthetics, History, and the Victorian Female Intellectual* (Athens, Oh., 2003), pp. xxiv, xxxi, 140–8.

[33] For valuable commentary on Lee and the supernatural as a means whereby she could experience the past at first hand, see Julia Briggs, *Night Visitors: The Rise and Fall of the English Ghost Story* (London, 1978), 111–23.

notions and ideals . . . it may take generations, even among the least hampered by the world's older generations, before other notions and ideals have become organic in young minds'.[34] Lee's struggle against such tribal memories and generational pressures was quickly to become that of Freud, her direct contemporary.

Lee's was an aesthetic philosophy predicated on the 'natural' as the source of all knowledge and wisdom, so that for her, as she had earlier noted in an essay on aesthetics published in 1883, 'the hostility between the supernatural and the artistic is well-nigh as great as the hostility between the supernatural and the logical'.[35] When acted upon by the imagination of the artist, the 'natural' transcends everyday experience into something stronger than the traditionally conceived supernatural of conventionally religious minds: 'This is the real supernatural, born of the imagination and its surroundings, the vital, the fluctuating, the potent, and it is this which the artist of every age, from Phidias to Giotto, from Giotto to Blake, has been called upon to make known to the multitude.'[36] If the supernatural was thereby rescued from the metaphysical realm favoured by Christianity, the ghostly was likewise redefined as a fundamentally modern aspect of a post-religious sensibility.

Lee's reasoning on this front was characteristically binary, as is apparent in her analysis of how it was increasingly the case that the modern world of post-Enlightenment reason could undo the potentially disastrous legacies of centuries of faith, both pre-Christian and Christian:

> We have forms of the supernatural in which we believe from acquiescence of habit, but they are not vital; we have a form of the supernatural in which, from logic and habit, we disbelieve, but which is vital; and the form of the supernatural is the ghostly. We none of us believe in ghosts as logical possibilities, but we most of us conceive of them as imaginative possibilities; we can still feel the ghostly, and thence it is that a ghost is the only thing that can in any respect replace for us the divinities of old, and enable us to understand, if only for a minute, the imaginative power which they possessed, and of which they were despoiled not only by logic, but by art. By *ghost* we do not mean the vulgar apparition which is seen or heard in told or written tales; we mean

[34] Vernon Lee, 'Introductory', in *Althea: A Second Book of Dialogues on Aspirations and Duties* (London, 1894), pp. ix–xviii, at pp. xii–xiii.

[35] Lee, 'Faustus and Helena' in *Belcarro, Being Essays on Sundry Aesthetical Questions* (London, 1883), 70–105, at p. 74.

[36] Ibid. 80.

the ghost which slowly rises up in our mind, the haunter not of corridors and staircases, but of our fancies.[37]

Lee's ghosts of the mind had a distinctly Enlightenment pedigree, but one in which, according to her narrative of intellectual and cultural history, figures such as Goethe had initiated a shift into Romanticism through their disillusionment with the worldly experience that had underpinned Enlightenment conceptions of reason:

It was from this sickness of the prosaic, this turning away from logical certainty, that the men of the end of the eighteenth century and the beginning of this century, the men who had finally destroyed belief in the religious supernatural, who were bringing light with new sciences of economy, philology, and history—Schiller, Goethe, Herder, Coleridge—left the lecture-room and the laboratory, and set gravely to work on ghostly tales and ballads.[38]

Lee's commitment to the truths of art had removed her from the merely reactive rationality of her grandfather's generation of freethinkers, allowing her to appreciate the full force of the shift initiated in Goethe's iconic *Faust*, with its return to the power of the supernatural and the uncanny.[39]

One has to infer, then, that, according to Lee, only a historicized imagination, which could appreciate what marked out the thinking of one era from another, could understand the nature and implications of the post-religious supernatural. By historicizing belief, Lee could seem to champion an age of faith over one of mere rationality, but it was a history considered as a branch of aesthetics and not a commitment to religious belief systems that allowed the student to understand such differences. The Victorian aesthete could value Christopher Marlowe's *Doctor Faustus* over Goethe's *Faust* precisely because she had gained from post-Enlightenment thought and experience an insight into earlier ways of believing; once again, in this intergenerational family romance, the granddaughter assumes for herself a depth of understanding denied to her grandfather's less imaginative generation:

The Mephistophilis of Marlowe, in those days when devils still dwelt in people, required none of Goethe's wit or poetry; the mere fact of his being a devil,

[37] Lee, *Belcarro*, 93. [38] Ibid. 97.

[39] 'It was from this rebellion against the tyranny of the possible that Goethe was charmed with that culmination of all impossibilities, that most daring of ghost stories, the story of Faustus and Helena. He felt the seduction of the supernatural, he tried to embody it—and he failed.' (Ibid. 97.)

with the very real association of flame and brimstone in this world and the next was sufficient to inspire interest in him; whereas in 1800, with Voltaire's novels and Hume's treatises on the table, a dull devil was no more endurable than any other sort of love.[40]

The devils and ghosts that Greenblatt observes swarming onto the Renaissance stage were, Lee observed, still part of an enchanted universe: the philosophers of the Enlightenment had disenchanted the world sufficiently to expel them from their imaginations, but it had failed fully to exorcize them, and they returned to disturb the comforts of the Victorians.

The ghostly is often present as a palpable metaphor for the richly imagined relationship between the past and the present in Lee's writings; it is particularly potent in her reflections on the power of art, especially music. In her last major work, *Music and its Lovers* (1934), a study in what she called 'psychological aesthetics', she characterized a phenomenon of hearing music that is not actually being played as 'haunting by music', instancing a visit to Delphi in 1908 when, as she was walking though the Sanctuary of Apollo, music from Gluck's operas *Alceste* and *Elena and Paride* 'haunted me'.[41] In an essay, 'Hearing Music', published four years before her experience at Delphi, Lee had related this sensation to a poet's insight:

'Tis in this sense, methinks, that we should understand the saying of Keats—to wit, that in a great many cases the happiest conjunction of music and the soul occurs during what the profane call silence; the very fact of music haunting our mind, while every other sort of sound may be battering our ear, showing our highest receptivity.[42]

The sensation of 'haunting by music' is something that went all the way back to her *Studies in Eighteenth-Century Italy*. Contemplating her cast of once celebrated but now neglected composers and musicians, the young Lee observed, with an elegiac tone that pervades much of her writing, 'all such ghosts of forgotten genius are poetical'.[43]

In a short chapter devoted to the Venetian playwright Carlo Gozzi (the influence of whose work would lead, ultimately, to Puccini's *Turandot*),

[40] Lee, *Belcarro*, 98. On Marlowe's *Doctor Faustus* as consciously secularizing, see Greenblatt, *Hamlet in Purgatory*, 154–6, 236, 258–9.

[41] Lee, *Music and its Lovers* (London, 1934), 451–2; she also used the phrase 'Chante Interiéur' to characterize such experiences: 113–14, 170–1, 508–9.

[42] Lee, 'Hearing music', in *Hortus Vitae: Essays on the Gardening of Life* (London, 1904), 45–54, at p. 49.

[43] Lee, *Studies of the Eighteenth Century in Italy* (1880), 120.

she observed that 'he had, unconsciously, evoked the grotesque world of the supernatural, and the supernatural world would not let its wizard go'. Again, for Gozzi, as for Lee, the worlds of the supernatural and of art fuse in the inspiration of the artist and the experience of the aesthete:

the indistinct voice in the wind, the hazy shapes in the moonlight, all this is incomprehensible to him; he wants *art*, and he is right; but below art, below the clear, the realized, the complete, is a limbo of fair unborn ghosts, shadowy and vague, of distantly heard memories, of vaguely felt emotions of pathos and joy. Let us not despise that limbo, that chaos; out of it emerges every masterpiece, and in it lies hidden many a charming or sublime shape which those who know the secret spell can evoke out of the midst of ever-changing forms which surround it.[44]

Meetings with such ghosts have something of the tryst about them, as witness her *envoi* to this instance of historical empathy (Lee, the consummate Europeanist, introduced this translation of Herder's notion of *Einfühlung* into English):

The men and women of the Italian eighteenth century are still mere ghosts, whom we have scared in our search after art; for whom we yet feel we know not what vague friendship and pity. And now we turn away from them with reluctance, from these men and women whom we have met in our rambles through the forgotten world of the Italian eighteenth century, these poets, and composers, and playwrights, and singers, to whom we have listened so long and so often; nay, even the poor crabbed little academic pedants and fops, at whom we have so often laughed, have become something to us, and even to them, with their absurdities as to the others with their greatness, we bid farewell with something akin to sorrow.[45]

Lee was preoccupied by 'that dead, forgotten world of art'.[46] It was her self-imposed task to act as a bridge from the aesthetically hungry present into that nostalgic landscape, to reanimate the shadows of disembodied ghosts for the understanding of the living present. In a suitably entitled essay, 'The Immortality of Maestro Galuppi'—with its deliberate echoes of Browning's 'A Toccata of Maestro Galuppi'—there is a moment of pre-Proustian synaesthesia, as a day in Venice given over to the composer's honour ends in grey light: 'It is,' writes Lee, 'the colour of the dead melodies . . . the colours . . . of the forgotten songs.'[47]

[44] Lee, *Studies*, 277, 283. [45] Ibid. 295. [46] Ibid. 139.

[47] Lee, 'The immortality of Maestro Galuppi', in *Juvenilia: Being a Second Series of Essays on Sundry Aesthetic Questions* (2 vols., London, 1887), ii. 2–17, at pp. 16–17. She refers approvingly to Browning's poem in *Studies*, 101, and, noting the once merely

Elsewhere, she referred to 'the embalming power of music'.[48] The same quality of the uncanny attached to buildings, as well as to music. In her essay, 'In Praise of Old Houses', Lee cited a Yorkshire friend's fear of such properties: '*There seemed to be other* people in it besides the living,' a reaction which Lee, a keen and perceptive traveller with a strongly developed sense of time and place, developed approvingly elsewhere.[49] A devotee of Rousseau, whom she admired as a music critic as well as a precursor of romantic sensibilities, Lee visited Les Chamettes, a house associated with the philosopher, with Jean-Jacques very much in mind. Her description of the house she visited is a process which reversed the fears of her friend, allowing Lee to instantiate her own secular and oddly pleasing sense of haunting:

> The house you enter stands empty, but with the air of having been inhabited till yesterday, though inhabited a little by ghosts: chairs and tables are in their places on the broken brick floor or dusty parquet; a big Louis XV sideboard also with a few coarse Strasbourg plates and a set of pewter; and beds, in their alcoves, with moth-eaten silk quilts; while on the walls, among mirrors cracked and dimmed, hang the portraits of the late owners.

It is a house, she observes, 'ready to be inhabited by any purchaser who should have the nerve to share a house with inmates not of this world'. The most perfect house she had ever seen, not the least of its becoming qualities was that it was: 'So completely and perfectly, also, of the Past!'[50] The whole essay is an oblique commentary on the worlds of Rousseau's *Confessions* and Goethe's *Wilhelm Meister*, works by two of her greatest eighteenth-century masters; others—besides the myriad of novelists she

quotidian nature of the past, in 'In praise of old houses', in *Limbo and Other Essays* (London, 1897), 19–41, at p. 40: 'Reading over Browning's *Galuppi* lately it struck me that this dead world of vanity was no more charming or poetical than the one we live in, when it also was alive.' On her view of the musical equivalences of 'A Toccata of Galuppi', see *Music and its Lovers*, 92, 96. Browning had referred admiringly to the young Vernon Lee in *Asolado* (1889): Gunn, *Vernon Lee*, 2. An association between haunting and synaesthesia is present in the opening of a 1904 essay, 'Sere and yellow': ' "Alors que je me croyais aux derniers jours de l'automne, dans un jardin dépouillé." The words are Madame de Hauterive's, one of the most charming among eighteenth-century letter-writers; but one of whom, for all the indiscretion of that age, we know little or nothing: a delicate, austere outline merely, a reserved and sensitive ghost shrinking into the dimness.' (*Hortus Vitae*, 151–63, at p. 151.)

[48] Lee, 'The love of the saints', in *Renaissance Fancies and Studies: Being a Sequel to Euphorion* (London, 1895), 1–63, at p. 30.

[49] Lee, 'In praise of older houses', 21.

[50] Lee, 'Les charmettes', in *The Enchanted Woods: And Other Essays on the Genius of Places* (London, 1909), 173–82, at pp. 177–9.

admired, from Richardson to Marivaux and Laclos—included Vico (to her the solitary 'thinker' of the Italian eighteenth century), and Winckelmann, who, following her mentor Walter Pater, she saw as the original creator of the type of aesthetic vision to which she devoted so much of her life and writings.[51] A Paterian to her core, Lee was particularly dismissive of Ruskin's dismissal of the plastic arts of the eighteenth century, answering his claim that the eighteenth century was morally bad in sardonic antitheses regarding:

> the fiendish wickedness of the 18th century, that abominable age which first taught men the meaning of justice as distinguished from mercy, of humanity as distinguished from charity: which first taught us not to shrink from evil but to combat it. And thus, because the 18th century is proved by its smirking fumbellowed goddesses and handkerchief-Garrotted urns to be utterly, morally, abominable, the one great art which flourished in this period, the glorious music of Bach, and Gluck, and Marcello, and Mozart, must necessarily be silently carted off to the dust heap of artistic baseness.[52]

The eighteenth century thus remained an immensely rewarding imaginative resource throughout Lee's life, so that when she developed her early interests beyond the neglected eighteenth century, backwards into the Renaissance—the study of which she pioneered, alongside Ruskin, J. A. Symonds, and Jacob Burckhardt—she did so under the imagined gaze of her eighteenth-century masters. She created in the process a sense of aesthetic genealogies not so unlike those promoted in the writings of her great contemporary, Nietzsche (with whose disavowal of the 'corrupt' Wagner she was in complete accord):

> For even so short a time ago, the Middle Ages were only beginning to be more than a mere historical expression, Antiquity was being only then critically discovered; and the Renaissance, but vaguely seen and quite unformulated by the first men, Gibbon and Roscoe, who perceived it at all, was still virtually unknown. To Goethe, therefore, it might easily have seemed as if the antique Helena had only just been evoked, and as if of her union with the worn-out

[51] Lee, *Studies*, 147 (on Vico); on Winckelmann, see the essay in *Belcarro*, 'The child in the Vatican', 17–48, at p. 24, 'Orpheus and Euridice', 49–69, at pp. 53–4; and 'A seeker of pagan perfection', in *Renaissance Studies and Fancies*, 163–231, at p. 202. On her debt to Pater, see 'The imaginative art of the Renaissance' and 'Valedictory' in *Renaissance Studies and Fancies*, 65–133, 233–60, at pp. 114 and note, 248–60. She had dedicated *Euphorion* to Pater, 'in appreciation of that which, in expounding the beautiful things of the past, he has added to the beautiful things of the present'.

[52] Lee, 'Ruskinianism: The would-be study of a conscience' in *Belcarro*, 197–29, at pp. 221–22. On Ruskin's highly critical position, see Dinah Birch, 'Ruskin's revised eighteenth century', in *The Victorians and the Eighteenth Century*, 163–81.

century of his birth, a real Euphorion, the age in which ourselves are living, might have been born. But, at the distance of additional time, and from the undreamed-of height upon which historical science has enabled us to stand, we can easily see that in this he would have been mistaken. Not only is our modern culture no child of Faustus and Helena, but it is the complex descendant, strangely featured by atavism from various sides, of many and various civilizations; and the eighteenth century, so far from being a Faustus evoking as his bride the long dead Helena of Antiquity, was in itself a curiously varied grandchild or great-grandchild of such a marriage, its every moral feature, its every intellectual movement proclaiming how much of its being was inherited from Antiquity.[53]

Goethe acted as the efficient guide through the many cultures Lee navigated in her evocative travel books; full of history and personal associations as they are, the guiding presence of Goethe gives them an overall formal consistency, a late Victorian absorption of Goethe's classicizing Romanticism acting as their ideal. It was a Goethean world that she created in her short romantic novel *Ottilie* (1883), which is essentially an elegiac essay on the world of *Werther* and *Wilhelm Meister*. Curiously, she claims to have been haunted by the figures of her novel both before and during its composition; novels, it would seem, just like myths, had their 'distorted phantoms, too hideous for reality, but which haunt and avenge'.[54] Not that the brother and sister who dominate what little action there is in *Ottilie* are anything other than sweetly imagined, Goethean figures, with more than a hint of Dresden china about them; the ghosts of her ghost stories are, however, altogether more sinister. Lee's best-known collection of short stories, *Hauntings* (1890), contains horribly lively spirits of the Renaissance and the seventeenth century—vampires and eerily androgynous men and women—but one of the most celebrated stories in the volume, 'A Wicked Voice', is very much a product of her earliest studies in the history of Italian music. It takes her haunted

[53] Lee, 'Introduction' to *Euphorion: Being Studies of the Antique and the Mediaeval in the Renaissance*, (2 vols., London, 1884), i. 1–13, at pp. 6–7. On Lee's standing as a historian and critic of the Renaissance, see Hilary Fraser, *The Victorians and Renaissance Italy* (Oxford, 1992), 234, 252, Zorn, *Vernon Lee*, 25–59, and Angela Leighton, 'Resurrection of the body: women writers and the idea of the Renaissance', in Chapman and Stabler, *Unfolding the South*, 222–38. Lee's Renaissance was, however, a truly European experience, allowing her to explore comparative themes over time and place, as instanced, most remarkably, in the essay in the first volume, 'The Italy of the English dramatists': *Euphorion*, i. 55–108.

[54] Lee, *Ottilie: An Eighteenth-Century Idyll* (London, 1883), 14; *Studies*, 188.

impressions of the past to a level of perfection that she would rarely reach again.

Lee's *Hauntings* are the result of the interpenetration of past and present, as she stated in the 'Preface' to the collection:

That is the thing—the Past, the more or less remote Past, of which the prose is clean obliterated by distance—that is the place to get our ghosts from. Indeed we live ourselves, we educated folk of modern times, on the borderland of the Past, in houses looking down on troubadours' orchards and Greek folks' pillared courtyards; and a legion of ghosts, very vague and changeful, are perpetually to and fro, fetching and carrying for us between it and the Present.[55]

The narrator of 'A Wicked Voice', a Norwegian composer, 'despised the new-fangled nonsense of Wagner, and returned boldly to the traditions of Handel and Gluck and the divine Mozart, to the supremacy of melody and the respect of the human voice'. This is, however, no coyly celebratory opening, for what the story will detail is how the dangerous voice of a long-dead castrato has come to haunt the composer's present, making the would-be creator of a nationalistic Wagnerian opera, *Ogier the Dane*, into a prisoner of 'the miserable singing-masters of the Past'.[56] The singer in question, Balthasar Cesari, nicknamed Zaffirino, is clearly based on the celebrated castrato Farinelli, by whom the young Violet Paget had long been obsessed. She had absorbed and accepted contemporary valuations of the legendary singer's talent:

His voice, it was universally acknowledged throughout Europe, had been infinitely more voluminous, extensive, and beautiful than any that had been heard before or since; his musical talent far more versatile and astonishing than any other; in short, the eighteenth century was unanimous in placing him alone and far above all its other great singers, his predecessors, contemporaries, and successors.

Farinelli was thus idealized by the young writer, who insisted that:

there is something nobler than romance in this man, who was neither a genius nor a wizard: modest and self-respecting in the most corrupting position, unselfish and forgiving amidst baseness; something which makes him appear like almost an idyllic hero among the artificial, worthless people around him.[57]

Zaffirino is, in these respects, the very reverse of Farinelli, but, in the fascination with the ambiguities of the castrato voice, he is still very

[55] Lee, *Hauntings: Fantastic Stories* (London, 1890), pp. x–xi.
[56] Lee, 'A wicked voice', in *Hauntings*, 195–237, at 195–6.
[57] Lee, *Studies*, 111, 113.

much its haunting representative. Lee was, perhaps, giving away more than she thought when she observed, in the preface to a new edition of *Studies in Eighteenth-Century Italy*, published in 1907, a quarter of a century after its first appearance, that it was the female, contralto voice that had preserved Handel's operatic arias;[58] the ambiguities of gender are central to her appreciation of voices and art. There is much of *fin-de-siècle* decadence in the mood evoked by the story, as in the way the male narrator collapses the worlds of the eighteenth and nineteenth centuries when gazing on a portrait of the singer:

> That effeminate, fat face of his is almost beautiful, with an odd smile, brazen and cruel. I have seen faces like this, if not in real life, at least in my boyish romantic dreams, when I read Swinburne and Baudelaire, the faces of wicked, vindictive women.[59]

The good Farinelli has become the wicked Zaffirino and, in the process, he has acquired a dangerously sexualized identity. One can also deduce, from an observation Lee made in her 1907 preface, that he has become positively vampiric:

> the musicians of former ages may be compared with the ghosts flocking hopelessly round the artificial trench of Odysseus, waiting in vain for the drink which restores their bulk and their voice; spectres, some of them, heroic or lovable, but who, for lack of that life-blood of attention, can never speak to posterity nor lay their hands on its soul.[60]

There is, then, a genuine sense of anxiety in Lee's disinterment of the purely physical traces of long lost voices; it is as if her writing is itself the blood for the ghosts that will bring them back, however fleetingly. Such a preoccupation with the dead appears to be indulged at the cost of the living. Zaffirino, in eighteenth-century life, had killed an admiring woman through the literal instrumentality of his wicked voice, and the composer sees the very moment in the singer's past when this event occurred: as in so many of her ghost stories, past and present are blurred

[58] Lee, 'Retrospective chapter: Preface to the new edition', in *Studies of the Eighteenth Century in Italy* (London, 1907), pp. xiii–xlix, at p. xxii.

[59] Lee, 'A wicked voice', 206. On the strongly Paterian nature of Lee's vivid imaginings of what many critics read as lesbian desire, see Ruth Robbins, 'Apparitions can be deceptive: Vernon Lee's androgynous spectres', in Ruth Robbins and Julian Wolfreys, *Victorian Gothic: Literary and Cultural Manifestations in the Nineteenth Century* (Basingstoke, 2000), 182–200.

[60] Lee, 'Retrospective Chapter', p. xlv.

in 'A Wicked Voice', and a harpsichord which accompanies a swelling voice one minute is seen to be broken and splintered the next.[61]

Three years after 'A Wicked Voice' was published, Lee, in a dialogue called 'Orpheus in Rome', had her alter ego Baldwin confess to his fascination with the original singer, Guadagni, 'for whom Gluck composed his *Orpheus*'. Guadagni, like Farinelli-Zaffarino, is an obsessive haunting, as Baldwin notes: 'It's odd by what caprice one singles out some particular forgotten creature of the past; or rather by what caprice some particular ghost chooses to manifest himself and haunt.' Guadagni is considered to be 'evidently . . . uncanny' by one of Baldwin's party, but so also is a musical instrument, the oboe-like hautboy, whose use in Gluck's opera leads to the claim that 'the hautboy, with its soft shrillness, its quivering breath, or at least this particular hautboy of Gluck's, is like the ghost of a human voice':[62] music, and the voices of singers especially, were potent sources of an aesthetic of the uncanny in Lee's writings. Haunting is an aesthetic metaphor, the aftertaste of immediate experience and sensation, in Lee's writings; aesthetics, acting as something very like the 'natural supernaturalism' of Romanticism, is the space in which to trace the actions of the uncanny in her stories and in her studies in the arts. Religion and its metaphysics are replaced by art and aesthetics in her vision of the spiritual life.

'A Wicked Voice' has also been read as a vividly imagined commentary on Lee's championing of eighteenth-century music over the Wagnerians, and as a subtle evocation of the homoeroticism that accompanied so much aesthetic thought in the 1890s, as well as being an immediately pre-Freudian essay on the fears of castration.[63] It is also a vivid reversal of that fascination with the eighteenth century which the younger Lee had felt. By 1907, in the introduction to a new edition of her first book, she was noting how the eighteenth century in Italy had been

[61] Lee, 'A wicked voice', 233–6. For a positive pre-echo of the image see her fairy tale, *The Prince of the Hundred Soups: A Puppet-Show in Narrative* (London, 1883), at p. 170: 'She was standing by the open spinet. She struck a chord, and, as she spoke the last words, burst into a wonderful, brilliant vocal phrase, triumphant, like her smile.'

[62] Lee, 'Orpheus in Rome' in *Althea*, 51–104, at pp. 51–6, 94. Signora Olimpia Fantastici, the good musical force in *The Prince of the Hundred Soups*, is the feminine reverse of the uncanny, sexually ambiguous male alto in 'A wicked voice', so that only positive results stem from the fact that she is 'the greatest, most beautiful, but also the most fantastic and unruly singer in the world' (*The Prince of the Hundred Soups*, 58).

[63] Carlo Caballero, ' "A wicked voice": On Vernon Lee, Wagner, and the effects of music', *Victorian Studies*, 35 (1992), 385–408; Patricia Pulham, 'The castrato and the cry in Vernon Lee's Wicked voices', *Victorian Literature and Culture*, 30 (2002), 431–7. Wagner is criticized, and Gluck praised, in 'Orpheus in Rome': 84–93.

the 'lumber-room' of her childhood, 'full of the discarded mysteries of lurking ghosts'; as a mature woman she could recognize what the younger woman had failed to see, that 'the Italian eighteenth century was humdrum'.[64] Humdrum in everything, that is, but its music, which she persisted in championing, usually against the admirers of Wagner, of whom the narrator of 'A Wicked Voice' was one.[65] Nonetheless, for all its charm, the eighteenth century can obsess the nineteenth century to a dangerously subversive degree, and Lee's readers are to take seriously the narrator's horror at 'this odious eighteenth century!', 'That cursed eighteenth century!', 'that hated eighteenth century!'[66] It had blunted his inspiration, effectively castrating his creativity: love of the past, even if it is a love created by a fascinating, if sexually ambiguous figure, can, Lee suggested, distort one's living relationship with the present. Ghosts are not exorcized in the therapeutic manner approved of by Freud in Lee's stories; they take over, and not the least of the reasons that they can fatally do so—as in such tales as 'Amour dure' and 'Oke of Okehurst'—is that the imagination can propel their existence in the mind into the external world.

Lee wrote another supernatural tale with an eighteenth-century Italian setting, 'Alberic and the Snake Lady', but it is more in the nature of a typically decadent fairy tale of the 1890s than the sort of complex psychological, aesthetically driven tale typified by 'A Wicked Voice'. 'Alberic and the Snake Lady' first appeared in Aubrey Beardsley's *Yellow Book*; it marks Lee's most obvious experiment with the literature of decadence. With its scenario of an effete, dying dynasty, finally undone by an enchanted and enchanting 'snake-lady', the story has been persuasively read as another of her castration fantasies, somewhere between E. T. A. Hoffmann's 'The Sandman', which Freud famously read as an instance of such anxiety, and Hans Andersen's similarly troubling 'Little Mermaid'.[67] 'Alberic and the Snake Lady', shivering

[64] Lee, 'Retrospective chapter', pp. xvi, xviii. [65] Ibid., p. xxx-liv.

[66] Lee, 'A wicked voice', 206, 218, 223.

[67] Lee, 'Prince Alberic and the Snake Lady', in *Pope Jacynth and Other Fantastic Tales* (London, 1907), 91–111. Freud, 'The Uncanny', in *The Uncanny*, trans. David McLintock (Harmondsworth, 2003), 121–62; Jane Hotchkiss, '(P)revising Freud: Vernon Lee's castration phantasy', in Carola M. Kaplan and Anne B. Simpson (eds.), *Seeing Double: Revisioning Edwardian and Modernist Literature* (Basingstoke, 1996), 21–38; Zorn, *Vernon Lee*, 152–7. On the polymorphous sexuality of snake imagery, see Martha Vicinus, 'The adolescent boy: fin-de-siècle femme fatale?' in Dellamora (ed.), *Victorian Sexual Dissidence*, 21–41. This was not the first time Lee had depicted the confrontation between a young man and a serpent: see also 'The three golden apples'

with sexual ambiguity, and quietly moralizing in tone, is very much a fairy tale for consenting adults; it is an effective evocation of the deadening effects of aestheticism turned decadent. Only the Beardsley who illustrated *The Rape of the Lock* could have hoped to depict the sinuous decor of the court of Luna, whose grotesquely made-up Grand Duke reminds one irresistibly of W. M. Thackeray's drawing, 'An Historical Study', depicting an ancient, spindly, pot-bellied Louis XIV being absorbed by a hitherto empty set of regal robes, and emerging in the process as a resplendently fat, beribboned, bejewelled, but monumentally dead, *Roi Soleil.*[68] Thackeray's *Grand Monarque* was drawn in the same year, 1840, that Carlyle dismissed him, fittingly echoing *King Lear*, as the very antithesis of the heroic: 'Strip your Louis Quatorze of his king-gear, and there *is* left nothing but a poor forked radish with a head fantastically carved;—admirable to no valet.'[69]

Whilst such effete yet masculine bodies figured all that was wrong with the eighteenth century in Lee's writings, the life-enhancing androgyny of Beaumarchais and Mozart's Cherubino represented all that was charmingly ambiguous about it. Cherubino:

> seems a delicate poetic exotic . . . this page, this boy who is almost a girl, with his ribbons and his ballads, his blushes, his guitar and his rapier . . . this is no delicate and gracious young creature of the stock of Elizabethan pages, no sweet exotic in the France of the 1780s; this Cherubino is merely a graceful, coquettish little Greuze figure, with an equivocal simplicity, an ogling *naïveté*, a smirking bashfulness, a hidden audacity of corruption; a creature of Sterne or Marivaux, tricked out in an imitation Medieval garb, with the stolen conscious wink of the eye, the would-be childlike smile, tinged with leer, of eighteenth-century gallantry.[70]

The eighteenth century lived for Lee in two extremes: on the one hand, rouged death; on the other, androgynous ambiguity. It was at once the troublingly aestheticized locus of pampered death, the world

in *Tuscan Fairy Tales* (London, 1880), 21–30. She was an admirer of Hoffmann, to one of whose most celebrated uncanny tales she devoted an essay which began with the assertion that 'There is nothing stranger in the world than music': 'Chapelmaster Kreisler: A study of musical romanticists', in *Belcarro*, 106–28.

68 The drawing, which dates from 1840, is fittingly reproduced in Peter Burke, *The Fabrication of Louis XIV* (New Haven, 1992), at p. 124. The baroque extravagances of the court of Luna are very easily rendered unstable by the interventions of a Gothic past into something very like a court of Lunacy.

69 Thomas Carlyle, *On Heroes, Hero-Worship and the Heroic in History* (1841: Lincoln, Neb., 1966), 184.

70 Lee, 'Cherubino: A psychological art fancy', in *Belcarro*, 129–55, at pp. 135, 137.

of Louis XIV's marmoreal absolutism, and the potential source for the escapist imaginings of a nervous chronicler of same-sex desire. It is not too much to say that Lee was engaged, in every sense, in queering the past. The eighteenth century was very much to Lee what the Renaissance had proved to be to Walter Pater, her much-esteemed exemplar of deeply imagined art historical reflection.

III

M. R. James, the Provost of King's College, is the best known of the three Cambridge heads of house who wrote ghost stories in the early twentieth century. Arthur Gray, the Master of Jesus College, Cambridge, published a short collection of ghost stories in 1919. The first of the stories, 'The Everlasting Club', gestures at the memories of costume that Grant Allen had thought so important in the cross-generational nature of haunting: Gray described a long-locked room in the college, in which 'legs have been stretched and wine and gossip have circulated in the days of wigs and brocade'. This was not, however, a happy memory of the eighteenth century, as Gray noted that the club was just one of the many dissipated societies that had once flourished in Cambridge, and which had 'in their limited provincial way aped the profligacy of such clubs as the Hell Fire Club of London notoriety'. The generally low morals of early eighteenth-century Cambridge were, Gray emphasized, lowered even further by the Everlasting Society, at least one of whose members had been 'in attendance on the Young Pretender in Paris'; these were in the 'graceless days of George II', which were succeeded 'by times of outward respectability, when religion and morals were no longer publicly challenged'. The last remaining member of the society could not, therefore, have expected to survive long into the reign of the pious George III, and, accordingly, away from them he was taken, seemingly by supernatural forces, though as Gray teasingly confided in his readers, 'Such superstitious belief must be treated with contemptuous incredulity.'[71] Plainly, Gray's heart was not in the eighteenth century, and his condemnation of it as immoral and profligate was fairly typical of his age. It would take the work of a Cambridge don of the next generation, D. A. Winstanley, to rescue

[71] Arthur Gray, 'The everlasting club', in *Tedious Brief Tales of Granta and Gramarye* (Cambridge, 1919), 1–8.

eighteenth-century Cambridge from its Victorian detractors.[72] A. C. Benson, the Master of Magdalene College, James's Eton friend and contemporary, wrote several ghost stories, but set none of them in the eighteenth century, unless an otherwise anonymous series of stories that appeared in the *Magdalene College Magazine* between 1911 and 1914 contributed by one 'B.', all but a couple of which concerned hauntings in eighteenth-century Magdalene, were his work, as their modern editor has speculated.[73]

James, like Leslie Stephen, was the product of an Evangelical family. Born in 1862, a couple of years before Stephen's religious doubts would compel him to leave Cambridge, James dedicated his life to his college and university before retiring in 1918 to the provostship of Eton. A consciously conventional churchman who was to remain solidly Protestant, James nevertheless moved some way from his father's committed Evangelicalism. His father was also both an Etonian and a former fellow of King's, where he had imbibed the Evangelical temper inaugurated in the college by Charles Simeon in the opening decades of the nineteenth century.[74] The younger James was never as sure of his sense of vocation as his father had been, and his decision not to pursue ordination has continued to prove something of a puzzle to his biographers. Nevertheless, whatever the certainties of his father's generation, from the date of his own election to a King's fellowship in 1887, James had settled into a changing and potentially turbulent academic atmosphere in a Cambridge in which the revolutionary New Testament scholarship of Westcott and Hort was making its mark on conventional belief; James's own explorations in what he called

[72] D. A. Winstanley, *The University of Cambridge in the Eighteenth Century* (Cambridge, 1922); *Unreformed Cambridge: A Study of Certain Aspects of the University in the Eighteenth Century* (Cambridge, 1935).

[73] Rosemary Pardoe (ed.), *When the Door is Shut and Other Ghost Stories by 'B'* (Runcorn, 1986). None of A. C. Benson's ghost stories, collected in *The Hill of Trouble and Other Stories* (London, 1903), and *The Isles of Sunset* (London, 1904), has an eighteenth-century setting. Benson's brothers also wrote in this vein. The two supernatural collections by R. H. Benson, a Catholic priest, are essentially a celebration of his religion, by turns morbid, in *The Light Invisible* (London, 1903), and quirkily apologetic, in *The Mirror of Shallot: Composed of Tales Told at a Symposium* (London, 1907). E. F. Benson, the most secular-minded of the brothers, has a sceptical friend of Voltaire suffer an agonizing death in 1760 as the result of seeing two seventeenth-century ghosts, in 'How fear departed from the Long Gallery' in *The Room in the Tower and Other Stories* (London, 1912), 133–55, at pp. 139–41.

[74] Pfaff, *James*, 62; Michael Cox, *M. R. James: An Informal Portrait* (London, 1983), 2, 72. On Simeon, see Charles Smythe, *Simeon and Church Order: A Study of the Evangelical Revival in Cambridge in the Eighteenth Century* (Cambridge, 1940).

'Christian archaeology' were also confirming suspicions common to many of his intellectual generation regarding the necessary relativity of religious beliefs.[75] Indeed, James's lifelong interest in the religiously ambivalent world of apocryphal scholarship may provide a clue to the distance he sometimes seems to have felt, however subliminally, from conventional Christian apologetics. As the literary critic Austin Warren noted, no one seems to have questioned James about his fascination with the apocryphal and the heretical, and he himself never openly questioned his own 'subterranean motives' in pursuing work on 'the Apocrypha', those otherwise forgotten books of the Christian Bible, whose ultimate, and sometimes arbitrary, exclusion from scriptural authority so suggestively questioned the status of holy writ.[76] Whether or not such apparently unconscious scepticism implies a refusal to be explicit about religious and metaphysical doubts, critics of the nineteenth-century ghost story have to take seriously Jack Sullivan's suggestion that the genre might well embody the very scepticism it ostensibly seeks to combat:[77] in this sense, James may have been much closer to such irreligious exponents of the form as Grant Allen (a journalistic favourite of Leslie Stephen, an excerpt from one of whose characteristically sceptical tales provides an epigraph to this chapter) than he would ever have cared to admit, either to himself or—still less—to others.

Furthermore, as Sullivan noted, James's ghostly tales are consciously addressed to readers with a sceptical turn of mind; and that scepticism is often implicitly eighteenth as well as explicitly twentieth century in orientation.[78] A great many of James's always malevolent ghosts are eighteenth-century revenants; and several of his tales take place during the long eighteenth century. His first collection, *Ghost Stories of an Antiquary* (1904), contained stories that dated back to the early 1890s. All but four of the eight stories assembled in this slim but influential volume either had eighteenth-century settings, or else involved the

[75] Pfaff, *James*, 90, 425. For another attempt at resolving the puzzle, see Cox, *James*, 72, 86–7, 165.

[76] Austin Warren, 'The marvels of M. R. James, antiquary' in *Connections* (Ann Arbor, Mich., 1970), 86–107, at p. 99. Julia Briggs has seen in his playfulness with textual authority in the ghost stories a parody of his work on biblical scholarship; the citation of learned texts—real or imaginary—is shown to be capable of proving almost anything: *Night Visitors*, 125.

[77] Jack Sullivan, *Elegant Nightmares: The English Ghost Story from Le Fanu to Blackwood* (Athens, Oh., 1978), 4.

[78] Ibid. 79.

actions in the nineteenth century of ghosts dating from the long eighteenth century. The tally is slightly smaller in the next collection, *More Ghost Stories* (1911), but even there three of the seven stories it contains had a markedly eighteenth-century provenance. No fewer than three of the five stories that constituted *A Thin Ghost and Other Stories* (1919) shared eighteenth-century associations. The pattern is also marked in the final collection, *A Warning to the Curious* (1925), with three of the six stories being firmly rooted in the experience of the long eighteenth century. A late story, 'Rats', contributed to Lady Cynthia Asquith's 1931 miscellany, *Shudders*, contains an unusually active eighteenth-century skeleton, kept more or less safely under lock and key in a nineteenth-century seaside inn.[79] Something like a half of James's published ghost stories are thus concerned with eighteenth-century hauntings; a story recently published from a manuscript at King's, 'The Fenstanton Witch', similarly concerns two eighteenth-century undergraduates of the college and the consequences of their ill-advised adventures in amateur diabolism.[80]

Certain patterns of association are discernible in James's preoccupations with the eighteenth century. The first theme concerns the nineteenth-century consequences of eighteenth-century necromancy. In 'Canon Alberic's Scrap Book', the opening story in his first collection, the nefarious dealings of a diabolically inclined French canon, who had died in 1701, come to afflict that most modern of personages, a Cambridge don with a taste for photography.[81] Similarly, in 'Mr Humphreys and his Inheritance', a story which first appeared in 1911, an eighteenth-century squire returned from the Grand Tour with a set of beliefs that had frightening consequences for his late nineteenth-century successor, Mr Wilson of Wilsthorpe, who had undertaken a great deal of building at his country seat, and had also been an enthusiast for pagan religion, a type that clearly fascinated James.[82] This was an associated theme that haunted his ghost stories, whatever their period settings, but it is especially visible in those with an eighteenth-century

[79] James, 'Rats', in Cynthia, Lady Asquith, *Shudders: A Collection of New Nightmare Tales* (London, 1930).

[80] James, *The Fenstanton Witch and Others*, ed. Rosemary Pardoe (Chester, 1999).

[81] James, 'Canon Alberic's Scrap-Book' in *Ghost-Stories of an Antiquary* (London, 1904), 1–28.

[82] James, 'Mr Humphreys and his inheritance', in *More Ghost Stories* (London, 1911), 215–74. A complex reading of the story as a religious allegory is offered by Martin Hughes, 'A maze of secrets in a story by M. R. James', *Durham University Journal*, 85 (1993), 81–93.

setting. In 'Lost Hearts', Mr Abney, a studious heathen revivalist with a pronounced interest in the mystery cults of the later Roman empire, allows his reading to get the better of him, leading to a bloody outbreak of antiquarian enthusiasm and sacrifical violence. Abney, who had contributed a description of an ancient statue of Mithras to the *Gentleman's Magazine*, succumbs to the results of his own horribly misplaced scholarship (when a comparatively old man) on his Lincolnshire estate in 1812; his peculiar scholarly tastes, allied with a penchant for child sacrifice, are, therefore, a much exaggerated variant of those of a post-Christian generation indebted to the work of writers such as Gibbon.[83] In the meticulous plotting and historical verisimilitude of 'Lost Hearts', James plainly relished taking the Gibbonian brand of gentlemanly semi-paganism to its logical limit. Eighteenth-century rationalism had transformed itself into irrationalism, a theme whose resonances Carlyle had enjoyed tracing in his *French Revolution*.

James was always suspicious of secularizing forces, and he seems to have exorcized some of these fears through ghost stories that detailed the grisly consequences of earlier repudiations of Christianity. A self-conscious Victorian moralist right up to his death in 1936, he saw himself as a fundamentally Christian scholar, and he heartily disliked the secular scholarship of such consciously post-Christian writers as Stephen, with whom he had stayed in Cornwall in 1888 as a friend of his stepson, George Duckworth. This was an occasion that greatly troubled James's mother, especially when she learned that her son thought his friend's sister, Stella Duckworth, extremely beautiful. She feared an unsuitable match, in which a pious James might marry a member of the irreligious Stephen clan, a religiously explosive variant of the Stephen family romance.[84] Her worries were excessive: James would never marry anyone, however beautiful, whether irreligious or devout, and his sexual ambivalence was least likely to resolve itself into companionship with a woman, though many of his friends tried to persuade him otherwise, especially when he became provost of King's.[85] Even when represented by Stella Duckworth, or her charismatic step-cousin J. K. Stephen, another young fellow of King's, with whom James

[83] James, 'Lost hearts', in *Ghost-Stories of an Antiquary*, 29–52.

[84] Cox, *James*, 87; Pfaff, *James*, 64, 88 n. 42.

[85] Pfaff, *James*, 62; Cox, *James*, 165. As Richard Holmes has noted 'it is the unspecifically feminine, the stiffening ectoplasm of *feminality* which seems to carry in the end the maximum emotional charge in James's fiction': 'M. R. James and others', in *Sidetracks: Explorations of a Romantic Biographer* (London, 2000), 161–71, at p. 170.

was on close terms, heathenism was anathema to him.[86] Whether it took the morally outrageous form of eighteenth-century paganism, or the morally serious, but no less distasteful, shape of nineteenth-century secularism, unbelief was for him simply unimaginable as a philosophy of life.

Such was the strength of James's dislike of the forces of secularization he saw at work around him that aspects of his Anglicanism assumed a vigorous, not to say vindictive, form in the sometimes repulsive logic of his fiction. Opponents of the Church of England at its most triumphant were wont to meet grisly ends. In 'The Uncommon Prayer-Book', an avaricious book-dealer, Poschwitch, is drained of his life blood by the indistinct but long-dead form of Lady Sadleir, an anti-Cromwellian who had dared to have Prayer Books printed during the Interregnum.[87] Another outsider, an Irish peer whose parents had given him the name Saul—' "whatever his godfathers could have been thinking of" '—meets a grisly end in 'The Residence at Whitminster' while still a child, the direct result of the witchcraft he had practised in his native land. The express liminality of Ireland in the British polity, and the suggestion that it had not been properly Christianized, is typical of James's insular variety of anti-Catholicism.[88] 'The Residence at Whitminster', a complex narrative, not only works on the level of geographical distancing—the young Irish peer dies in the environs of Whitminster, an English foundation which had contrived to survive in the interstices of the Dissolution and the Reformation up to the era of reform in the 1830s—but also in terms of temporal distancing.[89] The story begins with an Anglican clergyman disapprovingly surveying

[86] On his friendship with the notoriously unstable J. K. Stephen, the much loved son of Sir James Fitzjames Stephen, see Cox, *James*, 85, and Pfaff, *James*, 83. James was happy to recall his membership of J. K. Stephen's Coffee Club at Cambridge: M. R. James, *Eton and King's: Recollections, Mostly Trivial 1875–1925* (London, 1926), 170.

[87] James, 'The uncommon prayer-book', in *A Warning to the Curious and Other Stories* (London, 1925), 35–69. The story was inspired by the fanatically royalist Dame Anne Sadleir, who had donated to Trinity College, Cambridge, the Trinity Apocalypse, on which James quickly became an authority: Pfaff, *James*, 189; Cox, *James*, 144.

[88] He opposed Irish Home Rule, remarking in 1888 of Irish separatists: 'I have no patience with these people. Neither have I with the Home Rulers.' (Pfaff, *James*, 99; Cox, *James*, 107.) Such was his suspicion of Catholicism that, as provost in 1909, he refused permission for a performance in King's College Chapel of Elgar's *Dream of Gerontius*, a setting of Newman's poem, because, as he told A. C. Benson, it was 'too papistical': Cox, *James*, 72.

[89] James, 'The residence at Whitminster', in *A Thin Ghost and Others* (London, 1919), 1–47. Warren observes of James's attitude to time that: 'The antiquary and the mimic combine in the delight, and the skill, with which James varies the times of his

Lord Saul's behaviour in 1730, and it moves on to the haunting of the Residence by Lord Saul and his particularly repugnant familiars in the 1820s. A story published in 1919 thus examines the interrelations of two moments, divided by almost a hundred years, within the long eighteenth century, and it articulates in so doing a strong sense of the ineluctable and persistently troubling presence of the past in the present that is of the essence of 'haunting' in much nineteenth-century fiction. It is a story that resonates strongly with the theme of Henry James's *The Sense of the Past.*

'The Residence at Whitminser' gave James an opportunity for imaginative literary engagement with earlier historical sensibilities, providing him with a forum in which the imagination can be brought to articulate historical questions relating to such contentious issues as notions of historical progress and secularization. His stories demonstrate how a gothicized version of English history provides a different means of meditating imaginatively on the past, whether through Lady Sadleir's contempt for Cromwell, or, as instanced in 'The Rose Garden', via the haunting after-effects of Judge Jeffreys' trials in the West Country, that familiar staple of Whig historiography. The historical verisimilitude of his tales is at the centre of this spectral twist on the otherwise familiar. Vivid echoes of the language of Judge Jeffreys as recorded in the State Trials of the 1680s—a great favourite with Leslie Stephen—are registered in mock collations in 'The Rose Garden' and in 'Martin's Close', while in the enigmatic 'Two Doctors', he reproduced the style of a legal dossier from the reign of Queen Anne, and in 'The Diary of Mr Poynter' he performed the same service for an earlier type of the scholarly antiquarian don with a taste for an unlikely tale, Thomas Hearne.[90] The mosaic-like narrative of 'The Stalls of Barchester Cathedral', which details the terrible fate of a murderous late eighteenth-century cleric whose unconventional pursuit of preferment is fatally blighted by a curse on seventeenth-century cathedral carvings, allowed James to evoke the instantly recognizable cadences of the *Gentleman's Magazine.* The obituary notice for the unfortunate Dr Haynes is a small masterpiece of eighteenth-century pastiche, and merits lengthy quotation accordingly:

stories. The time is often double: the traditional device of the discovery and reading *now* of some document written in the remote or more recent past.' (*Connections*, 99.)

[90] James, 'The rose garden' and 'Martin's Close', in *More Ghost Stories*, 19–44, 169–213; 'Two doctors' and 'The diary of Mr Poynter', in *A Thin Ghost*, 135–52, 49–71. On Stephen's interest in such matters, see 'The state trials', in *Hours in a Library* (3 vols., London, 1904), iii. 287–315.

On February 26th, at his residence in the Cathedral close at Barchester, the Venerable Archdeacon Haynes, D.D. aged 57, Archdeacon of Sowerbridge and Rector of Pickhill and Candley. He was of—College, Cambridge, and where, by talent and assiduity, he commanded the esteem of his seniors; and when, at the usual time, he took his first degree, his name stood high in the list of *wranglers*. These academical honours procured for him within a short time a Fellowship of his College . . . His speedy preferments, first to a Prebend, and subsequently to the dignity of Precentor in the Cathedral of Barchester form an eloquent testimony to the respect in which he was held and his eminent qualifications. He succeeded to the Archdeaconry upon the sudden decease of Archdeacon Pulteney in 1810. His sermons, ever conformable to the principles of the religion and Church which he adorned, displayed in no ordinary degree without the least trace of enthusiasm, the refinement of the scholar united with the graces of the Christian. Free from sectarian violence, and informed by the spirit of the truest charity, they will long dwell in the memories of his hearers . . . The productions of his pen include an able defence of Episcopacy, which, though, often perused by the author of this tribute to his memory, afford but one additional instance of the want of liberality and enterprise which is a too common characteristic of the publishers of our generation . . . The urbanity and hospitality of the subject of these lines will not readily be forgotten by those who enjoyed his acquaintance. His interest in the venerable and awful pile under whose hoary vault he was so punctual an attendant, and particularly in the musical portion of its rites, might be termed filial, and formed a strong and delightful contrast to the polite indifference displayed by too many of our Cathedral dignitaries at the present time.[91]

The knowing bow to the complaint of all generations that their generation is lamentably less godly than its predecessors is a slyly ironic challenge to secular notions of progress. It was a complaint James, a passionate lover of King's and its music, would eventually and all too frequently make of his own successors in Cambridge. For James's reader of the generous tribute in the *Gentleman's Magazine* the irony is that Dr Haynes, the embodiment of charity, grace, and loyalty, is discovered to have been an ambitious, if troubled, murderer, and a suborner of witnesses in his household. He meets with a brutal end.

Language, as incarnated in texts recovered from a dangerous past, is a medium vivid with the presence of the uncanny in James's writings; it haunts his antiquarian heroes, who tend to come across exactly the appropriate text precisely in those terrified intervals that follow their

[91] James, 'The stalls of Barchester Cathedral', in *More Ghost* Stories, 135–67, at pp. 137–9. For a suggestive reading of the tale, see Martin Hughes, 'Murder of the cathedral: A story by M. R. James', *Durham University Journal*, 87 (1995), 73–98.

confrontation with otherwise unspeakable horrors. This symmetry of language and experience, at the very root of Freud's notion of the uncanny, is also apparent in James's evocation of the *Sortes Biblicae,* the technique of biblical divination, whereby divine exhortations were read into randomly selected texts, favoured by Moravians and once practised by John Wesley in the eighteenth century. (Wesley's experience of it was ambiguous; it nearly decided him against preaching to the colliers at Kingswood, a vital part of his field preaching career).[92] James makes appropriately effective use of this technique in 'The Ash-Tree', a story in which seventeenth-century witchcraft fatally haunts the dismissively worldly eighteenth century, as poisonous spiders, the unholy familiars of Mrs Mothersole—executed as a witch in 1690 on the evidence of Sir Matthew Fell—make away with Sir Richard Fell, Sir Matthew's direct descendant, in 1754. The disjunction in attitudes towards the supernatural evinced in the two periods is paralleled in the different resorts to the *Sortes Liturgicae* which the story describes as taking place in 1690 and 1754 respectively, indulged on both occasions by pious clergymen determined to make some sort of sense of the otherwise inexplicable events which have taken place.

Objects and places, no less than texts, are redolent sites of haunting in the tales of M. R. James. The disparity between the rational classicism of eighteenth-century houses such as that depicted in 'The Ash-Tree' and the horrible events that will occur within them was of some aesthetic moment. In 'The Mezzotint', the textual representation of a similar house resonates with a twofold sense of horror, the classic doubling of the uncanny experience. In this story, a Victorian don—for once at Oxford, rather than at Cambridge—witnesses the disappearance of a baby in 1802 in the clutches of a skeletal figure as the tragedy is replayed in a mezzotint of the scene, executed by the bereft father in 1805. Similarly, in 'The Haunted Doll's House' a macabre eighteenth-century murder is replayed *en miniature* in a reproduction of a mansion built in the style of Strawberry Hill Gothick.[93] 'The Haunted Doll's House'

92 For discussion, see Henry D. Rack, *Reasonable Enthusiast: John Wesley and the Rise of Methodism* (London, 1986), 190, and for Wesley's account of it, see his journal entry for 10 Mar. 1739 in W. Reginald Ward and Richard P. Heitzenrater (eds.), *The Works of John Wesley,* xix: *Journals and Diaries II (1738–43)* (Nashville, Tenn., 1990), 37. For a fascinating and moving parallel from his own clerical experience, see Owen Chadwick, *The Secularization of the European Mind in the Nineteenth Century* (Cambridge, 1975), 257–58.

93 James, 'The mezzotint', in *Ghost-Stories of an Antiquary,* 53–80; 'The haunted doll's house', in *A Warning to the Curious,* 9–34.

is an appropriately Walpolean fantasia, akin to (and the reverse of) the out-of-scale horrors of Horace Walpole's *The Castle of Otranto*, a work of which James was no great admirer, observing of it in a 1929 essay on ghost stories, 'I fear it is merely amusing';[94] he was, nonetheless, plainly fascinated by its narrative potential. His architectural tastes were decidedly not Walpolean, as is made clear in the opening to 'The Ash-Tree':

Everyone who has travelled over Eastern England knows the smaller country-houses with which it is studded—the rather dank little buildings, usually in the Italian style, surrounded with parks of some eighty to a hundred acres. For me they have always had a very strong attraction: with the grey paling of split oak, the noble trees, the meres with their reed-beds, and the line of distant woods. Then, I like the pillared portico—perhaps stuck on to a red-brick Queen Anne House which has been faced with stucco to bring it into line with the 'Grecian' taste of the end of the eighteenth century; the hall inside, going up to the roof, which hall ought always to be provided with a gallery and a small organ. I like the library, too, where you may find anything from a Psalter of the thirteenth century to a Shakespeare quarto. I like the pictures, of course; and perhaps most of all I like fancying what life in such a house was when it was first built, and in the piping times of landlords' prosperity, and not least now, when, if money is not so plentiful, taste is more varied and life quite as interesting. I wish to have one of these houses, and enough money to keep it together and entertain my friends in it modestly.[95]

James was fairly typical of his generation in his love of eighteenth-century vernacular classicism; it was to an altogether more modest specimen of such a house as the one he describes, Lamb House in Rye in Sussex, that Henry James moved from London, and in whose Garden House he dictated the later short stories and novels. The revival of the Queen Anne style, of what became known, borrowing an Arnoldian epithet, as 'sweetness and light', had begun in earnest in the 1860s, the decade of M. R. James's birth, would ultimately provide the style in which such new academic communities as Newnham College, Cambridge, and Lady Margaret Hall, Oxford, were to be built.[96]

James was not, then, drawn to the 'Gothick', be it in the tales or the buildings of Horace Walpole. James was in no doubt as to the tradition

[94] M. R. James, 'Some remarks on ghost stories', *The Bookman* (Dec. 1929), 169–72, at p. 170.

[95] James, 'The ash-tree', in *Ghost-Stories of an Antiquary*, 81–112, at pp. 83–4.

[96] On the fortunes of which style, see Mark Girouard, *Sweetness and Light: The Queen Anne Movement, 1860–1900* (New Haven, 1977).

in which his own stories belonged, and it was not the Walpolean Gothic, nor yet a contemporary vision of the supernatural tale, but rather that which had prevailed during his own childhood. As he observed in the 'Preface' to *More Ghost Stories*: 'I am well aware that mine is a nineteenth- (and not a twentieth-) century conception of this class of tale; but were not the prototypes of all the best ghost stories written in the sixties and seventies?'[97] James found the world of his childhood inescapable; his biographers have always cannily resisted any acceptance of a Freudian interpretation of his tales.[98] The writer from those decades whose work he most admired, many of the best examples of which he published in a small but effectively chosen collection with an affectionate introduction, was the Irish writer Joseph Sheridan Le Fanu. Many of Le Fanu's supernatural tales have an eighteenth-century Irish setting; his celebrated vampire story, 'Carmilla', from his collection *In a Glass Darkly*, is set in central Europe in the 1790s. He also wrote a novel of the uncanny, *The House by the Churchyard* (1863), set on the outskirts of eighteenth-century Dublin.[99] Le Fanu provides a signal instance of the phenomenon referred to by Terry Castle, that of an author whose love of the irrational and the supernatural prospered and took shape alongside Victorian rationalism. Lecky, the author of *The Rise of Rationalism in Europe*, was, like Le Fanu, a graduate of Trinity College, Dublin, and his vision of eighteenth-century Ireland was a decidedly different, infinitely more progressive, if less altogether entertaining one than that to be found in the spectral evocations, redolent of folk tales and superstitions, to be found in the popular stories of his contemporary, many of which had first been published in the *Dublin University Magazine*.[100]

97 *More Ghost Stories*, vi.

98 As recently as 1983, Michael Cox wrote of the stories that 'to dwell on them as vehicles of unconscious psychological investigation, to the exclusion of all other considerations, is to view them through a distorting lens' (*James*, 149 n.). This ought not, however, to disavow the usefulness of psychological readings *alongside* other considerations.

99 Joseph Sheridan Le Fanu, *Madam Crowl's Ghost, and Other Tales of Mystery* ed. M. R. James (London, 1923); *In a Glass Darkly* (3 vols., London, 1866); *The Purcell Papers* (3 vols., London, 1880); *The House by the Churchyard* (3 vols., London, 1863). He also wrote two historical novels set in Ireland both immediately before and two decades or so after the Williamite wars there. Both novels—*The Cock and Anchor* (1845) and *The Fortunes of Turlogh O'Brien* (1847)—though undoubtedly Protestant in flavour, are politically ambivalent.

100 For excellent studies of Le Fanu and his Irish context, see W. J. McCormack, *Sheridan Le Fanu and Victorian Ireland* (Oxford, 1980), and *Dissolute Characters: Irish Literary History through Balzac, Sheridan Le Fanu, and Bowen* (Manchester, 1993). Victor

In James's ghostly narratives the alleged rationality of the eighteenth century is similarly but an ill-conceived attempt at overcoming older and much darker forces that would dangerously re-emerge in the nineteenth century. As with Carlyle, James saw much greater strength in the religious (and supernatural) beliefs of the seventeenth century than he did in the cooler elements which thrived in the sceptical eighteenth century, and his stories frequently reflect this dimension of his historical thinking. Unlike Carlyle, however, there is reason to believe that James felt temperamentally more drawn to the equability of the eighteenth century than he did to the passions of the seventeenth century; passion, in James, is the force which frequently brings destruction in its wake. Just as 'The Ash-Tree' contained malevolent powers from the superstitious seventeenth century that would successfully overwhelm the complacent scepticism of the eighteenth century, so James's creation of that bridge into a nineteenth-century narrative would, nonetheless, question the ability of scepticism ever to dispel those instincts and intuitions that would continue to unsettle the secularizing elements in nineteenth-century thought. What would increasingly trouble James as he grew older was that twentieth-century unbelief would prove ever more invincible, and that his own quiet Anglicanism could not see it off; his war with the 'godless' party at King's obliged him to retreat from the world of Maynard Keynes, whose election to a strongly contested fellowship at King's James had approved, although the possibility of his later becoming Provost of the college would cause James much anxiety.[101] Disorientated by post-war Cambridge, James made his way back to the more comfortingly Christian ambience of Eton, where he would live out the final eighteen years of his life. It was at Eton that he had originally marvelled as a schoolboy at elderly survivors from the *ancien régime*; he had much enjoyed the fact that one elderly fellow of Eton, who lived on to witness the two jubilees of Queen Victoria, could remember the jubilee of George III.[102] It was the living generational perspective of the historian that informed James's reactions to the worlds in which he lived. The post-war generation was not one he found attractive; Victorianism was to serve as his favoured antidote,

Sage, *Le Fanu's Gothic: The Rhetoric of Darkness* (Basingstoke, 2004), offers a suggestive reading of many of the short stories and novels.

[101] On his increasing suspicions of Keynes and the 'godless party' which promoted him, and which he in turn promoted, see Pfaff, *James*, 214, 331–2, 340; Cox, *James*, 169–70, 187.

[102] James, *Eton and King's*, 80.

and he firmly adopted the mores and attitudes of the adult community, including its eighteenth-century remnants, who had presided over his schooldays.

His protest against the tone set by Lytton Strachey's classic of intergenerational revolt, *Eminent Victorians* (1918), further emphasized his desire to reinvent himself as a Victorian relic in a world with whose self-consciously mature adults he was markedly out of sympathy.[103] He described the situation in which he found himself in the sardonic opening of 'A Neighbour's Landmark':

> 'Remember, if you please,' said my friend, looking at me over his spectacles, 'that I am a Victorian by birth and education, and that the Victorian tree may not unreasonably be expected to bear Victorian fruit. Further, remember that an immense amount of clever and thoughtful Rubbish is now being written about the Victorian age. Now,' he went on, laying his papers on his knee, 'that article in *The Times* Literary Supplement the other day—able? of course it is able; but, oh! my soul and body . . . '[104]

As the tale that ensues demonstrates, 'Cursed is he that moves his neighbour's landmark,' and James, the pious antiquarian, was less than happy with those who would reform or denigrate that which they had inherited, be it the Henrician foundation of King's College, or the Victorian religion in which he had been reared. Indeed, not all the younger men produced by James's beloved Eton and King's would turn against the conservative interpretation of those institutions and their mores that their Provost had dedicated his singularly Victorian life to preserving, long after the old queen had died.

In the most powerful of his *Stoneground Ghost Tales* (1912), E. G. Swain, a former chaplain of King's (where he had written particularly bloodthirsty plays for the choristers in the 1890s), likewise plotted a story of eighteenth-century revenge around the biblical comminations, 'Cursed is he who moves his neighbour's landmark' and 'Remove not the ancient landmarks' (Proverbs 22: 28).[105] Fear of change and

[103] James told Sir Sydney Cockerell in 1923 that he couldn't stand Strachey: Pfaff, *James*, 392, Cox, *James*, 220. What would he have made of his brother, James Strachey, then busily translating the works of Freud for publication by the Hogarth Press?

[104] James, 'A neighbour's landmark,' in *A Warning to the* Curious, 70–96, at p. 71. Pfaff has identified the piece in question as 'The stricken years', which appeared in *The Times Literary Supplement* on the 11 Aug., 1921.

[105] James, *Eton and King's*, 235; Cox, *James*, 95; E. G. Swain, 'The rockery', in *The Stoneground Ghost Tales: Compiled from the Recollections of the Reverend Roland Batchel, Vicar of the Parish* (Cambridge, 1912), 103–21.

its consequences haunted James and his small band of conservative followers, chief of whom were Swain and R. H. Malden, later to become Dean of Wells and the author of an able collection of Jamesian tales, *Nine Ghosts* (1942).[106] The godless generation that James and Swain had feared would indeed transform King's some way from the godly college over which the Provost had presided, and the Victorian fear of Hanoverian worldliness would, in its turn, give way to the moral seriousness of Bloomsbury-inspired agnosticism. It was therefore fitting that the funeral of the elderly Provost of Eton, who had played Handel's funeral music on the organ rather than attend a May Ball when a young fellow of King's, should have been accompanied by the 'Dead March' from Handel's *Saul*; James's musical tastes were those of a Victorian discoverer of the eighteenth-century classics, a conventional taste for a man of his generation.[107] His was a Victorian funeral that took place towards the close of the Bloomsbury era; strikingly, his period as Provost at Eton was remembered by two writers, John Lehmann and Cyril Connolly, as having been decidedly eighteenth-century in atmosphere.[108] In thus uniting the eighteenth century and the Victorian age, the life and the writings of M. R. James marked the end of a tradition that would give way to the Modernist generation, and its own enthusiasms for the eighteenth century, often detailed through a deep detestation of the Victorian generation that preceded them. The eighteenth- and nineteenth-century portions of Woolf's own supernatural tale, *Orlando*, unpicking the bookmanship of her father, mark the same point from which Lehmann and Connolly had critically viewed M. R. James. The Victorian appreciation and construction of the eighteenth century had come to an end, and it was about to begin to be newly understood in their own terms by their successor generation.

[106] Cox, *James*, 95, 119, 123, 150; Pfaff, *James*, 267, 416 n. 77.
[107] Cox, *James*, 65; Pfaff, *James*, 37, 61, 147, 352, 399, 420, 421.
[108] Cox, *James*, 207; Ibid. 339, 348.

Index